Eric W. Sager
The Thinking Historian

The Politics of Historical Thinking

Edited by
Brigitta Bernet, Lutz Raphael, and Benjamin Zachariah

Advisory Board:
Caroline Arni, University of Basel
Amar Baadj, American University in Cairo
Berber Bevernage, University of Ghent
Federico Finchelstein, New School for Social Research, New York
Kavita Philip, University of British Columbia, Vancouver
Ilaria Porciani, University of Bologna
Dhruv Raina, Jawaharlal Nehru University, New Delhi
Jakob Tanner, University of Zürich

Volume 7

Eric W. Sager
The Thinking Historian

A Search for History as Understanding

DE GRUYTER
OLDENBOURG

ISBN (Paperback) 978-3-11-157085-3
ISBN (Hardcover) 978-3-11-156327-5
e-ISBN (PDF) 978-3-11-156380-0
e-ISBN (EPUB) 978-3-11-156425-8
ISSN 2625-0055

Library of Congress Control Number: 2024947340

Bibliographic information published by the Deutsche Nationalbibliothek
The Deutsche Nationalbibliothek lists this publication in the Deutsche Nationalbibliografie;
detailed bibliographic data are available on the internet at http://dnb.dnb.de.

© 2025 Walter de Gruyter GmbH, Berlin/Boston
Cover image: DrAfter123/DigitalVision Vectors/Getty Images
Typesetting: Integra Software Services Pvt. Ltd.

www.degruyter.com
Questions about General Product Safety Regulation:
productsafety@degruyterbrill.com

Acknowledgments

Although this book came into being in a little more than three years, beginning in 2021, it is the outcome of a long career in the dominion of History. There are, therefore, more debts than I can possibly acknowledge. Teachers, mentors, and friends at the University of British Columbia, the University of Winnipeg, Memorial University of Newfoundland, and the University of Toronto all have their place in my meandering journey. From 1983 to 2016, I had the good fortune to work in that extraordinary convivium of learning and geniality, the Department of History at the University of Victoria. Several colleagues have read parts or the whole of this book as it emerged, and I give warm thanks to Peter Baskerville, Gregory Blue, John Lutz, and Tom Saunders. I have learned more from my colleague Lynne Marks than she probably knows. I am especially grateful to John for his close reading of the manuscript and his editorial comments. Tom has a special place in my journey: many years ago, he persuaded me to teach our graduate historiography course. The students in that historiography class were an inspiration: at times brilliant, insightful, amusing, mischievous, and intellectually subversive, they were always challenging. In retirement, I miss them. I am very grateful to two students, anonymous to me at the time, who read an early draft of the book and offered insightful comments. One is Aaron Stefik; the other remains anonymous.

Others outside the History Department have assisted. Daniel Woolf of Queen's University gave wise counsel and encouragement in a moment of uncertainty. The anonymous readers for De Gruyter offered perceptive and deeply informed suggestions, and they did so with truly remarkable promptness. I am deeply grateful to the editors at De Gruyter for their respect, their enthusiasm, and their astonishing speed in responding to my communications. I give special thanks to Rabea Ritgerodt-Burke, the Senior Acquisitions Editor for History.

My children, Catherine and Zoë, and my grand-daughters Christina and Kaity, have encouraged me to think of historical futures. The artist who appears at the beginning of Chapter 8 is Jean Anne Wightman. In marriage, enduring love, and constant support, she has been with me throughout this venture of hope.

Contents

Acknowledgments —— V

1 **Introducing the Argument** —— 1

2 **A Knowledge Explosion** —— 7

3 **History as Understanding** —— 23

4 **Understanding Time** —— 33

5 **Argumentation** —— 45

6 **Parts and Wholes** —— 57

7 **Consilience** —— 62

8 **Perspectives** —— 72

9 **Analogy** —— 79

10 **Quantification** —— 95

11 **Abductive Reasoning** —— 108

12 **Reason and Imagination** —— 120

13 **The Future** —— 135

Suggestions for Further Reading —— 151

Index —— 153

1 Introducing the Argument

History is in peril. So we often hear, and those who sound the alarm offer plenty of evidence. Enrollments in university-level History courses are declining across North America and in the United Kingdom. The number of History professors has been declining for many years. University presses are under great pressure. Pessimistic warnings about the state of History teaching in schools abound. In 2022, for instance, the President of the Observatory on History Teaching in Europe declared that history teaching in Europe was "a field of ruins."[1] History teaching in the United States has become a political and ideological battleground. And another pessimism arises in our time: that in the wider culture of screen capitalism and social media, historical knowledge is dismissed or ignored in an expanding present-minded consciousness.

These declines, together with wider cultural changes that continue to challenge the authority of experts, have prompted a climacteric, a critical moment of inquiry into the value of history as a form of knowledge. Who now commands entry to the past? Who speaks of the past, and in what media? The past appears not only in text but increasingly in other evolving forms: film, games, reenactments, social media, virtual reality environments, and other immersive constructions. And what of verbal text itself, the preferred medium of scholarly history? What becomes of writing and text, when artificial intelligence can generate plausible historical accounts? What becomes of history itself?

What is history? What are historians doing, when we do our history-making? Why is history important? Can it be saved? The questions are more urgent than ever. I invite you into a conversation on these questions. In this conversation, I shall offer an argument about history as a way of understanding. The argument is this: if we are to mount new defenses of history for our time, we must turn not only to history as a body of theory-laden and applied knowledge, or to history as a set of skills, valuable these as undoubtedly are. We must also turn to history as

---

[1] Alain Lamassoure, quoted in an article by Stéphane Le Bars, *Le Monde*, 21 January 2022; cited in Jean-Philippe Warren, "A Revealing Shock?", *Intersections* (Canadian Historical Association), 7, 1 (2024), 4. The 2023 *General Report on the State of History Teaching in Europe* is on the web site of OHTE: https://www.coe.int/en/web/observatory-history-teaching/general-report. Lamassoure offers a fascinating summary of the work of OHTE in "L'enseignement de l'histoire en Europe," 7 February 2024, available on YouTube. Lamassoure portrays history teaching as a dangerous mix of chauvinism and amnesia. In 2019, the Social Sciences and Humanities Research Council responded to growing concerns by establishing the first comprehensive study of history teaching in Canada: *Thinking Historically for Canada's Future*: https://thinking-historically.ca/. See also note 352.

a way of thinking, as a specific type of imaginative reasoning. Thinking is here understood as the creative and analytical generation and organization of objects and ideas; it is an active and conscious process of cognition. I argue that historical thinking is necessary, not just to understand the past, but also to understand the present and the future.

In our conversation, my voice will remain clear, I hope, even when the subject becomes complicated, as it sometimes does. Here is one such complication: at a time when scholars speak of "plural histories," which history am I writing about? To which history does my argument apply? My answer is that I prefer to start with "plural pasts."[2] There are many ways of understanding past and present: these include myth, legend, folklore, oral traditions, and memory, to name a few. Academic history is one such understanding; it is the way of understanding to which my argument applies. It is important to specify this limiting frame because it places my argument in a necessary balance among different knowledge traditions. My history has its roots in Europe, whence it evolved and spread to other parts of the world, interacting in complex ways with other knowledge traditions, including many Indigenous oral histories. My focus, therefore, is on what we call "history" as a research-based discipline practiced by professional scholars and taught in schools, colleges, and universities in many places around the world. Does my argument – and do the elements of history that I seek to define – apply to non-historicist traditions? I am not sure how they would apply, but the question is an important one, and this book is, as I have said, the opening of a conversation and an invitation to join that conversation.

I begin with the kind of history I learned in my youth, presented here as a template, even perhaps a paradigm, that was soon subject to radical challenges. I entered the domain of Clio, the Muse of History,[3] in the 1960s, and I have carried the marks of that decade for the rest of my career. I absorbed a history framed in an epistemology – a theory of knowledge – that I scarcely perceived and rarely questioned. In Chapter 1, I seek an understanding of that history, that way of knowing the past. I suggest briefly how that history came to be challenged and how much of it was shattered in the last decades of the twentieth century. My reflections in Chapter 1, and later in the book, are personal and also historical: I am following an intellectual tradition which holds that every historian is a historical subject. All of us, in doing our history, exist in our own historicity. As the historiographer Stefan Berger has shown so persuasively, the writing of history is closely linked to the

---

2 Arthur Alfaix Assis, *Plural Pasts: Historiography Between Events and Structures* (Cambridge: Cambridge University Press Elements Series, 2023).
3 The ancient Greeks credited Clio, daughter of Zeus and Mnemosyne, with the special power of historical memory and the ability to inspire historians.

building of identities.[4] Since that is so, we must try to stand aside and observe ourselves in our history-making presence. Our reflections on history and meaning "must endeavour to acquire as much historical self-transparency as possible" (the words are those of the German philosopher Hans-Georg Gadamer).[5]

This book is not, however, another history of the major intellectual trends and "turns" of the last decades of the twentieth century. The opening chapters are the preface to my argument. My understanding of history emerges from the young person that I was a half century ago. I was always a keen defender of Clio, the Muse that adopted me, but the ground on which I stood proved to be unstable. I needed to grow up, and I have tried to do so. There may be a lesson here for young historians: pause, as I did not, to reflect on what you are doing and why. The reflection will be worth the effort. Out of my own pause for reflection came the steps taken in Chapters 2 through 5: gradually, I moved beyond the history of my youth. I moved toward something I refer to as "understanding," toward new ways of thinking with time, and toward history as a thinking enterprise.

Historical thinking is not a new subject. In recent decades "historical thinking concepts" have preoccupied many experts in the field of education theory. These scholars were concerned above all with the way in which history was taught in schools. History was too often contained in textbooks that presented one event after another, as facts that students were expected to memorize. Such history was boring. Furthermore, it fell prey to the illusion that "the way things are told is simply the way things were."[6] History education, argued the education theorists,

---

4 Helge Jordheim, Lisa Regazzoni, and Chiel van den Akker, "Introduction. On the Need for Theory in History," *Journal of the Philosophy of History*, 17, 3 (December 2023), 351–2. Stefan Berger, *History and Identity: How Historical Theory Shapes Historical Practice* (Cambridge: Cambridge University Press, 2022).

5 Hans-Georg Gadamer, *Truth and Method*, 2nd revised edition, trans. Joel Weinsheimer and Donald G. Marshall (New York: Continuum, 2004) (first published 1975), xxiii. A powerful argument for deploying the first-person self in historical investigation and writing is offered in Ivan Jablonka, *History is a Contemporary Literature: Manifesto for the Social Sciences*, trans. Nathan J. Bracher (Ithaca: Cornell University Press, 2018); for a concise statement, see Jablonka's "The New Frontier: Preface to the Cornell Edition," viii. There is a genre of "l'ego histoire" or self-history: among other works on this genre see Jaume Aurell, *Theoretical Perspectives on Historians' Autobiographies: From Documentation to Intervention* (London: Routledge, 2016); Jeremy D. Popkin, *History, Historians, and Autobiography* (Chicago: University of Chicago Press, 2005); Enzo Traverso, *Singular Pasts: The "I" in History* (Columbia University Press, 2023).

6 Sam Wineburg, *Historical Thinking and Other Unnatural Acts: Charting the Future of Teaching the Past* (Philadelphia: Temple University Press, 2001), 12. Wineburg is citing what the French literary theorist and philosopher Roland Barthes referred to as the "referential illusion." Roland Barthes, "Historical Discourse," in Michael Lane, ed., *Introduction to Structuralism* (New York: Basic Books, 1970), 145–55.

must turn to first principles: if history is not a collection of information or "facts" about the past, what is it? Answers varied, but a frequent answer was that history is a cognitive process, a way of thinking. As the Canadian educators Peter Seixas (pronounced SAY-shas) and Tom Morton put it: "Historical thinking is the creative process that historians go through to interpret the evidence of the past and generate the stories of history."[7] Peter Seixas had already defined the process as consisting of the "big six" thinking concepts: historians establish historical significance; historians use primary source evidence; historians examine continuity and change; historians analyze cause and consequence; historians use historical perspectives; historians attempt to understand the ethical dimensions of history. Other scholars emphasized other competencies, including such things as contextual reasoning, creative reading, critical reading of non-textual histories, and narrative competence.[8]

I say to my student readers: you would learn much from reading the works of education theorists; and if you are likely to become teachers, such reading is surely essential. I need, however, to say why and how my understanding of historical thinking differs from that of most education theorists. For one thing, their target was history teaching in classrooms in schools. It followed that their emphasis was very much on sets of critical skills or competencies. Indeed, it often seems that they were equating history, as a discipline, with such skills or competencies. My argument in this book is that history is much more: it is a fluid and evolving set of thinking modes that cannot be reduced to skills or methods. Historical thinking is not, as the title of Sam Wineburg's book suggests, an "unnatural act." We perform many of the elements of historical thinking naturally, although the full assembly of historical thinking requires education and practice.

Furthermore, there is a tendency among education theorists to see a clear demarcation between past and present: the past has gone and we cannot enter it;

---

[7] Peter Seixas and Tom Morton, *The Big Six Historical Thinking Concepts* (Toronto: Nelson Education, 2013), 2.
[8] See especially Wineburg's discussion of "contextualized thinking" in his *Historical Thinking*, 89–112; Michael Douma's chapters on creative reading and writing in his *Creative Historical Thinking* (London: Routledge, 2018), 51–69; and Stéphane Lévesque's chapter on "Narrative Competence" in *Thinking Historically: Educating Students for the 21st Century* (Toronto: University of Toronto Press, 2009), 135–54. Other works include: Kadriye Ercikan and Peter Seixas, eds., *New Directions in Assessing Historical Thinking* (New York: Routledge, 2015); Jannet van Drie and Carla van Boxtel, "Historical Reasoning: Towards a Framework for Analyzing Students' Reasoning about the Past," *Educational Psychology Review*, 20, 2 (June 2008), 87–110; Jeffery D. Nokes, *Building Students' Historical Literacies: Learning to Read and Reason with Historical Texts and Evidence* (New York: Routledge, 2022); Sam Wineburg, *Why Learn History (When It's Already on Your Phone)* (Chicago: University of Chicago Press, 2018).

the past is therefore different and distant from the present. To understand the past, therefore, we must avoid "presentism" – allowing our present views and biases to shape how we write history. In this view (not shared by all education theorists!), a set of thinking procedures or competencies will allow students to bracket, or stand aside from their own present world views as they scrutinize evidence, thereby to see the past on its own terms, in all its many differences. Do you see a problem here? I hope so. The problem is this: it is not possible to set aside, or step out of, our present values or cultural contexts when we do history. We historians are also historical beings. Our interpretations are made within "the horizons of social and cultural contexts that affect our perception of what is meaningful, relevant, and valid."[9] Thus, there is an unresolved problem in much of the education literature, a problem that may be related to its acceptance of empiricism. Empiricism, put simply, is the idea that knowledge comes from experience and the evidence of experience. And that by applying the correct procedures and competencies, one can overcome the distance between the present and the past. There is another fascinating problem for curious students that I leave in a footnote.[10] Clearly, any proposal for historical thinking should strive to overcome these problems, even if the result may not satisfy all readers.

I will propose specific elements of historical thinking. I present these not as skills or competencies, but as constituent parts or components of historical thinking, in the absence of which the thinking would be different or might not exist in its current form. I define these elements mainly in Chapters 6 through 11: mereology (parts and wholes), consilience, perspective, analogy, quantification, and abductive reasoning. I do not claim that my list of elements is complete or exhaustive. On the contrary, I believe that historical thinking is so plastic and so expansive that no list may be complete. Likely my readers will be able to suggest other possibilities. Already, prior to publication, one reader asked: is not emo-

---

9 Robert Thorp and Anders Persson, "On Historical Thinking and the History Educational Challenge," *Educational Philosophy and Theory*, 52, 8 (2020), 896.
10 Return to the statement by Seixas and Morton that "Historical thinking is the creative process that historians go through to interpret the evidence of the past and generate the stories of history." This follows from their introductory definition of history itself: "Histories are the stories we tell about the past." Seixas and Morton, *The Big Six*, 2. Do you see a problem here? I accept that in an introductory work, concise statements are necessary and underlying assumptions need not be fully discussed. Nevertheless, a problem remains. What is meant by "stories"? Is story the same as narrative? If so, is all history narrative in form? If you answer affirmatively, then are you dismissing all history whose authors declare their work to be "postnarrative"? Is there a way in which the authors might have anticipated such questions, and answered them, even tentatively? On narrative see also footnote 44.

tional reasoning an element in historical thinking?[11] It may be so, and by way of excuse, I plead only that this book is the opening of a conversation. The conversation is necessary, in my view, because if we are to defend history persuasively, we must defend it as a necessary form of thinking and reasoning. It follows that we have a duty to identify and define the elements contained in that form.

I have tried to write the kind of book that I never had when I was a graduate student in history in the late 1960s and early 1970s. My search for history as a way of thinking is that of a particular kind of historian, as readers will see. I have studied a strange mix of subjects, including peace movements, sailing ships, seafaring labor, families, unemployment, and economic inequality. A late-comer to the field of historiography, I bring something unusual and, I hope, valuable: the perspective of a Canadian social science-oriented practitioner who has dabbled in quantitative methods, database construction, and economic history. I do not enter this conversation equipped with the credentials of a career-long historiographer. My qualifications instead lie in many years of teaching a graduate-level historiography course, and in the reading and hard thinking that such teaching demands. My students were my constant and committed teachers. I come to this subject from a rigorous school.

And so, I invite you to meet my Clio, the wandering Muse whose song it has been my destiny to sing.

---

11 Emotions and senses have a claim to be included, not least because recent studies argue that emotions are more than past experiences deserving of historians' attention; they raise epistemological issues if one accepts that, as Rob Boddice puts it, "We are our worlds. We are biocultural." Rob Boddice, *The History of Emotions* (Manchester: Manchester University Press, 2018), 156. Emotions also raise the potential of "languages of feeling" in historical discourse: see Rob Boddice and Mark Smith, *Emotion, Sense, Experience* (Cambridge: Cambridge University Press, 2020), 9–17. One might make an even stronger case for including empathy among the elements of historical thinking. See Tyson Retz, *Empathy and History: Historical Understanding in Re-enactment, Hermeneutics, and Education* (New York: Berghahn, 2018).

2 A Knowledge Explosion

History tells us things about the past that those living at the time did not know. Few of us born soon after the Second World War knew that in the first three or four decades of our lives, there occurred an explosion of historical knowledge that was unprecedented in human history. I refer to the European-origin history that moved beyond Europe to the Americas and many other parts of the world, where it was variously absorbed, deflected, and often rejected. Never before had there been such a rapid growth in the population of historians as occurred in the third quarter of the twentieth century. The numbers do not tell the whole story, but they serve as indicators of a sudden and explosive change (I am a social science historian, so I do some counting!).

Consider my own alma mater. The 1949–50 Calendar of the University of British Columbia lists eight professors in the Department of History; among them was "Miss Margaret Ormsby, Assistant Professor." A mere twenty years later, when I was in the PhD program and Dr. Ormsby was the Head of the Department, the count of professors was closer to forty. Similar growth appeared in other established universities. And across Canada, as in other countries, many new universities were established, with their own History departments.

Australia, where they count such things, offers another example. Australian universities employed sixty historians in 1954. By 1973 universities and colleges employed about 750 academic historians.[12] I have not found comparable estimates of the number of academic historians in Canada, but there can be no doubt that rates of increase were unprecedented. Membership in the Canadian Historical Association increased five or six times between the early 1950s and the late 1970s.[13] In the United States, the number of PhD graduates in History offers another measure. There were around 300 History doctorates awarded each year in the early 1950s. By 1971–72, the number was over 1,100. One of the remarkable things in this period was that the growth of History doctorates was more rapid than the growth of doctorates in social science fields, including Economics. In the early 1970s, there were 11 new History PhDs for every 8 new Economics PhDs.[14]

---

[12] Martin Crotty and Paul Sendziuk, "The Numbers Game: History Staffing in Australian and New Zealand Universities," *Australian Historical Studies*, 50, 3 (August 2019), 355.
[13] Reports of the annual meetings listed all annual members in the 1940s and 1950s: there were slightly over 400 in 1950. By the late 1970s, according to the CHA, membership was around 2,200. Of course many members were not university-based academics.
[14] Robert B. Townsend, "Precedents: The Job Crisis of the 1970s," *Perspectives on History* (newsmagazine of the American Historical Association), April 1, 1997; Robert B. Townsend, "Number of History PhDs Rising Again, But Job Openings Keep Pace," *Perspectives on History*, January 1, 2008.

The publication of scholarly papers and books in History certainly followed a similar path. In three or four decades, more new historical knowledge was created in Europe and the Americas, and more history was written, than had appeared in the entire history of Western culture before 1950. The growth entailed an expansion of the objects to be historicized: as Dipesh Chakrabarty (the Indian historian and postcolonial theorist) has said, the "imperious instinct of the discipline" meant that *"everything* can be historicized."[15] An alarming decline in numbers followed in the 1970s and 1980s, but the History explosion was not over. By the early 2000s, the number of new History doctorates in the United States was not far off its previous peak.

Historians in the future will be better positioned than we are to understand why this explosion occurred; we are still too close to the eruption. Those historians would do well to begin by asking: what *was* the history that so consumed my generation? Looking back from my fragile perch in the third decade of the twenty-first century, I remember something of the History that I learned in my youth. Undergraduate classes were lecture courses that said nothing about history as a way of knowing. History was a matter of piling up evidence, or facts, relevant to a subject. That's what professors did in lectures. And that is what I did in writing History essays, those exercises in strangled originality. In an essay I could address a specific subject or problem; I could marshal evidence and draw a clear, if simple, conclusion. The test of merit was the sufficiency of footnoted evidence – sufficient, at least, to satisfy the professor or whoever graded the essay. I had no sense of History as a matter of interpretation, and certainly no idea that there was an epistemology at work here. I was good at writing essays: I could control the assembly and plausible ordering of things in sentences and paragraphs.

My undergraduate courses were all lecture courses; the few seminars were restricted to Honors students. So there was no real introduction to different ways of viewing the same evidence – to History as interpretation. Nor was there any real introduction to *doing* History. As my friend Chad Gaffield has often said: imagine if tennis were taught in the same way that History was taught then (and even later). Students of tennis would spend four years watching experts play the game and taking notes. Then, in their first year as graduate students, they would watch even more intensively, and read about the physics and biomechanics of

---

On growth in the "Golden Age" (1945–75), see Thomas Bender, Philip M. Katz, Colin Palmer, and the Committee on Graduate Education of the American Historical Association, *The Education of Historians for the Twenty-First Century* (Urbana and Chicago: University of Illinois Press, 2004), 4–10.

15 Dipesh Chakrabarty, *Provincializing Europe: Postcolonial Thought and Historical Difference* (Princeton: Princeton University Press, 2000), 112.

tennis swings and ball propulsion. Then, in their next year as graduate students, they would be given a tennis racket for the first time and told to hit the ball.[16]

This peculiar mode of teaching a scholarly discipline was related to a commonplace understanding of what History *was*, even among professional historians. How many of them had read the great philosopher of history, R.G. Collingwood?[17] Probably only the "intellectual historians." For those who lectured in History in the postwar decades, history consisted of a body of knowledge contained mainly in the works of great historians, virtually all of them male. The first task of students was to acquire some familiarity with that body of knowledge. I can hear them saying: one cannot begin to introduce students to different interpretations of the French Revolution until the students have some minimal understanding of what the French Revolution was. And if History is indeed interpretation, and students must present interpretation in essays and theses, they can only learn to do that by reading great historians to see how it is done. After that, they can be let loose in the archives to collect evidence – a task which they can learn only by doing it. This largely unexamined intellectual-pedagogical edifice relates in turn to the durable faith in something called objectivity – a concept later explored, historically, in an important book by Peter Novick (*That Noble Dream*, 1988).[18]

It is easy, in retrospect, to be critical and condescending. We must remember that many who operated in that world were superb teachers, and that students did learn things. But we need to understand the historiographical context in which multiple disruptions and discontents were born within this edifice of knowledge. The History that I was absorbing soon confronted a series of challenges and subversions. The loudest of these took place, at first, in Europe. But Canada too was a tinder box, even if Canadian students were spared compulsory reading of such ancient texts as the history of the English people by the Venerable Bede, written in the eighth century.[19]

The history that my generation inherited rested upon a mix of realism and empiricism. Empiricism holds that knowledge or truth claims come from sensory

---

16 Chad Gaffield, "Primary Sources, Historical Thinking, and the Emerging Redefinition of the B.A. as a Research Degree," UOttawa Publications (2000): https://doi.org/10.20381/ruor-20545.
17 R.G. Collingwood, *The Idea of History* (London: Oxford University Press, 1977 reprint; first published 1946).
18 Peter Novick, *That Noble Dream: the "Objectivity Question" and the American Historical Profession* (Cambridge: Cambridge University Press, 1988).
19 Bede's eighth-century *Ecclesiastical History of the English People* was standard fare for Oxford undergraduates in the 1960s. It was, according to Geoff Eley, part of the "unimaginative Oxford pedagogy, which sought to dampen the intellectual ardor of youth in the cold shower of antiquated knowledge." Eley, *A Crooked Line: From Cultural History to the History of Society* (Ann Arbor: University of Michigan Press, 2008), 1.

experience or observation of things in the world around us, including traces of the past. Thus, objects in the past had an existence, and that existence was independent of our beliefs, linguistic practices, and conceptual frames. Empiricism was loosely conjoined with realism in a simple correspondence theory of truth: there is a reality in the past, and the historical representation of that reality is dependent on the surviving traces of that reality.[20] This fact- or evidence-based correspondence theory takes its origins in the writings of David Hume, John Stuart Mill, and others. It acquired full currency in the "metaphysical realism" of the early twentieth century. The philosopher Bertrand Russell stated the case succinctly: "Thus a belief is true when there is a corresponding fact, and is false when there is no corresponding fact."[21]

Of course there is more to be said about our undigested philosophical assumptions. As a graduate student, I was a very ambivalent empiricist and so, I suspect, were many of my peers. In the 1960s, and even earlier, there were prominent voices that questioned our naïve empiricism. "We are not mere purveyors of fact!" we proclaimed. "We deal in interpretation!" Interpretation was confirmed for me by a famous introduction to theories of history: E.H. Carr's *What Is History?*, lectures published in 1961 and still worth reading today. In *What Is History?* Carr (1892–1982) offered an elegant and often amusing critique of empiricism (although you should notice that he did not answer the question in the title of his book).[22] Although the book was never included in any reading list in my undergraduate or graduate courses, I read *What Is History?* at some time in the 1970s. I readily accepted Carr's insistence on "the dichotomy of fact and interpretation" and shared the privilege he accorded interpretation. "By and large, the historian will get the kind of facts he wants. History means interpretation."[23] And Carr taught us that causation necessarily involved value: "It is precisely this notion of an end in view which provides the key to our treatment of causation in

---

[20] Kuukkanen introduces correspondence theory in Jouni-Matti Kuukkanen, *Postnarrativist Philosophy of Historiography* (New York: Palgrave Macmillan, 2015), 132–42. See the recent discussion of realism and anti-realism in Branko Milovic, "What Is Historical Anti-Realism and How to Define It?", *Journal of the Philosophy of History*, 18, 2 (June 2024), 113–24, and other articles in this issue. Recent defenses of realism include Adrian Currie and Daniel Swaim, "Past Facts and the Nature of History," *Journal of the Philosophy of History*, 16, 2 (July 2022), 179–206.
[21] Bertrand Russell, *Problems of Philosophy* [1912] (Oxford: Oxford University Press, 1971), 129.
[22] In his first lecture Carr says: "I shall not embark on a philosophical discussion of the nature of our knowledge of the past." Carr, *What Is History?* (London: Penguin Books, 1990) [1961], 10. Does it need to be said that there is no answer to the "what is" question outside a discussion of the nature of knowledge created, and that any such discussion is necessarily philosophical?
[23] Carr, *What Is History?*, 23, 29.

history; and this necessarily involves value judgments."[24] And since causation was interpretation, interpretation also entailed value judgments.

Rejecting fact in favor of interpretation was not as easy as I realized at the time. Our cherished "interpretation" was itself seriously under-examined. Most obviously, many or most of us were unaware of the deeply gendered lens through which our interpretations were enclosed; certainly, I was unaware, at least before the 1980s. It would take years before the lens began to be perceived.

History as interpretation had to be a kind of creative undertaking. But what kind of creativity was at work in it? We are observing, I suggest, an important moment in the long history of history since the Enlightenment. A troubling question kept re-appearing: was history art, or was it science? In 1903, J.B. Bury (1861–1927), Regius Professor of History at Cambridge University, stated bluntly that history is a "science, no less and no more." In saying this, he was contradicting predecessors and contemporaries who insisted that history was an art, a branch of literature that required imagination. The first comprehensive reply to Bury came from another English historian, G.M. Trevelyan (1876–1962), who insisted that history, even where its methods of source gathering and critique were thorough and rigorous, could not be a science akin to the physical sciences. The object of inquiry in history was simply too variable, Trevelyan said; causal laws of general application could not be deduced.[25]

The question about history as art or science endured into the mid-twentieth century. One common answer was that history, if not exactly a science, was scientific in its methods; at the same time, it was a literary art at the point when representation and interpretation began. This answer did not settle the issue. For one thing, if history was indeed a literary art, then why was it such bad art? Why was this literary art confined to a poor imitation of late-nineteenth-century realism in fiction? Such questions were merely one of the unresolved problems of history's status in the third quarter of the twentieth century.[26] And in our current era of anthropogenic change, the question of history's relation to science surfaces again.[27]

---

24 Carr, *What Is History*, 107.
25 The long conversation over art and science is summarized in Ann Curthoys and John Docker, "History, Science and Art," in *Is History Fiction?* (second edition, Sydney: University of New South Wales Press, 2010), 69–89.
26 Hayden White dissected the ambiguity of history's position between art and science in "The Burden of History," *History and Theory*, 5, 2 (1966), 111–34.
27 Among many examples, see Z.B. Simon's call for scientific literacy in Zoltan Boldiszár Simon, Marek Tamm, and Ewa Domańska, "Anthropocenic Historical Knowledge: Promises and Pitfalls," *Rethinking History*, 25, 4 (2021), 415–9.

Whether understood as art or science or some sort of hybrid, history began to splinter and fracture even as it expanded. The fracturings were multiple and often painful, but not debilitating because the practice of history grew and won new followers. Rifts, schisms, and "turns" proliferated, but often their philosophical underpinnings went unseen. Callow youth, embarking on advanced degrees in History, rarely stopped to examine the assumptions on which their intellectual endeavor was based. I daresay that in the early 1970s the young Sager would have accepted all of the following statements if anybody had presented them to me. Although I cannot be sure, I suspect that many, if not most, of my generation would also have accepted these assumptions. What do you think of these seven propositions?

1. Meaning requires that a statement be verifiable (achieving the status of truth). Methods exist in historical analysis to achieve verification.
2. Although the past is not subject to experimental treatment, nevertheless, history can aspire to be a science, or science-like, in its methods of verification.
3. Knowledge and truth claims in history are a posteriori, not a priori; they are derived from experience or observed phenomena (traces surviving from the past).
4. Since truth claims and knowledge are derived from experience, knowledge cannot extend beyond the experience on which it is based.
5. A priori knowledge exists, as in mathematics, but this knowledge is non-empirical; it is about the logical consequences of our definitions.
6. Concepts and theories, including those in historical analysis, derive ultimately from experience in the real world. They are distillations by scholars of an accumulation of observed phenomena. They can be tested against further compilations of evidence.
7. Empiricism is the servant of skepticism. There are no repeatable laws in human society, as there are (or may be) in the natural world. To this extent, history, even if scientific in its methods, differs from the natural sciences.

Such assumptions – there were undoubtedly others – were derivatives and amalgams of empiricism and its ally, logical positivism (truth claims must be based on empirical observation and logical proof). But all of these assumptions were being questioned or rejected; any residues that survived were also being challenged. All that seemed solid was melting beneath me, although my "training" limited my capacity to see what was happening. A form of positivism endured in many places, as in the social science of the Annales group in France. The Annales historians were enormously influential: they stood at the birth (perhaps re-birth) of social history, interdisciplinarity, the history of mentalities, and the use of quantitative methods. Elsewhere, positivism was dissolving, and so was the simple empiricism that underlay my understanding of history as representation or recreation of the past. Even the natural sciences were being transformed. Many came to see that natural phenomena do not exist independently of the observer; in the act of observing, we change what we see.

Writing in 1966, in an oft-cited essay on "The Burden of History," the American historian Hayden White offered a stinging critique of the historian's training. At the time, White was still a relatively young historian. He would become one of the most important theorists of history and narrative in my lifetime. He was an intellectual provocateur, and despite the gender-specific mode of this passage, his critique resonates with me:

> What is usually called the 'training' of the historian consists for the most part of study of a few languages, journeyman work in the archives, and the performance of a few set exercises to acquaint him with standard reference works and journals in his field. For the rest, a general experience of human affairs, reading in peripheral fields, self-discipline, and *Sitzfleisch* [stamina] are all that are necessary. Any-one can master the requirements fairly easily. How can it be said then that the professional historian is peculiarly qualified to define the questions that may be asked of the historical record and is alone able to determine when adequate answers to the questions thus posed have been given?[28]

Needless to say, White's essay lay far outside the boundaries of my education or reading: it was hidden in a journal with the (at the time) off-putting title *History and Theory*. More seriously, the assumptions that underpinned my work as a historian were unknown to me. I had never been asked to perceive them, still less to question them. To be blunt: I did not know what I was doing.

It is easy, with the gift of hindsight, to be critical and complacent. We may guard against complacency by casting a critical gaze upon our own time. Do we possess a better understanding of what we are doing, and if so, of what does that "better" consist? What is the current status of undergraduate or graduate courses on historiography, history and theory, historical logic, or historical methods? At another level: even in the wake of the many disruptions and transformations of the last half-century, how far has history moved from that edifice of realism and naïve empiricism that stood unyielding amid the questions that were cracking its foundations? And are we able to answer Hayden White's question in our own era?

In the last decades of the twentieth century, history encountered a multitude of challenges. These included postmodernism, poststructuralism, gender, postcolonialism, semiotics, narrativism, and other "turns," as we often called them. There is no need here to review or summarize all of these challenges; they are

---

28 White, "The Burden of History," 124.

covered extensively in many textbooks and original works. I will do no more than draw out specific implications that remain with us today. Above all, these intellectual, philosophically rooted challenges struck at the foundations of the epistemology that I had absorbed in my youth. Gradually, and often reluctantly, I was compelled to accept new understandings of the relation between past and present, of temporality, and of history itself. And eventually the impulse to search for new understandings would lead me to the subject of historical thinking.

Among other things, the history that I had learned in the 1960s told me that I must respect the alterity of the past; I must transcend my personal location in the present in order to observe the past "on its own terms." My history should be, as far as possible, independent of my identity and of my present ethics and politics; I should write in the third person, as though I were a neutral observer. Such wisdom could not stand beside a new and more deeply grounded understanding: history is always the outcome of situated knowing. It is something created in the present, by a present-located knower, whose values are inescapably embedded in the knower's research and writing. Moreover, the history itself may be constituted in those values.

Today, history faces a host of new challenges at the same time as scholarly history expands its scale and range. We speak now of plural histories, plural temporalities, or, as I prefer, plural pasts. E.H. Carr's question, "what is history?", if it were asked today, would be qualified or re-phrased because it proposes a singularity that no longer exists. I cannot say what philosophers can make of an attempt to define a discipline, or a way of knowing, that exists in such pluralities. And how can historians, when meeting an introductory History class for the first time, honestly answer the "what is history?" question?[29] I confess now that in my teaching I usually evaded the question.

A crucial question arises: if there are only plural histories or plural pasts, then are histories necessarily relative to the knower? Ninety years ago the American historian Carl Becker gave us a gender-specific aphorism: "everyman his own

---

[29] There are many books on the "what is History?" question. I urge students to consider the definition offered by the great historian J.G.A. Pocock, writing about history and time in 1985. History, said Pocock, is time experienced as public being. His definition is historically grounded: he was writing about history as an outcome of history. J.G.A. Pocock, "Modes of Political and Historical Time in Early Eighteenth-Century England," in *Virtue, Commerce, and History: Essays on Political Thought and History* (Cambridge: Cambridge University Press, 1985), 91. See also the argument in his magisterial book *The Machiavellian Moment: Florentine Political Thought and the Atlantic Republican Tradition* (Princeton: Princeton University Press, 1975). See also R.G. Collingwood's essential book *The Idea of History* (1977 reprint).

historian."[30] Today, this notion arises again with renewed egalitarian force. When multitudes outside our academies say they are doing history, how can we respond without appearing to be self-serving elitists? If we do have a special and justifiable claim to knowledge, what is that claim, and can it be made plausibly?

Histories, in the plural, admit a wide degree of diversity in behaviors, norms, values, and beliefs across societies and cultures. To this extent history accepts a specific relativism – the recognition of such diversity. But if we accept diversity in the practice of history, and in the values that underpin those practices, does it follow that history must admit a high degree of *ethical* relativism? Surely we historians must be able to say whether there is a boundary beyond which an acceptable cultural relativism does not give way to an unacceptable ethical relativism. In my lifetime, the problem of relativism has arisen in a number of contexts, and most obviously in responses to Hayden White's influential book *Metahistory* (1973). In his re-thinking of history, White urged that historians' work was an act of "figurative imagination." "Descriptive language," he wrote, "is, in fact, figurative and emplots events to suit one or other type of story."[31] White urged that we read historical works for their literary and tropological forms (trope: a figure of speech or metaphorical expression).

Then White went even further. Since the same facts could be used to produce different narratives, "when it is a matter of choosing among these alternative visions of history, the only grounds for preferring one over another are *moral* or *aesthetic* ones."[32] To some this implied an unacceptable ethical relativism, and White was accused of enabling denials of the Holocaust, an accusation that he vigorously rejected.[33] The problem of relativism also arose from White's charge that academic history, in its stubborn claims to objectivity or neutrality, "has sold

---

[30] Carl Becker, "Everyman His Own Historian," *American Historical Review*, 37, 2 (January 1932), 221–36.
[31] Hayden White, "Historicism, History, and the Figurative Imagination," *History and Theory*, 14, 4 (December 1975), 48–67. The words quoted are from the Abstract.
[32] White, *Metahistory: The Historical Imagination in Nineteenth-Century Europe* (Baltimore: Johns Hopkins University Press, 1973), 433. See also Hayden White, "Historicism, History, and the Figurative Imagination," 48–67.
[33] Hayden White, "The Politics of Historical Interpretation: Discipline and De-Sublimation," *Critical Inquiry*, 9, 1 (September 1982), 113–37. "As far as I am concerned, cultural relativism can lead to many different ethical and political positions, but leads more often to tolerance and efforts to understand the other, rather than to intolerance, xenophobia, and fascism." White, "The Public Relevance of Historical Studies: A Reply to Dirk Moses," *History and Theory*, 44 (2005), 337. For the early stages of the debate with White over representation and the Holocaust, see Saul Friedlander, ed., *Probing the Limits of Representation: Nazism and the 'Final Solution'* (Cambridge, Mass.: Harvard University Press, 1992).

out any claim to relevance to present existential concerns of the societies in which it is practised."[34] He then embarked upon a search for a "practical past" and he acknowledged that his practical past entailed "a relativist position."[35] Upon all of us, now as then, there fell a crucial question. Does the search for a "practical history" mean that history offers no enduring or stable truths, but only relative truths – statements valid only in and for specific times and places, in and for specific ethical or political commitments?

Postcolonial histories gave a new urgency to the problem of relativism. Respect for the "other" was a necessary ethic. But scholars in both history and anthropology were aware of enduring contradictions. Acceptance of difference and diversity did not cancel, but could still coexist with epistemic violence – the many forms, for instance, of ethnocentrism, orientalism, and exoticism. The question endured: what respectful practices, what perspectives, and what methods were commensurate with an ethically and historically acceptable cultural relativism?[36]

The traces of the past that survive into the present limit what can be said; to this extent, evidence is a *sine qua non* of historical truth claims. But our truth claims can no longer rest upon a sufficiency of evidence alone. Any diligent researcher can assemble immense troves of "fact" and build arguments upon those facts. The validity of the arguments rests not upon the putative "evidence" but on the procedures and forms we deploy in using the evidence.

My on-going, life-long conversation with my Muse needed to change, and so it did. I say to Clio: you are the Proclaimer, daughter of Zeus and Mnemosyne, goddess of memory. You are also a Greek and a gendered image deployed through the ages as the inspiration of male creativity.[37] And I have conversed with Clio as though she were an identity separate from me. But that is an illusion: the illusion that history is a part of my life – my "day job" – and only a part, however large. Now, in the eighth decade of my life, I have a different understanding of the

---

[34] White, "The Public Relevance," 337.
[35] White immediately qualified his position: his argument did not imply an acceptance of "universal relativism." Hayden White, *The Practical Past* (Evanston Illinois: Northwestern University Press, 2014), xi.
[36] See, for instance, Bruce Kapferer and Dimitrious Theodossopolous, eds., *Against Exoticism: Toward the Transcendence of Relativism and Universalism in Anthropology* (New York: Berghahn Books, 2016).
[37] In *The Gender of History: Men, Women, and Historical Practice* (Cambridge Mass.: Harvard University Press, 1998) Bonnie G. Smith dissects the gender-specific languages and assumptions of nineteenth-century historians. What is the gender of my imaginary Clio? The answer is that the Clio who comes from antiquity is a female Muse. Clio would be better invoked in as many identities as we may impart. The apt pronoun for such a plural Muse would be "they."

Muse who speaks through me. Now I say: I think, therefore I think historically. Thought and being are one.

I ask: what is history, and what are histories? I began by seeking an answer in epistemology: history is this or that way of knowing, this or that episteme. Perhaps in this way of seeking, there is too much Clio and too little Hermes. Hermes is a complex deity, the winged messenger of the gods, the god of travelers, the god of translation and interpretation. Hermes is often associated with hermeneutics, although the etymological association of hermeneutics with Hermes is disputed. Hermeneutics is a branch of philosophy concerned with the conditions of understanding. Hermeneutics emphasizes interpretation as the path to understanding. Biblical hermeneutics, for instance, refers to the interpretation of biblical texts. Hermeneutics is about how we grasp meaning or come to an understanding of something.

Does it take hermeneutic philosophy to tell us that history is about interpretation? It is an unspoken common sense: we are not purveyors of fact; we deal in interpretation. But use a term frequently and unreflectingly, and it is certain to be problematic. What do we mean by interpretation? When I look back at my first two books, I find only a few appearances of the word in each book. But I use the word in three distinct senses. In a few places, it refers to the book as a whole: the total content is an "interpretation." Elsewhere, it refers to the historian's reading of a small fragment of text and acknowledges that more than one reading or "interpretation" may be possible. The word refers also to the understanding of something by a historical agent: a shipmaster could interpret the law in one way or another, for instance. One gets the impression of a very serviceable word, the precise meaning of which depends on the context of its use.

Clearly, interpretation does not mean translation. It is not the conversion of texts from the past into another text, with the original meaning preserved as far as possible. Much more is going on. But what? One older way of answering this question is to distinguish interpretation from other procedures; in other words, to say what is *not* interpretation. Long ago, when I was an apprentice historian, I took for granted a distinction between interpretation and description. Simple descriptions might be necessary, but only as a preface to the major task, that of interpretation. Then, I cannot remember when, the American philosopher Arthur C. Danto (1924–2013) knocked that idea out of my head. There is no such thing as pure description, independent of interpretation. "I wish to maintain that history is all of a piece. It is all of a piece in the sense that there is nothing one might call a pure description in contrast with something else to be called an interpretation.

Just to do history at all is to deploy some overarching conception that goes beyond what is given."[38]

Another distinction made by earlier writers was between interpretation and explanation. For some, interpretation is a procedure that precedes explanation. Thus, in the case of the Industrial Revolution, according to Michael Flinn, "until the nature of the revolution was established, explanation of its origins was unlikely to be rewarding."[39] Interpretation means establishing the existence and nature of a large conjuncture – an Industrial Revolution, a Scientific Revolution, a Reformation – which then requires an explanation, with specific emphasis on causes or origins.[40] There are at least two problems here. First, what separates explanation from interpretation? Why is explanation, if it can indeed be isolated, not also interpretation?[41] A second problem is that the distinction tends to reserve interpretation for large-scale events or phenomena. And this simply does not happen: historians also refer to their writing about localized or micro-historical events as interpretation.

Sometimes interpretation appears as the set of systematic rules, procedures, and methods used in the historian's analysis of sources from the past. It is what turns fragments from the past into "evidence." If so, we might then agree with the German historian Jörn Rüsen that "historical interpretation ... is the decisive cognitive procedure of historical studies."[42] Here, then, is how historians create meaning, in a way that is fundamentally different from the procedures and methods of the natural sciences. We cannot conduct experiments; so we engage in interpretation. Perhaps because of this very centrality, interpretation – a process or procedure – easily becomes conflated with something else. Marxism offers an *in-*

---

38 Arthur C. Danto, *Analytical Philosophy of History* (Cambridge: Cambridge University Press, 1965), 115.
39 M.W. Flinn, *The Origins of the Industrial Revolution* (London: Barnes & Noble, 1966), 16–17.
40 Marvin Levich, "Interpretation in History: Or What Historians Do and Philosophers Say," *History and Theory*, 24, 1 (February 1985), 48. Maurice Mandelbaum also makes a distinction between "interpretive" accounts and the sequential or explanatory accounts that lie within the overall interpretative account. "Where one part of an interpretative account comes into conflict with specific facts or relationships that have been generally agreed upon by competent historians, it will presumably be the interpretive account, not the sequential or explanatory ones, that will be damaged." Mandelbaum, *The Anatomy of Historical Knowledge* (Baltimore: Johns Hopkins University Press, 1977), 42.
41 There is an intriguing discussion of interpretation and explanation in Peter Munz's, *Shapes of Time: A New Look at the Philosophy of History* (Middletown, Conn.: Wesleyan University Press, 1977), 62–112. Munz accepts the presence of covering laws in the historian's thought.
42 Jörn Rüsen, *History: Narration, Interpretation, Orientation* (New York: Berghahn Books, 2005), 65. Rüsen immediately acknowledges that the meaning of interpretation "has remained ambiguous."

terpretation of modern history: Marxism is also a *theory*, and it offers a *metanarrative*. Are these terms synonymous? Sometimes interpretation is conflated with the form or mode of history as communication. This tendency was most apparent among narrativists, for whom interpretation *was* narrative. Rüsen again, in his summary of a narrativist position: "Historical interpretation is fundamentally committed to this form; it has to bring the empirically evident information of the past into a narrative. Only in this form is the information of the past specifically 'historical,' and only in this form can historical knowledge fulfill its cultural functions." "Interpretation brings the historical relationship between the facts into a narrative form." And it follows that the "sense-generating process of historical interpretation" appears as "an essentially poetic act."[43] At this point, interpretation has lost all independent status. If all history is narrative in form, and all interpretation is narrative, why bother with interpretation at all?[44]

My ruminations on interpretation are a confession. I have used the term many times, as a foundational concept in my practice and writing as a historian. I do not remember stopping to ask what I meant. When a concept is so plastic and variant, it may be best to avoid it altogether. One might reserve its use for situations where there is little chance of uncertainty. Perhaps interpretation means the reading of a text or situation in a context, so as to derive sense or meaning. To interpret is to allow a text to speak and to take meaning in the present horizon of the reader. If so, then interpretation is a beginning to something much larger: understanding.

Let us return, therefore, to hermeneutic understanding. In this tradition, we find F.D. Schleiermacher (1768–1834), Wilhelm Dilthey (1833–1911), Martin Heideg-

---

43 Rüsen, *History: Narration, Interpretation*, 66, 67.
44 History may not always appear in narrative form. Remember Hayden White's qualification: "Historians do not have to report their truths about the real world in narrative form. They may choose other, nonnarrative, even antinarrative modes of representation . . . ." White, "The Value of Narrativity in the Representation of Reality," in *The Content of the Form: Narrative Discourse and Historical Representation* (Baltimore: The Johns Hopkins University Press, 1987), 2. Remember also that a great deal of history is communicated in the form of essays, and essays are often non-narrative in form. Even where narrative is present, other forms and cognitive procedures may also be present. A postnarrativist philosophy seeks to identify grounds for truth claims or justification that lie outside narrative. Jouni-Matti Kuukkanen, for instance, sees "the historical text as an informal argumentative entity" that contains "reasoning for theses of history." The "central suggestion" of his book on postnarrativism "is that historiography is about making rational, argumentative speech acts. This is based on the idea that well-performed argumentative speech acts are rationally persuasive and that historiography is ultimately a rational practice." Kuukkanen, *Postnarrative Philosophy of Historiography* (London: Palgrave Macmillan, 2015), 191–2.

ger (1889–1976), Hans-Georg Gadamer (1900–2002), Paul Ricoeur (1913–2005), and many others. Hermeneutics is neither a specific theory of knowledge nor a theory of interpretation, and it does not offer a set of rules or methods. It is about the conditions of meaning or understanding; it is about what happens when understanding occurs.[45]

Understanding, at its simplest, means to grasp something, to see something more clearly, to integrate an object within a larger frame. Understanding cannot be reduced to specific knowledge. Some formulations emphasize understanding as an ability or capacity to realize a possibility of being or doing: it is not specific knowledge but rather understanding that enables a swimmer to swim or a philosopher to discern meaning in Plato. Understanding may involve applications: thus the German philosopher Hans-Georg Gadamer follows Aristotle's concept of practical understanding or practical wisdom (the Greek word is phronesis). Understanding does not mean having an abstract notion of the Good; it means having the ability to do good in human affairs.[46] Understanding must itself be understood as historical: it is always situated within a context or temporal condition. Gadamer says that "understanding proves to be an event."[47]

This brief introduction barely scratches the surface of many discussions in a large literature. But the reader will see where I am going. How many times have you heard that history is a body of knowledge? I have even been asked, by non-historians, whether my field of study is coming to an end: surely you must be close to knowing it all by now? How much remains to be discovered? A more sophisticated appreciation of history says: yes, of course, the body of knowledge requires up-dating and constant interpretation and re-interpretation, in order to

---

[45] For introductions to hermeneutics, see: Theodore George, "Hermeneutics" (2020) in the *Stanford Encyclopedia of Philosophy*; Lawrence K. Schmidt, *Understanding Hermeneutics* (London: Routledge, 2006); Jens Zimmermann, *Hermeneutics: A Very Short Introduction* (Oxford: Oxford University Press, 2015). On social sciences: Zygmunt Bauman, *Hermeneutics and Social Science: Approaches to Understanding* (London: Routledge, 2010) (first published in 1978).
[46] Catalin Vasile Bobb, "The Place of Phronesis in Philosophical Hermeneutics: A Brief Overview and a Critical Question," *Hermeneia*, 25 (2020), 29–36; Darren Walhof, "Phronesis and Solidarity," in Robert Dostal, ed., *The Cambridge Companion to Gadamer* (Cambridge: Cambridge University Press, 2021), 117–38. On understanding, useful introductions are Stephen R. Grimm, "Understanding," *Stanford Encyclopedia of Philosophy* (6 May 2021); Grimm, "Understanding, Know-How, and Wisdom as Forms of Knowledge," in Lucy Campbell, *Forms of Knowledge* (forthcoming, Oxford University Press). Jörg van Norden offers a summary of the different meanings of understanding in German and Anglo-American discourses: Van Norden, "Against the Historicist Tradition of Historical Understanding," in Zoltán Boldizsár Simon and Lars Deile, eds., *Historical Understanding: Past, Present, and Future* (London: Bloomsbury Academic, 2022), 217–25.
[47] Gadamer, *Truth and Method*, 308.

improve the knowledge and make it more relevant. A still more sophisticated appreciation holds that history is an ever-changing representation of past experience in the present, achieved according to rules of method and confirmation; it is, therefore, a human science, albeit very different from the natural sciences.

Yes, I have lived with and through these and other ideas about history. Let me now see history as a way of understanding: neither a body of knowledge nor a body of methods and practices, but a way of seeing, a way of integrating parts into wholes, an active discipline of the mind, a phronesis. And is that not what I have been seeking from the beginning of my career? One does not surmount disruptions, or connect the disconnected, or acquire a modest control over hidden mysteries through a body of superior knowledge or a set of methods allowing us to measure things previously unknown. To the extent that I pursue these ends, I do them within historical thinking as a path to understanding. And it is a historical thinking project that I seek.

Hermeneutic approaches to understanding offer an escape from naïve empiricism, and at the same time, they help to answer the problem of relativism: if historical understanding is different for each observer, how do we tell good history from bad history? (and there is more than one answer). Of course, understanding can only occur within the subject-position of the historian as observer. But this does not mean that only individual perspectives exist, and that all such perspectives have equal value.[48] Objectivity, if it exists at all as a usable concept, can only refer to claims that withstand critical scrutiny within a shared context of meaning. In our history, that shared context includes acceptance that there can be no final or definitive truth. The necessity of reference to traces and clues from experience allows only probable readings of texts, and truth claims that are always hypothetical and defeasible.

We have only begun to explore what might lie within this understanding. One point needs to be clarified: how do I get from understanding to thinking? These are not the same things.[49] My answer is that thinking refers to our process of cognition, the creation and organization of objects, ideas, and senses. History contains specific forms of thinking that exist in cultural contexts. Our task is to seek those forms of thinking: what are they, and what is the understanding that they inhabit and sustain?[50]

---

[48] See, for instance, the elegant summary of approaches to relativism in Zimmermann, *Hermeneutics*, 16–18, 59–66.
[49] Nevertheless, at one point, Gadamer says that hermeneutics is "a theory of the real experience that thinking is." *Truth and Method*, xxxiii.
[50] Gadamer again: "Understanding proves to be an event, and the task of hermeneutics . . . consists in asking what kind of understanding, what kind of science it is, that is itself advanced by historical change." *Truth and Method*, 308.

I could proceed in the style of those who have written many fine books about the value or meaning of history. Following that tradition, I might offer a chapter about the evils of misinformation in our time and the need for evidence-based argument; a chapter about the necessity of history for community and identity; a chapter about history and fiction; a chapter about the relationships between theory and evidence; and perhaps a chapter about causation. I choose to proceed in another way.

3 History as Understanding

In 1982 an American businessman named Sam Bittner published a short article in the *Chronicle of Higher Education*.[51] Bittner told a personal story about a contract his company made to extract beryllium from a mine in Arizona. He consulted mining engineers and asked whether they could provide him with a chemical or electrolytic process to refine directly from the ore at the mine site. The engineers said that such a process was probably impossible. At this point, Bittner paused and did something unusual. He thought as a historian might think. Then he hired a History student, gave him or her a credit card, and told the student to find the beryllium refining process. Within a week the student came back with the details of the refining process, as well as processes for the refining of other minerals that often accompany beryllium ore.

A non-historian might be surprised by this story. Most historians will find nothing surprising, although they are likely to question the details and ask for more supporting evidence. Some might say that the story merely illustrates a point hardly worth making: the first step in answering Bittner's question, or any such question, requires investigative research, whether the question is about mining technology, a political event, or a plane crash. With Bittner's question, the answer was that one must look in the archives of the Bureau of Mines in Denver, and perhaps other archives as well. That answer is obvious – to a historian. But we need to ask: what is the thinking process that precedes this obvious answer? The thinking involves placing a single object within a contextual whole, and that whole is temporal. An ore is a physical substance existing in specific locations. But it is more than that: it is a substance that humans seek to move, change, and deploy for specific purposes. This being the identity of the substance, the substance exists in time as well as in space. In other words, it has a history. And Bittner's question was, therefore, historical, to be answered in the first instance by a historian, not by an engineer.

A point hardly worth making? Not at all. For too long, historians have struggled to find ways to explain to non-historians what it is that we do. Perhaps we have placed our explanations in the wrong containers.

At a much grander scale, consider the following.

> As we have noted, during the first thousand years before Christ, the culture of the vine and olive spread from the eastern regions of the sea to the West. The Mediterranean, by its climate

---

[51] Sam Bittner, "I forgot to tell him that I was sending him for the impossible," *Chronicle of Higher Education* (14 April 1982).

24 — 3 History as Understanding

> *was predestined for shrub culture. It is not only a garden, but, providentially, a land of fruit-bearing trees.*
>
> *On the other hand the climate does not favour the ordinary growth of trees and forest coverings. At any rate it has not protected them. Very early the primeval forests of the Mediterranean were attacked by man and much, much too much, reduced. They were either restored incompletely, or not at all, hence the large area covered by scrub and underbrush, the debased forms of the forest. Compared to northern Europe, the Mediterranean soon became a deforested region. When Chateaubriand passed through Morea, it was 'almost entirely bereft of trees.' The traveller crossing from the bare stones of Herzegovina to the wooded slopes of Bosnia enters a very different world, as Jean Brunhes has noted. Almost everywhere, wood was expensive, often very expensive indeed. At Medina del Campo 'richer in fairs than in montes [i.e., wooded mountains]', the humanist Antonio de Guevara, reflecting on his budget, concluded 'all told, the wood cost us as much as what was cooking in the pot.*[52]

I have selected one small passage from the monumental history of the Mediterranean by the great French historian Fernand Braudel (1902–1985). I could have chosen many other such passages. What should we say about this excerpt? We might say that this is clearly a work of both geography and history. We might say that the erudition, sustained across three weighty volumes, is staggering, seemingly beyond the capacity of any single individual. But if we wish to say something about history, as a scholarly discipline, do we then note that this discipline is characterized by inter-disciplinary or cross-disciplinary knowledge? Do we say that history is a discipline of deep and extensive research into sources surviving from the past, and that the first requisite of history is research skill of a high order? We might indeed say such things, and they would be true. But we would be misrepresenting and devaluing history.

What we observe in that passage is historical thinking – a specific and definable process that leads to understanding. That process involves seeing parts and wholes: seeing an object as part of a whole, and seeing a whole as composed of multitudes of parts. An individual is looking at his budget, and he notes the price of wood. Another person passes through Morea and notes the scarcity of trees. These instances are parts of an immense whole, something that becomes whole and new in the gaze of the historian – something we may call "the Mediterranean." And in that thinking, indeed fundamental to it, is temporality – the process of *thinking* parts and wholes *into* the dimension of time. The historian is thinking in temporal planes: in the case of Braudel, geographical time, social time, and individual time. The Mediterranean world exists in these planes of time; indeed, the Mediterranean *is* this assembly of parts and whole in time.

---

[52] Fernand Braudel, *The Mediterranean and the Mediterranean World in the Age of Philip II*, vol. 1, trans. Sian Reynolds [1972] (Berkeley: University of California Press, 1995 edition), 239.

Braudel leads me to another element in historical thinking that is so obvious that it may go unobserved. Historical thinking is the cognitive recognition of increasing complexification in the arrow of time. To put it another way, in any situation, past or present, the degrees of freedom are expandable. This mode of thinking is so normalized that it becomes unconscious and ubiquitous. It appears in the mental reflexes of graduate students in History courses, when they respond to proffered explanations by asking: what is missing here? They mistrust even plausible accounts and explanations because they know that something is likely to be missing. They know that there is no simple answer and that any answer on offer is likely to be too simple in one way or another.

Once again it helps to proceed by example. There is perhaps no better example of complexification in historical thought than the sustained, evolving thinking about fertility decline since the eighteenth century (fertility decline, defined simply, means the decline in birth rates in a population). Explaining this decline has involved enormous intellectual resources over generations; this was one of the great historical problems of the twentieth century. In the mid-twentieth century, there was a theory called demographic transition theory. Put simply, this theory held that there were stages in the transition: from high mortality and high fertility, through a stage of lower mortality and high fertility, to a stage of low fertility and low mortality, with causal links connecting each stage. The story of what followed is a story of complexification.

> *Teams of demographers, such as those involved in Princeton University's well-known European Fertility Project, tested a range of 'explanations', including modernization theory and rational economic choice theory, in order to find a common thread which would illuminate the timing and magnitude of the drop in fertility in Western countries. Marshalling a huge range of aggregate statistics from 700 départements, counties and provinces, they were forced to the conclusion that there was no simple answer, that fertility change resulted from as yet unspecified cultural and linguistic factors. Failing to find one universal law underlying this particularly fascinating human map-making, the authors of this vast and extremely useful project turned to the process by which lower fertility spread, suggesting the diffusion hypothesis whereby various cultural forces helped to disseminate the knowledge of fertility control. This hypothesis has the virtue of opening up a space into which a number of other explanatory factors can be introduced.*[53]

Note the language: the expansion of "factors" is a "virtue." The number of relevant conditions or factors was expanding to embrace information flows, internal family dynamics, schooling, religion, and much more, and so the complexification

---

[53] Alison Mackinnon, "Were Women Present at the Demographic Transition? Questions from a Feminist Historian to Historical Demographers," *Gender & History*, 7, 2 (1995), 225.

continued. Alison Mackinnon furthered the complexification when she asked: "Were women present at the demographic transition?" Mackinnon was foregrounding questions already being asked about gender, women's agency, choice, and power in the context of heterosexual relationships.[54]

It is the recognition of complexity and expandable degrees of freedom that makes historians suspicious of generalizable laws or statistical modeling that appears to turn complexity into reductive simplicity. The suspicion may sometimes be misplaced, since the modeling is often a search for that which is *not* contained in the model; it is itself a recognition of complexity. Complex thinking also helps to explain the historian's resistance to metanarrative and teleology, as well as our belief that reductionism is a cardinal sin.

Complexity is a much-theorized subject of its own, and it is important to say something, however briefly, about complex systems theory. Put simply, complex systems theory is about conditions of multi-state and variable dynamics characterized by interactions and feedbacks. In referring to complexification in historical thought, I am not suggesting that historians are working, however tangentially, with complex systems. There are affinities of thought and language: complex systems involve temporality; they are characterized by large degrees of freedom, nonlinearity, and multiple interactions. But complex systems remain systems, and for most analytic purposes, they are treated as closed. Living organisms, including humans, exist in open systems. Historical thinking treats its objects as existing in open, unbounded contexts: there is complexity, but there is no system. In Canadian historiography, we have a telling example in Harold Innis (1894–1952). Innis is known, among other things, as the co-originator of the staples thesis – the idea that historical change, especially in colonial societies, is closely related to the production and export of raw materials. John Bonnett's impressive ingenuity and analytical acuity give us Harold Innis as a pioneer of complex adaptive systems.[55] If you find Bonnett persuasive, as I do, then Innis is thoroughly idiosyncratic. He is that rare bird in our species of winged messengers – a sys-

---

[54] Among those already asking questions about women in the context of family was Nancy Folbre, "Of Patriarchy Born: The Political Economy of Fertility Decisions," *Feminist Studies*, 9, 2 (summer 1983), 261–84. There are many surveys of the literature, but a useful introduction to 1996 is in the early chapters of Simon Szreter, *Fertility, Class and Gender in Britain, 1860–1940* (Cambridge: Cambridge University Press, 1996).

[55] John Bonnett, *Emergence and Empire: Innis, Complexity, and the Trajectory of History* (Montreal & Kingston: McGill-Queen's University Press, 2013). For the ways in which certain European social theorists sought to understand and strategize complexity, see Carl Dyke, "No One in Charge and No End in Sight: Strategizing Complexity in the European Early Twentieth Century," *Journal of Austrian Studies*, 54, 4 (Winter 2021), 119–34.

tems theorist – and as such helps to confirm that our complexification is non-systemic.[56]

A corollary of complexification is the historical thinker's detection of reductive error. Of course, history is often reductive, most obviously in historical teaching. We engage in specific forms of reduction through summary, pertinent instances, analogy, and visualization; we seek to make the complex understandable. As we do this, we seek reduction without reductionism. By reductionism, I mean the interpretation of complex phenomena in terms of, or by reference to, constituent elements of the phenomena. Historical thinking is anti-reductionist in this sense, in that it resists explanation or representation that attributes wholes to parts. Change in historiography often comes from the repeated detection of reductive error, and there are many instances of such change.

Consider what has been referred to as the "classic" interpretation of the French Revolution, associated especially with the French historian Albert Soboul (1914–1982). Here is William Doyle's summary of that interpretation:

> The Revolution is the culmination of a long social evolution, itself economically driven. It marks a turning point in economic history, too: the transition from feudalism to capitalism. The social manifestation of this transition is the defeat of a declining feudal aristocracy living off the surplus extracted from the peasantry by a rising bourgeoisie enriched by capitalism and characterized by moneyed rather than proprietary wealth. The Revolution is thus the decisive engagement in a class struggle in which, at a crucial moment, the bourgeoisie is able to mobilize the support of the masses in order to achieve victory. This is inevitably a very bald summary of complex matters, and the sources of the classic interpretation are complex in themselves.[57]

In the decades prior to 1990, this classic interpretation collapsed. Why? It is important to note that the interpretation was persuasive and powerful for a long time. It generated an enormous volume of research. The many parts of the overall conception were not wrong. There was capitalism; there were social classes; there was a peasantry; and so on. What happened was that questions were asked outside the frame of the classic interpretation, and those questions made the whole appear reductive. I do not accept Doyle's explanation that "only empirical research" of an original kind was likely to challenge the classic interpretation. The anti-reductionist thinking came first; the new research followed.

I confess that some of what I wrote in the past now seems reductionist. Forty years on, I look back on my early work on the history of pacifism. My emphasis

---

[56] David J. Staley introduces "the future as a complex adaptive system" in Staley, "The Future as a Domain of Historical Inquiry," in Simon and Deile, *Historical Understanding*, 160–1.
[57] William Doyle, "Reflections on the Classic Interpretation of the French Revolution," *French Historical Studies*, 16, 4 (Fall 1990), 744.

on the material and class-specific conditions of pacifist thought now seems to attribute wholes to parts, despite my attention to religious and intellectual contexts.[58] But behold that word! *Contexts.* If there were a motto for historical thinking in my lifetime, it might be: context is everything! And context is always plural. Historical thinking links past actions, objects, and persons to proximate and connected situations or conditions, and these may be cultural, social, economic, political, environmental, and much more. Each element in the contextual circle will be weighted and connected to other elements. Discussions and debates in history often revolve around the weightings, and whether or not specific contexts have been missed or under-emphasized.[59]

Are those sentences clear? If so, the clarity is specious because context and contextualism are enormously complex concepts, continuously evolving and contested. As an example of the complexity, let me begin with an example that is well known, instructive, and controversial. On 14 February 1779, Captain James Cook was killed in Hawaii. In his book *Islands of History* (1985), Marshall Sahlins puts Cook's death into the "contexts" of Hawaiian culture, ritual, and myth, wherein Cook was understood as the dying god Lono, who undergoes an annual death and rebirth. The contexts, however, are multiple and inter-acting. To add to the complexity, there is also a present context: the intellectual context of anthropological and historical reasoning in the 1980s.

> *Events themselves bear distinctive cultural signatures. Captain Cook fell victim to the play of Hawaiian categories, or more precisely to their interplay with his own – which inadvertently led him into dangerous 'risks of reference.' So one might read Chapter 4 [of this book] . . . . wherein the famous navigator meets his end by transgressions of the ritual status the Hawaiians had accorded him . . . An event is not simply a phenomenal happening, even though as a phenomenon it has reasons and forces of its own, apart from any given symbolic scheme. An event becomes such as it is interpreted. Only as it is appropriated in and through the cultural scheme does it acquire an historical significance . . . . The other [theoretical] move, perhaps more original, is to interpose between structure and event a third term: the situational synthesis of the two in a 'structure of the conjuncture'. By the 'structure of the conjuncture' I mean the practical realization of the cultural categories in a specific historical context, as expressed*

---

[58] Eric W. Sager, "The Working-Class Peace Movement in Victorian England," *Histoire sociale/Social History*, XII, no. 23 (May 1979), 122–44; "The Social Origins of Victorian Pacifism," *Victorian Studies*, XXIII, no. 2 (Winter 1980), 211–36; "Religious Sources of English Pacifism from the Enlightenment to the Industrial Revolution," *Canadian Journal of History*, XVII, no. 1 (April 1982), 1–26.

[59] The contextualism of Quentin Skinner prompted much discussion in the 1980s and after. See James Tully, ed., *Meaning and Context: Quentin Skinner and His Critics* (Princeton: Princeton University Press, 1988).

in the interested action of the historic agents, including the microsociology of the interaction.[60]

This is all about contexts, in the plural. The context of structure/conjuncture is inseparable from the "historical context" within which there are interacting "cultural signatures." Among other things, this passage from Sahlins points to the plasticity and fluidity of "context." Sahlins does not use the term indiscriminately, and his analysis rests on other key concepts, such as structure and conjuncture.

Among historians there is the risk that "context" becomes a kind of default category, a mental reflex. We all know that we do it – we contextualize. But what do we mean when we refer to context? Students would do well to begin by reading Peter Burke's valuable attempt to put "context" into context.[61] The word and its affiliates go back a long way. In the Enlightenment, Burke observes "an expansion of meaning" and a shift "from what might be called the micro-context of local circumstances to the macro-context of an entire culture, society, or age."[62] The nineteenth century saw other shifts in meaning, as in the historical thinking of Karl Marx, but Marx was certainly not the only contextualist. The twentieth century is the great era of contextualism, and the social history explosion of the third quarter of the century was an outgrowth of earlier contextualisms. In E.P. Thompson's *The Making of the English Working Class* (1963), experience and class appear in multiple contexts, including social context, industrial context, and even "real historical context."[63] The great surge of microhistory reflected in part a more refined search for specifiable contexts.

The problem is that if context is everywhere, it is also nowhere. It can be anything at all that is alleged to be relevant to an object in view. It can be small and very local, or even global. It is a property of the historian's gaze and a property of that which is seen. As the French historian Alain Boureau has noted, there is a danger of circularity: "Too often the context is implicitly or unconsciously constructed as a function of the explanation it is called on to provide."[64] If one were to take the concept to an extreme – one can understand a past event or text *only* in its context – then understanding would be impossible: as Peter Burke says, to understand Plato we would have to live in an ancient Greek city-state. Furthermore, does our attribution of context assume a set of conditions that existed in its

---

60 Marshall Sahlins, *Islands of History* (Chicago: University of Chicago Press, 1985), xiii–xiv.
61 Peter Burke, "Context in Context," *Common Knowledge*, 8, 1 (2002), 152–77.
62 Burke, "Context in Context," 158.
63 E.P.Thompson, *The Making of the English Working Class* (London: Gollancz, 1963), 11.
64 Alain Boureau, "Richard Southern," *Past and Present*, 165 (1999), 221–2, cited in Burke, "Context in Context," 172.

own past, already there (in the words of Peter E. Gordon) as a "sphere that pre-exists the act of interpretation"?[65]

Context is not going away. But we need to think harder about what we mean by it. Is it a method, or merely a sensitivity to situation and perspective? Is it something exterior to the past events or actions being observed, or is it a component of them? An answer to this question is necessary. Take, for instance, the history of "Indian" residential schools in Canada and the United States. We may understand residential schools *in the context of* a colonizing project by the state and specific institutions, including churches. If so, it is not enough to display the mechanisms of cultural colonialism *within* the schools, important as that is; one must also establish the context as it existed outside the schools, a context which then engendered and enveloped the schools, imparting to them the meaning that the historian seeks to confer.

For intellectual historians of the future, the history of the idea of context would be a challenging and rewarding project. The evolution of the idea in the last half of the twentieth century relates to deep cultural and historiographical changes that lie beyond my understanding. I suggest that contextualism is connected to changing approaches to causation. One might even say that contextualism is a transcendence of causation. When I was a young apprentice historian, I assumed that history was about causes. E.H. Carr told me that "the study of history is a study of causes."[66] Causation meant the explanation of an event or outcome by reference to prior conditions, and these were necessarily plural. The task of the historian was to identify the conditions and then to weigh them.

With the growth of social and cultural history in the last half of the twentieth century, event-oriented causation lost purchase. Social and cultural changes were temporal processes that could not be explained by the selection and weighting of prior events or precipitating agents. Instead, historians came to think in terms of conditions that were both prior to and coincident with the processes being observed. The older model of causation was supplanted by a model of multivariate inter-acting conditions within which an explanandum resided.

Cause was also supplanted by something called "contingency." Contingency has become another oft-cited ingredient in historical thinking. The word has many associations: search online and you will find it associated with free will, chance, probability, and counter-factualism ("things might have been different").

---

[65] Peter E. Gordon, "Contextualism and Criticism in the History of Ideas," in D.M. McMahon and S. Moyn, eds., *Rethinking Modern European Intellectual History* (New York: Oxford University Press, 2014), 37, 43, cited in Victoria Fareld, "Framing the Polychronic Present," in Simon and Deile, eds., *Historical Understanding* (London: Bloomsbury Academic, 2022), 26.
[66] Carr, *What Is History?*, 87.

But what is it? If pressed, I would have said that it means close connection or even dependence; two events or processes are so closely connected that one requires the other (thus among humans, reproduction is contingent upon insemination). But is that all there is to it? If we are to use the term in a way that is not haphazard or imprecise, we might begin by referring to the careful reasoning of the philosopher Yemima Ben-Menahim.[67] For Ben-Menahim, contingent truth refers to something different from necessary truth. Necessity means that something is inevitable, regardless of any initial conditions; thus death comes to us all, within certain time limits (the timing and circumstances of any individual death are, by contrast, contingent). Contingency means a high degree of sensitivity to initial conditions; small changes to initial conditions would make a significant difference to outcomes.[68] Historical contingency is not the same as chance: E.H. Carr was correct when he rejected the idea that an accidental or chance condition had historical effect.[69] Contingency does not mean the rejection of causation, however; contingency is a separate category.

On first reading, this may sound like a call for counter-factual reasoning, or even speculation. What happens if we change the initial conditions? Suppose we extract railways from the American economy for much of the nineteenth century: in this counter-factual situation, what would the rate of economic growth have been?[70] Ben-Menahem's discussion contains no such appeal. The definition says that the historian is assuming that if there had been a difference in the set of initial conditions, the outcome would have been different; thus the set of initial conditions is just so – it is not otherwise than what I claim it to be – and the outcome follows. If any of the initial conditions had been different, the outcome would have been different. Contingency means that any specific change in the past was not inevitable; changes do not follow as necessary consequences of specifiable laws; changes do not follow a path toward a knowable future.

How useful is contingency? Does it help us to think about the nature of historical explanation? Yes, it makes sense to see a difference between necessity and

---

67 Yemima Ben-Menahim, "Historical Contingency," *Ratio*, 10, 2 (1997), 99–107.
68 There are other senses of contingency. In one definition, contingency refers to the unpredictability of outcomes from earlier conditions, or the "causal insufficiency" of earlier conditions for later outcomes: John Beatty, "Replaying Life's Tape," *Journal of Philosophy* 103 (2006), 336–62. Beatty is discussing Stephen Jay Gould.
69 At the same time, we need to note possible objections to Carr's critique of "what if" counterfactualism. Carr's brief comments on the "Cleopatra's nose" argument hardly settled the issue. See Quentin Deluermoz and Pierre Singaravélou, *A Past of Possibilities: A History of What Could Have Been*, trans. Stephen W. Sawyer (New Haven: Yale University Press, 2021), 28–9.
70 The argument is in Robert W. Fogel, *Railroads and American Economic Growth: Essays in Econometric History* (Baltimore: Johns Hopkins Press, 1964).

contingency. But one might well ask: is the historian ever interested in any questions to which necessity might apply? We are not interested in those outcomes which always or inevitably follow from a given set of initial conditions (people who are unable to swim, when they fall into fast-moving rivers while wearing no lifejackets and in the absence of rescuers, invariably drown). We are very interested in outcomes where prior and adjacent conditions are highly variable, where even small variations will change the outcome. But is this not self-evident? Of course a difference in those conditions would have yielded a different outcome. For this reason the historian is always sensitive to context, and history is about context, however defined. So do we need contingency at all? What does it give us that context-sensitivity does not? I suspect that it is for such reasons that Ben-Menahem's valuable discussion led to more discussion, in efforts to invest her contingency with more compelling substance. In doing so, writers fall back on theories of causation (necessary and sufficient conditions, tipping points, etc.), or on evolutionary science and paleontology, where contingency continues to resonate.[71]

I have not quite done with contingency. Small changes in initial conditions may have large or lasting consequences. If so, then surely the change was not a small thing at all. How am I to know what is small and what is lasting? To be sure, everything is contingent – it exists "only if." But this contingency is, at best, only a beginning to my thinking. I recall – the memory will not go away – that neo-colonial Vietnam War that preoccupied me in my youth. My country, Canada, was complicit. I knew that such complicity existed "only if" certain prior conditions also existed. But how, by what processes of thought and analysis, could I identify those conditions, either then or now? Our journey toward understanding has only begun.

---

[71] See, for instance, Rob Inkpen and Derek Turner, "The Topography of Historical Contingency," *Journal of the Philosophy of History*, 6, 1 (2012), 1–19. They add "description sensitivity," a "catchment metaphor," and "conditional inevitability" to the mix. A useful summary of definitions of contingency is in Alison K. McConwell and Derek D. Turner, "Historical Contingency: A Special Issue on Epistemic and Non-Epistemic Values in Historical Sciences," *Journal of the Philosophy of History*, 17, 1 (June 2023), 1–8.

4 Understanding Time

Historians think with and about time. But what is this time that resides so firmly in our sensibility? Perhaps we may see it more clearly if we visit a place where the sense of time is very unlike our own.

On a clear day in July 1992 I was in Australia, on a flight from Sydney to Darwin, looking down upon the central red desert. The land below is a canvas of mottled reds and browns, speckled with flecks of white and orange, with dark lines meandering across the landscape. Gone forever is my misconception that a desert takes a uniform light sandy hue. But then I have seen this desert before, haven't I? I have seen it in Aboriginal art. But how did they do it? Did Aboriginal painters get into aircraft and look down on the land? To my very English-Canadian mind, there is a mystery here. There is a way of seeing in this art, a sense of space and time, of which I know nothing.[72]

I found much to learn in my Australian sojourns. One lesson was this: if you wish to understand history, begin by looking where it does not exist, as we know it. Only then may you begin to understand. Listen, for instance, to the following voice from a place where our history does not exist: *how do you European-origin people communicate your history? By writing it. In doing so you confess that it is not important. If you have to write something down, it is not important to you. If it really is important to you, then you will remember it. And if it is important to others, they will remember it already.*[73]

Our idea of history is a tiny and recent thing. It goes back a few hundred years; or if you go back as far as Thucydides, then 2,400 years. Brief moments in time. Now, in Australia, I have come to a place where understandings of time and space go back fifty thousand years or more.

Try, therefore, to step outside a European-origin dualism of nature and culture; try to step outside our ontology of human and non-human. What is the Aboriginal understanding of time? Do Aboriginal people think that human beings

---

[72] I wrote this opening paragraph in 2022, before I came across a similar vision by Marnie Hughes-Warrington and Anne Martin. Hughes-Warrington and Martin flew over the same landscape and saw "the patterns of Australian Aboriginal dot paintings." They connect the vision to ethics: "Doing what is good, fair and just has no singular timestamp in Aboriginal Australia and no place for authority derived from distance or objective detachment." I have left my paragraph unchanged. Marnie Hughes-Warrington with Anne Martin, *Big and Little Histories: Sizing Up Ethics in Historiography* (London: Routledge, 2022), 174.
[73] Where did I hear this voice? I cannot remember for sure. It may have come from something told to me many years ago by the historian Judith A. Allen, but I take full responsibility for any distortions in my echoing of that voice.

exist in a framework of time?[74] And, by the way – is it possible to translate meaning from an ancient oral culture into the language of a literate people? If we can translate, however imperfectly, then imagine that time is not geometric. There is no arrow of time, no linear time, and possibly not even circular time.[75] There is no past, as we understand past, because that would imply a separation between present and past. Where ancestral powers are constant in the material environment, past and present are immersed in each other. The Dreamtime did not occur in a remote past, because it is not absent, as past would imply. There is a "when" – "when crocodiles lay their eggs" – but it refers to something spatial and seasonal; it refers to departures and returns. Time exists within the departures and returns of nature, within its rhythm. Time is rhythm. We cannot "tell time"; instead, we may dance time. People may enter the rhythms of time-place by repeating nature's pulse in ceremony.[76]

Imagine that "where" and "when" do not exist in language. They exist in songlines, the sung contours of the land. Songlines were brought into being in the Dreamtime, when ancient but present beings sang the world into existence. To know where you are, you must know your place in the songline. "Music is a memory bank for finding one's way about the world," said Bruce Chatwin's friend Arkady.[77] Nganyinytja, a Pitjantjatjara woman elder, said: "We have no books, our history was not written by people with pen and paper. It is in the land, the footprints of our Creation Ancestors are on the rocks. The hills and creekbeds they created as they dwelled in this land surround us. We learned from our grandmothers and grandfathers as they showed us these sacred sites, told us the stories, sang and danced with us the Tjukurpa (the Dreaming Law). We remember it

---

74 Tony Swain argues that Australian Aboriginals "did not understand their beings in terms of time" (which is not to say that they had no concept of the temporal): Swain, *A Place for Strangers: Towards a History of Aboriginal Being* (Cambridge: Cambridge University Press, 1993), 2. See Anna Clark, "Just a Matter of Time: Reviewing Temporality in Australian Historiography," *Rethinking History*, 28, 1 (2024), 1–27.

75 Some may see the Dreamtime as circular because of its recursive presence, but the circular metaphor may be a misleading imposition. On time and spatial representation: Lera Boroditsky and Alice Gaby, "Remembrances of Times East: Absolute Spatial Representations of Time in an Australian Aboriginal Community," *Psychological Science*, 21, 11 (November 2010), 1635–9.

76 I am drawing on Veronica Strang, "On the Matter of Time," *Interdisciplinary Science Reviews*, 40, 2 (2015), 101–123; Deborah Bird Rose, "To Dance With Time: A Victoria River Aboriginal Study," *Australian Journal of Anthropology*, 11, 3 (2000), 287–96. On the relationships among time, historical thinking, and cultural difference see the essays in Jörn Rüsen, ed., *Time and History: The Variety of Cultures* (New York: Berghahn Books, 2007).

77 Bruce Chatwin, *The Songlines* (New York: Penguin, 2012 [1987]), 108.

all; in our minds, our bodies and feet as we dance the stories. We continually recreate the Tjukurpa."[78]

Catch a glimpse of this other world, and from that vantage point, look back on our own. And our own becomes a little clearer, a little sharper in its outlines. Our understanding of time, inherited from agricultural pasts, is a skinny sprig, a thin tendril whose blooms are uniflorous. We historians know a lot about time, but the time that we understand is primarily linear time, although it may also be circular. Linear time is sequential: one thing happens after another. The arrow of time points in only one direction. Of course, time may appear to speed up, as in revolutions (which is both a temporal and spatial metaphor). But it is still linear, and even a dimly conceived notion of circularity is bound within the linear (the sequence continues but returns to its starting place). Time, for us, may also be detached from human consciousness: it is something that exists in intervals and the intervals are measurable; they are assumed to be independent of human control. Time is distinct from space, but it is *like* space because it is a measurable thing. We may stand outside it and observe it.

I did not see clearly at the time that I was receiving an introduction to decolonization. Australia was giving me a crash course in thinking outside European understandings of time and space. Time, I was learning, is not just linear. Time is known for its polysemy – the coexistence of many meanings in one word or phrase.[79] In our Anthropocene era, the entire concept is being re-thought and polychronicity is entering our sensibility.

I retreat for the moment to my older mental framework and to linear time. I try to see it with fresh eyes. William Sewell gives us a clear introduction in his *Logics of History*. Time, he says, is fateful: it ushers into being a consequence that is irreversible; the outcome cannot be returned to any prior state. Time is also sequential: acts occur; "every act is part of a sequence of actions"; and the effect of an act is dependent on its place in the sequence. Linear time is also event-oriented: it tends to privilege specific acts or moments or occurrences, things that may be placed within a sequence. The sequence ushers the act into being and into our vision. This time, says Sewell, is also complex, because many different sequences may converge and interact. An event may lie at the confluence of many social processes in time, and it is the task of the historian to uncover the social processes and to assess them (some may be short-term, some long-term;

---

[78] Quoted in Diana James, "Tjukurpa Time," in Ann McGrath and Mary Anne Jebb, eds., *Long History, Deep Times: Deepening Histories of Place* (Acton, Australian Capital Territory: Australian National University Press, 2015), 33.
[79] François Hartog, "*Chronos, Kairos, Krisis*: The Genesis of Western Time," *History and Theory*, 60, 3 (September 2021), 427.

some may have more weight than others). It follows that time, even if linear, is also heterogeneous: it is a mix of continuity and change, of distinct processes with their own rates of movement.[80]

I would add another characteristic of time that historians know, even if they rarely state the knowledge explicitly. Linear time has end points. There are beginnings and endings; between the end points there are punctuation points, moments when change over time speeds up or slows down. The end points become vantage points: places from which change can be observed, either prospectively or retrospectively. Most obviously, a narrative contains a sequence, and the end point in the sequence is a resolution, a closure. In that closure the moral content – the point of the story – becomes apparent.

Linear time favors the movement of persons and things toward ends. In this sense, it tends to the teleological. Even if older notions of human progress are displaced, nevertheless, linear time registers the empowering of human agency. Linear time also tends to favor consequentialism: the ethical principle holding that the grounds of right or wrong are to be found in the consequences of acts. We observe, retrospectively, the separation of Indigenous children from their families; we know the action to be evil because, looking forward in time from the separation, we observe its effects on the families, the children, and their children. History, however, is an on-going movement between consequential ethics and its alternatives. Historians are not ethicists, and they can be opportunistic and pluralist when viewing and assessing human behavior in the past. Many, if pressed, would no doubt think consequential ethics to be compatible with its alternatives. These include virtue ethics, which holds that moral judgment must be based on the virtue of an agent or an action; thus, the separation of Indigenous children from families is an evil because a benevolent consideration is absent among the agents. Another is rule ethics, which places the emphasis on adherence to principles or rules; thus, we know the separation of children to be evil because such separations violate specific principles of equality of treatment and consideration that apply to all regardless of race.

Whether or not history occurs in narrative mode, linear time sustains ethical reasoning. In the example of Indigenous children, that reasoning is retrospective. Looking back along the trajectory of time, events occur, either in sequence or cycles. The events, actions, and outcomes are placed in ethical containers. And there is another ethical dimension – a prospective one. History looks forward,

---

[80] William H. Sewell Jr., *Logics of History: Social Theory and Social Transformation* (Chicago: University of Chicago Press, 2005), 6–11. Lynn Hunt discusses the appearance of modern conceptions of time in *Measuring Time, Making History* (Budapest: Central European University Press, 2008).

from distant events and conditions, to the present and future. The prospective ethic may not be prescriptive in an explicit way, but it is still present.

As a practicing historian, I continued to operate with that older understanding of linear time. But even within that frame, there were ambiguities. Once we admitted the notion that time could accelerate, as in revolutions, it followed that time could never be uniform. It was necessarily perspectival: time was different for economic structures than it was for media, and different again for various technologies. Time differed among societies and cultures. The great French historian Fernand Braudel had already introduced us to multiple coexisting temporalities. In the longue durée, temporal processes move slowly and change is stretched over centuries. In the conjuncture, or cyclical time, the temporal process is quicker, and in this temporality industrial revolutions could occur. In the short time span, or *histoire événementelle*, singular events occur.

The implications of Braudel's conception of time were clear enough for historical practice: its applications were evident in his writings and those of other *Annales* scholars. The implications were less clear when it came to the more complex multitemporalities that followed. The German historian Reinhart Koselleck (1923–2006), in *Sediments of Time* and other works, transcended the linear-cyclical conception in a new multiple temporality that embraced spatial or geological metaphors.[81] In Koselleck's layers of time, different temporal patterns can coexist and interact, opening the possibility for "nonsynchronous synchronicities" (as Simon and Tamm put it).[82] It remains unclear how such complex temporalities might influence the writing of history.

Koselleck made an effort to incorporate multiple temporalities in his own historical writing, but his theoretical reflections seem to have had a more enduring impact than any applications of his temporality in historical writing. Historiography also registered Koselleck's impact. Especially important was his argument about Sattelzeit (saddle time or threshold time). This was a temporal shift at the core of modernity, occurring between roughly 1750 and 1850. A "new time" appeared in European culture. Previously, "nothing fundamentally new would arise" and so "it was quite possible to draw conclusions from the past for the future."[83] Now, in the new consciousness of time, the past was always strange and different, and so the past did not allow easy prediction of the future. History in its

---

[81] The key works are: Reinhart Koselleck, *Futures Past: On the Semantics of Historical Time*, trans. Keith Tribe (Cambridge Mass.: MIT Press, 1985); *Sediments of Time: On Possible Histories*, trans. Sean Franzel (Stanford: Stanford University Press, 2018).
[82] Zoltán Boldizsár Simon and Marek Tamm, *The Fabric of Historical Time* (Cambridge: Cambridge University Press Elements Series, 2023), 23.
[83] Reinhart Koselleck, *Futures Past*, 203.

modern form arose as a way of submitting the new temporal complexity to empirical and even scientific control.

This meant that new and variable temporal sensibilities were at the core of historicism. It also meant that temporality could be immensely complex. Temporality was easily identified and understood where there were obvious affinities, as between linear time and narrative history. Narrative easily accommodated linear time because it reflected sequence. Where such affinities were less obvious, temporality may be more difficult to define and even discern. In ethnographic historical writing, the synchronic might seem to have displaced the diachronic, and temporality may be indistinct.

I can illustrate the point by referring to a small book I published in 1993.[84] Readers will not know the book, but the point can still be made, as a prompt to similar readings or re-readings of other, more scholarly works. During my Australian sojourn in 1992, I wrote a short, impressionistic "discovery" of the town of Darwin in the 1930s, based mainly on a very large oral history collection. The book is organized around themes: houses, the outdoor cinema, sports, trains, animals, taverns. The whole thing appears to be in an ethnographic mode: a description of material things, culture, habits, and parts of an environment. Interviewees quoted from an oral history collection may tell stories, but the book is not written in a narrative form (in the sense of a sequence of events culminating in a closure or resolution).[85]

Revisiting the book almost three decades after its writing, I saw, as I did not see when writing it, that its meaning rested in a deep structure of temporality. A multitude of small memories, turned into anecdotes, are constructed from an end point in the present. From that end point "old Darwin" emerges – a place where things could happen only in that time and place. Sometimes change over time occurs from a beginning, a significant new arrival, such as the building of the North Australia Railway in the 1880s. More often, the change over time is registered as a contrast with a later or modern Darwin. Houses in old Darwin did not have ceiling fans. The cinema, the Star Theatre, had no roof (one evening in 1935, the Flying Doctor flew his plane by the screen to see what movie was showing). Even football (Aussie rules, of course) was different then, and men of different classes and races could have a bash at each other on the field. Trains sometimes got

---

84 Eric W. Sager, *Discovering Darwin: The 1930s in Memory and History* (Darwin, NT: The Historical Society of the Northern Territory, 1993).
85 Of course, readers may infer a narrative in which the founding of Darwin is a beginning, the appearance of the town in the 1930s is a middle, and the more recent and "modern" Darwin is an end. To that extent a narrative may exist. I would argue, however, that the text of the book does not take narrative as its form or structure.

"lost," and the station master would phone the post office to ask the postal clerk if she knew where his train was. The town was a "community" where everybody knew everybody else, or knew who they were. Consciousness of time is registered as difference – everything was different then. Historian and speakers share in this construction of temporal difference. From a vast oral archive, the historian is selecting fragments of speech that bear witness to temporal contrast. The memories recorded in the book are not chosen at random, or by reference to a detached criterion of what is curious, amusing, or colorful. The selections are purposeful.

The temporality is mainly linear, but not entirely so. Aboriginals appear in the book, much too briefly, to register their memories of change from their own points of beginning: dispossession, or the arrival of strange new crops, for instance. There are moments when Aboriginals speak and the listener cannot apprehend meaning: objects appear to have no location, or events are juxtaposed but seem unconnected. Multiple temporalities are present, but some are obscure to the reader or listener. Jump ahead three decades or more, into our own time, and imagine re-writing the book in our digital era. What complexity might an algorithm detect when applied to the entire corpus of oral interviews? Temporality, I conclude, is durable but an elusive trickster. It may be the most commonplace element in historical consciousness and also the most inscrutable.

Now, in the third decade of the twenty-first century, we witness another burgeoning of time studies. In this context, my old linear thinking appears more constricted than ever. New metaphors (such as fabric) replace the geological metaphor. New terms appear, such as "chronocenosis": "a way of theorizing not simply the multiplicity but also the conflict of temporal regimes operating in any given moment."[86] New understandings of our present begin to bear upon historicity. Is our present awareness of the speed and diversity of transitions into the future (climatic, technological, political) changing the way we frame the temporalities that we apply to the past? It may be, as Simon and Tamm have suggested, that new "transitional concepts" have emerged beside more familiar ones, "producing new kinds of historicities."[87] It might also be the case that our sense of lightning-speed change in the present is profoundly destabilizing: Dipesh Chakrabarty refers to a new "sense of the present that disconnects the future from the

---

[86] Dan Edelstein, Stefanos Geroulanos, and Natasha Wheatley, eds., *Chronocenosis: How to Imagine the Multiplicity of Temporalities Without Losing the Emphasis on Power and Conflicts* (Chicago: Chicago University Press, 2020), 4. See the "Review Essay" on this book by Margrit Pernau, *History and Theory* (June 2023), 1–9. For a useful introduction to "chronopolitics," see Fernando Esposito and Tobias Becker, "The Time of Politics, the Politics of Time, and Politicized Time: An Introduction to Chronopolitics," *History and Theory* (September 2023), 1–21.
[87] Simon and Tamm, *The Fabric*, 41–2.

past by putting such a future beyond the grasp of historical sensibility." This sense is destabilizing because "the discipline of history exists on the assumption that our past, present, and future are connected by a certain continuity of human experience."[88]

That continuity of human experience may be lost in the Anthropocene. I am referring to the contested idea of a geological-temporal age in which human activity is the dominant force in climate and environment, an age in which nature and humanity collapse into each other. For theorists such as François Hartog, the Anthropocene entails an unprecedented disorientation because of its radical discontinuities, its "gigantic differences in temporal scales," and its movement toward catastrophe and perhaps even extinction, or an end to human time. Hartog says: "It is no longer, as it was in the good old days, a matter of simply articulating the past, present, and future but of taking into account pasts, presents, and futures whose impacts may differ, diverge, or even contradict each other but which nonetheless form a nexus or a web of temporalities in which, to one or another degree, we act and are acted upon. The first challenge is to orient oneself in a knot of temporalities that no Alexander will sever."[89] Hartog proposes "an Anthropocene regime of historicity" that "may help to orient us, unravel things, create order so as to release the order of times defining the new human condition." It is important to note that Hartog is not prophesying the end of history. He says: "the Anthropocene, far from being yet another end of history, could lead toward a revival – and a new concept – of history."[90]

Postcolonial history has also contributed to time studies by expanding our awareness of multiple temporalities. Postcolonial scholars came to see European-origin clock time and temporality as colonial impositions that were incommensurable with the temporal understandings of the colonized. In his *Provincializing Europe* (2000), Chakrabarty embedded temporality in the European historicism that justified and even "enabled European domination of the world in the nineteenth century."[91] Yet the imposition was not one-sided, because colonial subjects had their own temporalities and even "countertemporalities." On Barak, in his

---

[88] Dipesh Chakrabarty, *The Climate of History in a Planetary Age* (Chicago: University of Chicago Press, 2021), 23, 68.
[89] François Hartog, "Chronos, Kairos, Krisis: The Genesis of Western Time," *History and Theory*, 60, 3 (September 2021), 438.
[90] Ibid., 434.
[91] Dipesh Chakrabarty, *Provincializing Europe: Postcolonial Thought and Historical Difference* (Princeton: Princeton University Press, 2000), 7. On time see also, among others, Mohammed S. Ali, "Marking Time and Writing Histories," *History and Theory*, 60, 2 (June 2021), 271–91; Adib and Paul Emiljanowicz, "Colonial Time in Tension: Decolonizing Temporal Imaginaries," *Time & Society*, 28, 3 (August 2019), 1221–38; Frederick Cooper, "Decolonizations, Colonizations, and More

fascinating study of temporality in Egypt, gazes upon multiple intersecting temporalities. "The abstraction of 'time'," he argues, "took a path that was ultimately dependent on, yet inherently distinct from, Western time.... Like Western time, Egyptian time was historically constructed and made durable by railways, telegraph lines, and various other artifacts, big and small; confusingly, both times were constructed as essential, ahistorical phenomena concealing the circumstances of their making, albeit in different ways."[92] There are other examples.[93] Postcolonial studies continue to challenge our understanding of time and also, therefore, of history. They offer instructive examples of how to observe time- and place-specific temporalities, as they interact with and resist the European variants.

But what are the implications of the new time studies for historical thinking and writing? Are we seeing new temporalities informing a renovated historical thinking? It is probably too early to detect many reflections of time studies that are often schematic and abstract as well as very recent. If we attend carefully to recent historical writing, however, we are likely to discover that complexity and diversity in temporal thinking already exist. We are likely to see a temporal thinking very unlike that among my mentors half a century ago. If this is so, then historians are well prepared to confront the "knot of temporalities" that Hartog refers to, and perhaps also to create new historicities in and for the Anthropocene.

If we look carefully, we can detect historians thinking with plural and even conflicting temporalities. Take any work of history that you are currently reading, and ask, "what understanding of time is contained in this work?" Here is an exercise: read the first paragraph of the first chapter of *The Great Plague Scare of 1720* by Cindy Ermus, published in 2022. The words "time," "temporality," and "change" do not appear in that paragraph. Now ask: is temporality present? In what form or forms is it present? (Answer for yourself before you look at my suggestions in the footnote.)[94] Note that many of the nouns and verbs connote time

---

Decolonizations: The End of Empire in Time and Space," *Journal of World History*, 33, 3 (September 2022), 491–526.
92 On Barak, *On Time: Technology and Temporality in Modern Egypt* (Berkeley: University of California Press, 2013), 239–40.
93 For instance, Amanda Lagji, *Postcolonial Fiction and Colonial Time: Waiting for Now* (Edinburgh: Edinburgh University Press, 2023). This book is about both literature and history.
94 The paragraph begins with a temporal short frame or *histoire événementelle*: "From 1720 until 1722...." "Ultimately taking" in the third sentence implies a slightly longer duration. Later in the paragraph, there is a long duration, when the plague leaves an "indelible mark" that becomes an enduring part of "collective memory." The word "epidemic" connotes temporal disruption and acceleration: something spreads quickly in time and indicates an acceleration of mortality. The words "traditional" and "traditionally" imply a certain kind of long duration: a story

and change in time. In fact, Ermus's paragraph offers a clear demonstration of the multiplicity of times: it is not about simple linear time, although linear time is certainly present.

There is no way to choose examples that are representative, and readers may see in my next example a tendentious and self-serving choice. If so, I respond by saying that the exceptional may open our eyes to elements borne by the commonplace.

Trickster Travels (2006), by Natalie Zemon Davis (1928–2023), is a history of a sixteenth-century Muslim traveler "between worlds." The travels of Leo Africanus (to use one of his names) are spatial and temporal, and temporality is basic to his identities. Here is historical thinking and writing: Davis's text gives us a "trickster bird" in multiple overlapping temporalities. For the purpose of fixing specific actions and events in time, we are given two measured times: the Muslim lunar calendar and the common era calendar. Short-term events in measured time interact with long durations: a book published in 1550 endures and attracts attention for centuries.[95] Al-Hasan al-Wazzan is presented in "crossings" that are concurrently spatial and temporal. The temporality is linear and much more. Circular time is frequent: thus, for instance, the teachings on jihad, the responsibility of holy war, enter at one time and then return in another time.[96]

Al-Wazzan's travels as a diplomat between 1504 and 1518 are not recounted as a chronicle, one after another across parts of Africa. They are located in contexts, including, crucially, temporal contexts. His diplomatic encounters occur between sultans, courtiers, and officials who are themselves historical subjects, their relationships, powers, and religious beliefs enduring for centuries and sub-

---

endures for a very long time, even into the present. There are differing human time scales, but the paragraph hints at the possibility of natural or non-human time: a plague proceeds on its own time scale governed by the movement of a bacillus. There is another dimension of temporality here, indicated by the reference to Hurricane Katrina, which occurred in 2005. Note also that this book was published in 2023, immediately following the COVID-19 pandemic. There is a collapsing of time, or bridging of temporal locations, when the past enters the present in this explicit way. "The present is haunted by the past," as Jan Assmann says in *Moses the Egyptian: The Memory of Egypt in Western Monotheism* (Harvard University Press, 1997), 9. It may be also that the present is haunting the past that the book gives us. In reading the rest of Ermus's book, one will need to consider what the book does with the relationship between present and past that arises from this movement across time. Furthermore, the distinct temporalities interact with each other. There is more, but enough has been said to indicate that polychronicity is present here. Cindy Ermus, *The Great Plague Scare of 1720: Disaster and Diplomacy in the Eighteenth-Century Atlantic World* (Cambridge: Cambridge University Press, 2022), 1.
95 Natalie Zemon Davis, *Trickster Travels: A Sixteenth-Century Muslim Between Worlds* (New York: Hill and Wang, 2006), 4.
96 Davis, *Trickster Travels*, 21.

ject to change over longer and shorter time spans. Time locators are as frequent as spatial ones.

The identity of the man is time-dependent. In certain temporal zones he is al-Hasan al-Wazzan. In others he is Giovan Lioni Africano. In others he is Yuhanna al-Hasad. There are subsets of these: thus Giovan Lioni Africano changes with time and space.[97] His Christian name rendered in Arabic was Yuhanna al-Asad, and it becomes for Davis a temporal construct: "It suggests the entanglement of values, perspectives, and personae in his life in Italy in the next seven years."[98] The same applies to his writings. Thus al-Wazzan's best-known book, *The Description of Africa*, has multiple identities that vary with time. *The Description of Africa* that he finished in 1526 is not the same as *The Description of Africa* published in Venice in 1550.[99] There is yet another temporal location of *The Description*: it is located in the centuries-old tradition of geographies in Islamic culture.[100] The contents of *The Description* are located in temporal movement and time-shifting views among al-Wazzan's contemporaries. Commenting on his disdainful remarks about features of Black persons, Davis says: "here he is following old expressions of color prejudice found among Berbers and Arabs, though by the time he was writing those words a more appreciative view of Black appearance had long since emerged in the travel literature and elsewhere." Different interventions upon the text "broke the *Description* into fragments."[101] And as the book changes, so does the man: changes in his book "suggest what kind of man Europeans preferred him to be." Even in the silences that Davis is able to detect, al-Wazzan is a time-shifting being: "What kind of a person invites silence in his own societies and times?"[102]

Inferences about what "might" have happened to al-Wazzan are projections across time. The likely and possible conversations between curious scholars in Rome and their Muslim guest are full of questions about people and events in recent times, projected into al-Wazzan's present in Rome in the 1520s.[103] Davis's careful analogical reasoning uses temporal shifts or displacements to infer things about al-Wazzan, as for instance from Ibn Khaldun (1332–1406), and from known

---

[97] Davis, *Trickster Travels*, 4.
[98] Davis, *Trickster Travels*, 65.
[99] Davis, *Trickster Travels*, 95.
[100] Davis, *Trickster Travels*, 98–105.
[101] Davis, *Trickster Travels*, 5, 146.
[102] Davis, *Trickster Travels*, 13.
[103] Davis, *Trickster Travels*, 73.

activities or practices of other North Africans in previous times. A known marriage custom of the 1300s is carried forward and imputed to the early 1500s.[104]

There is even an imagined temporal consciousness attributed to the man himself: "his strategies of flying back and forth" give to al-Wazzan a consciousness of time and of the future. He manipulates and uses stories and images that were "circulating in variant forms" over time. He imagines unknown and anonymous future readers of his *Description*, should the book eventually be rendered in print.[105]

In the Epilogue Davis proposes a temporal zone that did not exist. "If only François Rabelais had got to Italy a decade earlier . . . ."[106] This is counterfactual history, imagining events that did not happen or events that occurred in time zones other than their known ones. Finally, the history presented here is of another time – the present, as of the 1990s and early 2000s, and the future from that moment. "In the mid-1990s the relation between European and non-European populations was at the centre of things, and polar ways of thinking were being challenged." In this temporal context, "It seemed a fine moment to return to Jean Léon l'Africain."[107] *Trickster Travels* is a momentous historical work: it is about a multitude of fine and transient moments.

We historians are the keepers and recorders of time. We place our subjects in their time, which are also our times, because we control their movements in and through times. The temporality in historical thinking is indeed plural – linear, circular, recurrent, chronometric, calendrical, kairotic, accelerating, frozen, deep, geological, planetary, Dreamt, and many more. These times may occur simultaneously and also antithetically.[108] We historians are time travelers, in a specific sense: we place times from our discovered pasts into our present. Those meetings of times are our histories.

---

104 Davis, *Trickster Travels*, 39.
105 Davis, *Trickster Travels*, 111, 124.
106 Davis, *Trickster Travels*, 271.
107 Davis, *Trickster Travels*, 10–11.
108 Simon and Tamm quote Chris Lorenz in making the case for plural temporalities in Simon and Tamm, *The Fabric*, 54–5.

5 Argumentation

The past is contained in song and dance. It is present in an ancient language that I cannot understand. Of the several hundred people gathered together in this place, I know only two. I have left my place in the world, or so it seems. Where am I? I am in a longhouse of the Kwakiutl nation, a guest and witness at a modern potlatch. I am here to share a feast and to witness sacred ceremonies, transfers of rights, commemorations of the dead, a wedding, the giving of gifts, and much more. I am stunned by an awesome display of cultural and material riches. I am honored to be here, but also conscious of being an outsider.

I am wrong to suggest that I have left my place in the world. My hosts would not say so. I have a place here, as a witness, as a settler, as an invited guest on their land. I am a witness to the survival of a people and a culture. I am made aware that survival embraces change: the modern potlatch is not the same as the pre-contact potlatch. Survival requires change, and survival happens despite the massive disruptions of disease, death, and settler land grabs. As a witness and guest, I am reminded that my way of knowing is contained within a recent European heritage of thought and learning.

In my way of knowing and seeing, there is much that lies beyond my understanding. I am a distant descendant of the European Enlightenment, which bestows upon us its faith in reason and its categories of nature and culture. This heritage has the power to silence, to delegitimize, to relegate other ways of knowing to myth, folklore, or superstition. This heritage leaves me unprepared for many questions. Among them, for instance, is the question: "do glaciers listen?" Such is the title of a brilliant study of knowledge and colonial encounters by the Canadian anthropologist and historian, Julie Cruikshank. From her, I learn that my way of knowing is not a prison. It is possible for Indigenous knowledge and Western science to speak across boundaries that are "permeable," and to speak in "entangled narratives." This speaking does not mean that "different cultural perspectives are bridgeable by concepts in English language." It means that we can listen to the dialog, and we can witness, as we "listen for different stories."[109]

---

[109] Julie Cruikshank, *Do Glaciers Listen? Local Knowledge, Colonial Encounters, and Social Imagination* (Vancouver: University of British Columbia Press, 2005), 220, 256, 259. In my view, Cruikshank's work is one outstanding example of an emphasis on "articulations." "We might think, then, of tracing multiple articulations of settler colonialisms and Indigeneities, across time and space, in transformative relations with one another." Ben Silverstein, "Theoretical Frontiers," in Ann McGrath and Lynette Russell, eds., *The Routledge Companion to Global Indigenous History* (London: Routledge, 2022), 69.

https://doi.org/10.1515/9783111563800-005

I am learning about the scope and the limits of my situated understanding. I have inherited a historical consciousness. My culture gives me a deep awareness of change, disruption, and discontinuity, and together with these, a yearning for stability and permanence. I call upon the tools available to me, and prominent among these are my capacity to reason, to think in time, and to think with values. My situated understanding also tells me that none of these tools is universal; all are local and contingent, however powerful I wish them to be. And I have learned that my understanding is a recent import among settlers in an ancient land.

From my untutored historical consciousness emerged a search for historical explanation, or historical argument. But what is argument? It may mean debate or dispute, or one side in a disagreement. I think of argument in a different sense: it is two or more statements leading to a conclusion or a new meaning, and it is intended to persuade. An argument may be tentative and provisional, but it seeks to give intellectual resolution, to solve a problem, to make whole things that have been incomplete.

I did not realize until recently that there is an entire field of scholarly inquiry called argumentation theory. Although interdisciplinary, the field has a long history in philosophy going back to Plato's dialectics. Argumentation theory is about the complex activity of speech or communication in which reasoning is used to support claims or defend positions. One might think that the field has some relevance to history and historical thinking. Apparently not. Douglas Walton and other specialists tell us that argumentation theory straddles philosophy, communication studies, linguistics, psychology, and artificial intelligence. Argumentation is important for "everyday life, law, science, politics, and business."[110] History is not mentioned.

I find the omission of history surprising. I am also surprised at how rare the mention of argumentation is in the era of postmodernism and the linguistic turn. Is there not a connection between argument, as defined here, and language or discourse? The absence of connection probably reflects the fact that argumentation theory emerged within philosophical traditions very different from those that spawned postmodernism.[111] Argumentation theory did not wholly depart

---

110 Douglas Walton, *Methods of Argumentation* (New York: Cambridge University Press, 2013), 1. See also Catarina Duthil Novaes, "Argument and Argumentation," *Stanford Encyclopedia of Philosophy* (updated 2021); Novaes offers similar lists but also omits history.
111 A useful history of the subject from classical times is "The History of Schemes," Chapter 8 in Douglas Walton, Christopher Reed, and Fabrizio Macagno, *Argumentation Schemes* (Cambridge: Cambridge University Press, 2008), 275–307. See also Frans H. Van Eemeren, R. Grootendorst, R.H. Johnson, C. Plantin, and C.A. Willard, *Fundamentals of Argumentation Theory: A Handbook of Historical Backgrounds and Contemporary Developments* (New York: Routledge, 1996).

from positivism. It also related directly to logic, and especially something called informal logic (non-formal rules of reasoning in ordinary language). Logic entails an acceptance of empiricism, and it is often associated with positivism, as "logical positivism" indicates.

These are deep waters indeed, and I venture no further than to pose a question: is there something in argumentation theory that might help in understanding what historians are doing when they do history? The question is worth asking, even if a fully developed answer must be left to younger and better minds. There are clear risks here. Argumentation theory tends to become highly abstract and even taxonomical. An argument is "like an organism," says the English philosopher Stephen Toulmin (1922–2009); it has a gross "anatomical structure" as well as a finer "physiological one."[112] Argumentation theory risks giving priority to form over content. It is possible to map or diagram the anatomical structure of an argument while saying nothing about the value or significance of the argument and each element within it. We may apply the same caveat to logic. Logic is about the rules and forms of reasoning; logical reasoning is independent of the significance of the statements or truth claims in that reasoning. An argument may comply with basic rules of logic at the same time as its ethical or political truth is rejected.

So why bother with argumentation theory at all? And why bother with logic? A simple answer to the latter question is: there is more than one test of value in historical thinking. Informal logic is one such test. There are other criteria of value; this fact in no way makes logic irrelevant. On the contrary, fallacious reasoning fails to persuade, however laudable the values informing that reasoning. History does have a logic of reasoning, derived and adapted from the wider domains of logic in other disciplines. Mark Bevir says: "The logic of an academic discipline consists of an analysis of the forms of reasoning appropriate to it."[113] More than half a century ago, David Hackett Fischer gave us an invaluable pioneering study of that logic in his *Historians' Fallacies* (1970).[114] Fischer's subtitle was "Toward a Logic of Historical Thought." It is one of the great mysteries of historiography in my life-time that the challenge implied in that subtitle was never extensively met, despite a few valuable attempts. Only if history is limited to a type of poetics is logic irrelevant to our thinking and reasoning.

---

112 Stephen E. Toulmin, *The Uses of Argument* [1958] (Cambridge: Cambridge University Press, 2003), 87.
113 Mark Bevir, *The Logic of the History of Ideas* (Cambridge: Cambridge University Press, 1999), 7.
114 David Hackett Fischer, *Historians' Fallacies: Toward a Logic of Historical Thought* (New York: Harper and Row, 1970).

What about argumentation theory?[115] An answer can begin with what Stephen Toulmin said in his seminal work long ago: the "patterns of argument" in one field are different from those in another, even if certain general rules of logic are shared. Standards of validation and even applied logic are intra-disciplinary processes, he said: they are different in optics than they are in jurisprudence, and so they must be different in history. It follows that the form of reasoning in an argument cannot be separated from the content of the argument. Uncover the anatomy of argumentation in history, and we come closer to historical thinking.[116] Argumentation theory provides models or templates against which the observable patterns of reasoning in history may be clarified.

Toulmin's oft-cited model has six components, including a claim or conclusion.[117]

Backing: you know that your neighbour has two large German shepherds.

Warrant: dogs are animals that bark.

Grounds: you hear barking in the distance.

Qualifier: so it is probable that . . .

Claim: there are dogs somewhere nearby.

Rebuttal (or reservation): unless there are wolves or coyotes nearby.

---

[115] An introduction to argumentation in history is offered by P. David Pearson, Vicki Griffo and Catherine Anne Miller, "Argumentation Across the Disciplines" (May 2018). Their focus is on the teaching of History: https://www.researchgate.net/publication/324857504_Argumentation_Across_the_Disciplines. Jouni-Matti Kuukkanen introduces argumentation and reasoning in his *Postnarrativist Philosophy of Historiography* (New York: Palgrave Macmillan, 205). He says that "the transition from narrativism means regarding historiography as a type of *rational* practice and not as a kind of narrative storytelling" [his italics]. "Historiography attempts to produce *synthesizing* or *colligatory* views on the past" (198). In my view, his book leaves much to be said about the form or content of such reasoning practices. For an argument about "narrative as a rational practice," see Mariana Imaz-Sheinbaum, "Principles of Narrative Reason," *History and Theory*, 60, 2 (June 2021), 249–70.
[116] Stephen E. Toulmin, *The Uses of Argument*, 235–6.
[117] The schema is adapted from Toulmin, *The Uses of Argument*, 87–102. My summary is also indebted to the summary at the Purdue University Online Writing Lab: https://owl.purdue.edu/owl/general_writing/academic_writing/historical_perspectives_on_argumentation/toulmin_argument.html (accessed 9 July 2024).

Toulmin's model was merely the beginning. Elaborations and other field-specific models have appeared ever since. There are superficial similarities to historical reasoning. There is a claim – a statement or conclusion that follows from preceding elements, including, crucially, the evidential grounds behind the claim, as well as the assumption (warrant) that links the grounds to the claim. In both the qualifier and rebuttal, there lies an implied or explicit acknowledgment of the provisional nature of the claim. So far, the historian may be on familiar ground.

But this schema does not take us very far on its own. The relationships among the elements remain unspecified. The reasoning that links "warrant" to the elements that follow is unstated: is it inductive, deductive, or something else? The example is simplified for illustrative purposes, and so it is over-simplified. Replace "dogs nearby" with a historical claim of even modest complexity, and the schema appears merely question-begging.

How to proceed? One could refine and elaborate the schema endlessly, as argumentation theorists have done (in 1996, Walton proposed 25 argumentation schemes for presumptive reasoning) and try to adapt it to history.[118] I propose to move beyond schematic representation and instead try to discern the forms and procedures of reasoning in an actual work of history. In doing so, I am not pretending to peer into the mind of a historian. This is not an exercise in psychology. Rather, the point is to display, in a very tentative way, the reasoning that appears in a text. There is an obvious limit to such an exercise: it will not be possible to discover patterns or modes of reasoning that are applicable to all works of history. Any observations can only be suggestive.

Such an effort to discover the reasoning in a specific work is not unprecedented, of course. Allan Megill, for instance, offers a valuable essay on abductive reasoning in writings about Thomas Jefferson.[119] More recently, the French historian Ivan Jablonka examines history as a way of reasoning and discusses specific "approaches to veridiction" in historical reasoning (I return to Jablonka in Chapter 12).[120] My approach here is somewhat different, and again I proceed by attempting to demonstrate historical reasoning in specific examples.

But what work should I choose, and by what criteria? One cannot propose a criterion of representativeness – that would be impossible. I will propose a work that is recent and deals with questions that most historians would agree to be cur-

---

118 Douglas Walton, *Argumentation Schemes for Presumptive Reasoning* (New York: Routledge, 1996), 46–110.
119 Allan Megill, *Historical Knowledge Historical Error: A Contemporary Guide to Practice* (Chicago: University of Chicago Press, 2007), 125–50.
120 Ivan Jablonka, "Approaches to Veridiction," Chapter 7 in *History Is a Contemporary Literature*, 132–54.

rent and even urgent. Quality is a criterion: I will choose a book that has won awards and has earned high praise for its quality. And to avoid being deflected by any interpretative commitments of my own, I choose a work distant from my own research interests.

In 2020, the American historian Thavolia Glymph published *The Women's Fight: The Civil War's Battles for Home, Freedom, and Nation*. The first chapter of the book is titled "Home and War."[121] Here are the first two paragraphs of that chapter.

> "It seems strange that we should be in the midst of a revolution so quiet, and plentiful and comfortable does it seem up here," Margaret Ann Meta Morris Grimball wrote in her diary in early December 1860. "Every thing [sic] goes on as usual, the planting, the negroes, all just the same, and a great Empire tumbling to pieces about us, and a great pressure in the money market in all parts of the country, we strange to say, were never so easy, and I hope thankful."[1] By the following December, Grimball's world had changed dramatically. "We are on the Frontier," she wrote in December 1861, invoking the colonial settler language of a world bereft of civilization. She soon faced "a great calamity" when eighty-four of her family's slaves left "all together" for Edisto Island in the Union-occupied lowcountry.[2] From the start of the war to the end, enslaved people resisted efforts to force them to help build a slave-owning nation-state, and by March 1862 the resistance had come to Grimball's home. Her life was no longer "so easy." Enslaved women and men, supported unwittingly by the arrival of U.S. military forces, staked their claim to freedom on the destruction of the foundation of her claim. As a refugee, she also faced the hostility of poor white women. The language in which Grimball voiced her anguish betrayed her familiarity with violence against one's personhood, family, dignity, humanity, and home, the kinds of violence directed at enslaved and poor white people and their homes. Her anguish and the words in which she voiced it became a familiar refrain in the letters and stories of slaveholding women as the war bore down on them and their homes.
>
> The Civil War set women across the South in flight. The flight of lowcountry slaveholding women and their lives as refugees at the heart of this chapter was unique in many ways, particularly in its timing, the manner of its initial presentation, and to some extent, the particular nature of the conflict it generated with nonslaveholding women. The increasingly common experience of white women on the run and homeless challenged proslavery ideology. As their numbers grew, the "claims of home and country, wife and children" that had supported Southerners' call to war succumbed to this reality. By the end of the war, enough "terror-stricken" white women and children had been forced into the streets and were "wander[ing] aimlessly from place to place" to embarrass the battle cry that called men to die for home but sent them to fight and die for slavery, as if the two things everywhere meant the same thing. The embarrassment was visible in the sight of white men clinging "to the tops of the coaches as they

---

121 Thavolia Glymph, *The Women's Fight: The Civil War's Battles for Home, Freedom, and Nation* (Chapel Hill: University of North Carolina Press, 2020) 19, 20. Among the many awards for this book were the Darlene Clark Hine Award of the Organization of American Historians and the Albert J. Beveridge Award of the American Historical Association.

pulled out" of railroad stations in the final days as Union forces closed in. In the cars below, the women they had gone to war to protect mingled indiscriminately with cows and baggage.³ In such scenes, slaveholding ideology and the slaveholders' revolution lay among the ruins. All around the departing women and men were strewn the remnants of the institution of slavery that had made a special place for white women no less than for white men. In the coming years, the war that arrived in South Carolina slaveholding country in 1861 spread everywhere that the U.S. army placed its flag, as well as far beyond the areas of contact. In war, "the very foundation of the classic Southern household – a household resting on slave labor – would crumble."⁴

The first thing to note is something so obvious it might be missed: this is not the opening of a narrative. It is, rather, the opening of an argument. As Carol Faulkner states in her review of the book: "At the moment when many historians prioritize narrative, Glymph's book is a sustained argument."[122] Yes, it is possible to detect short narratives within the book. It might even be possible to re-configure the sustained argument into a narrative and to present it in that form. But that would mean throwing out the form of reasoning that Glymph has chosen. At the same time, temporality is in the foreground: the sustained argument is a temporal argument. Note the temporal signals: "By the following December," "From the start of the war to the end," "as the war bore down on them," and others. The active verbs also underline temporality: they indicate action occurring in time. The nature of the temporal logic remains to be discerned. But that logic is not contained within a narrative in which one action or condition follows from preceding ones. Temporality does not require narrative.

The second observation is that there is more than one claim or conclusion. Indeed, the second paragraph contains a series of claims. Three stand out. First, the Civil War set women across the South into flight. Second, the experience of white women in flight and homelessness challenged proslavery ideology (and to this claim are attached quantitative claims). Third, the foundation of the classic Southern household would crumble (and presumably did crumble). If there are grounds, warrants, and backing behind these claims, they are not fully stated. Herein lies an important point about historical argumentation: it does not proceed in a neat and formulaic order of the kind that we can see in scientific argumentation. The claims, as here, may precede the justification and may only hint at the logic connecting justification and claim.

My next observation is that there is no interrogative sentence in these two paragraphs. Every sentence is declarative, and each exhibits a declarative confidence. This text is not ordered around a question or questions followed by an-

---

[122] Carol Faulkner, "The Women's Fight," *Journal of Interdisciplinary History*, 51, 3 (Winter 2021), 486.

swers. It could be, of course, that the question is implied. The question could be: why (or how) did the foundation of the Southern household crumble during the Civil War? And the author might be assuming that readers will easily see the implied question. Long ago, R.G. Collingwood stated that every explanation is an answer to a logically prior question: "Every statement that anybody ever makes is made in answer to a question."[123] But surely, in the example before us, it would be presumptuous and misleading to attribute an implied question. We are not in the business of revising Glymph's text. Why does the text not take a question-and-answer form (there is a word for the question-and-answer form: erotetic)? Presumably because the argument and the logic are not erotetic and some other logic is at work. For instance, if the text were to begin with a "why" question, or even a "how" question, the reasoning would entail some form of causal logic. "Why" implies an "effect" or "consequence" to be "explained" by reference to specific necessary and sufficient conditions. The reasoning in the argument before us does not go down that path. It does not go down any path demanded by erotetic logic.

Declarative confidence, however, does not mean certainty. The claims presented here are provisional, not final and definitive. A few qualifiers gesture toward provisionality: "in many ways" but not all ways; "to some extent." But the reasoning here, and in the text that follows, is *probabilistic* in a particular way. In order to understand why this is so, we need to back up a step and ask another question: does the reasoning in this text involve deductive logic?

Deductive logic, simply defined, refers to a process of reasoning in which two or more statements (premises) lead to a conclusion. If the premises are valid, then the conclusion follows *necessarily* (as in the syllogism: All men are mortal/ Socrates is a man/Therefore Socrates is mortal). This reasoning allows certainty (by contrast, inductive reasoning allows only probable or possible conclusions). If I try hard, I can reduce Glymph's opening statements to a deductive syllogism:

- The classic Southern household depended for its survival on the presence of women.
- During the Civil War, large numbers of women in Southern households were displaced.
- The foundations of the classic Southern household crumbled.

But this logic does not work, and it is not the logic in the text. The conclusion does not follow from the two premises. It follows from ancillary conditions to the premises: the unique characteristics of specific women ("lowcountry slaveholding

---

[123] R.G. Collingwood, *An Essay on Metaphysics* (Oxford: Clarendon Press, 2002 [first published 1940]), 23.

women"); the particular nature of the conflict arising between slaveholding and nonslaveholding women; the nature of the experience of women on the run; and other conditions specified later in the book. An argument depending on such multiple conditions cannot be reduced to syllogistic logic. To put it another way: syllogistic logic allows a formal validity that historical logic does not.

There is a logic of probability in historical reasoning. We take this for granted, don't we? We seek only probable or likely truth, not absolute truth. But is that all there is to it? It is actually quite difficult to define what probability means, and even more difficult to estimate the probability that an outcome will occur. A well-known procedure is Bayesian probability, named after an English philosopher named Thomas Bayes (1701–1761). Bayesian logic means to estimate the probability that an outcome will occur, and to estimate the change in probability as more evidence becomes available. In a very simple way, you might be using this kind of reasoning when you try to estimate the chances that your favorite sports team will win its next game. There is a connection to historical thinking: Bayesian reasoning means the probability that a hypothesis is acceptable given the relevance and quantity of available evidence. In a book published in 2004, the philosopher Aviezer Tucker argued that a form of Bayesian reasoning "is the best explanation for the actual practice of historians."[124] His argument raised in a new way the entire question as to whether history can be considered a science.

Whether or not we accept Tucker's argument, I suggest that there is a difference between probability in history and probability in mathematics or science. Probability in the latter is predictive and prospective. Thus, behind weather forecasts is the science of meteorology, and the forecast is stated in terms of probability: there is an eighty percent chance of rain in this time period. Probability in history is not predictive or prognostic in this way. It is retrospective probability: given this specific outcome, it is probable that some condition or conditions were contributory. In Glymph's text, there is an outcome: the foundation of the classic Southern household crumbled. The statements that precede the last sentence of the second paragraph are conditions to that outcome, and they are *probable* conditions. It is highly probable that the ending of slavery was a condition directly related to this outcome. Furthermore, there is a strong probability that a related condition was "the increasingly common experience of white women on the run and homeless." The probabilistic reasoning is not stated explicitly, but it is present, for instance, in the conditional verbs used in the text. Probability is basic to

---

[124] Aviezer Tucker, *Our Knowledge of the Past: A Philosophy of Historiography* (Cambridge: Cambridge University Press, 2004), 134.

historical thinking: where there is no certainty, there is probability, as truth claims are always provisional and subject to revision.

There are other differences between probability in science and probability in history. In history, the spaces for error are different. Thus, in history retrospective probability cannot be stated as a percentage. At the same time, the degree of permissibility for error is low. Thus, if the weather forecast states an 80% probability of precipitation, and there is no precipitation, the "mistake" is forgiven. Only if such a "mistake" occurs in several repetitions is the probability estimate subject to questioning and possible revision. Not so in history: the retrospective probability is held to be very high; the truth claim is provisional but held to be beyond any easy or easily perceptible challenge. It has a high level of confidence. If we choose to see a relationship between conditions and conclusion in Glymph's text – and this is certainly one way of reading the text – the relationship is certainly probabilistic. The rest of her chapter will provide an edifice of support, linking conditions and claims, in order to raise the confidence levels of probabilistic truth claims.[125]

Does this mean that the history we are looking at involves inductive logic? Inductive reasoning is reasoning from the particular to the general; in an inductive argument, it is claimed that the premises provide support for the probable truth of the conclusion. This sounds like historical reasoning: the work of history presents a series of particulars, cited as evidence, and the particulars serve as premises leading to a plausible conclusions. If I try to discern this form of logic in *The Women's Fight*, however, I encounter serious problems. First, I have to work very hard to identify and isolate premises and conclusion. I see major conclusions to chapter one stated on page 50 ("In the end, the war transformed the homes of all Southerners . . . ."). But what of the last two sentences of the chapter (page 54)? "Many lowcountry slaveholding women and their families would never return from the journeys of exile begun in 1861. Others returned, broken financially and in spirit, to homes no longer secured by the labor of slaves and unrecognizable in other ways." I take these sentences to be conclusions as well, but within a

---

[125] It might be objected that there is an important exception to this description of probability in History. In the statistical modeling or testing of a hypothesis, there is a form of probability that is predictive. Thus, in a model of fertility decline, in which the dependent variable is the number of births, one may enter a number of independent variables to observe (predict) an estimated strength of the relationship between independent variables and the number of births. The observed result is subject to a significance test: a p value, or probability value, says how likely the observed result could have occurred under the null hypothesis of no relationship among the variables in the model. When applied to data from the past, however, this probability is still retrospective: the historian is looking backward from an array of outcomes (births) toward the conditions that are provisionally associated with those outcomes. Retrospective probability remains intact.

specific perspective – the gaze of lowcountry slaveholding women. Conclusions exist here, but they are deeply embedded in a vast pointillist collage of voices and actions and experiences. An assembly of micro-level instances becomes a holistic image in the mind of the reader. The conclusions do not follow from premises. Rather, evidence and conclusions are seamlessly interwoven in a vast canvas of intersecting images.

As the psychologist Ivana Markova points out, inductive thinking "treats fragments or elements of phenomena as units that, themselves, are considered to be stable variables."[126] In historical thinking, by contrast, units of action or thought in the past are relational and embedded; they cannot be extracted from the larger canvas or context in which they exist, to be treated as variables or premises. Markova's example is Le Roy Ladurie's *Peasants of Languedoc* (1974), but we can apply her observation to Glymph's *Women's Fight*.[127] Inductive reasoning draws conclusions from aggregations of data treated as unique or distinct phenomena; in historical reasoning, by contrast, past phenomena may have a distinctness but they are also interdependent and embedded, parts of wholes.

A related problem is that of causation. Where we see cause-and-effect argument and causal logic in some form, then we would have to ask if inductive reasoning was present. But is there a logic of causation in *The Women's Fight*? Perhaps there is an outcome or effect: the crumbling of the foundation of the southern country home. The "causes" would be a long series of inter-acting conditions presented as prior or concurrent conditions and serving as premises to the conclusion about cause. But this is simply not happening in the text. When "cause" appears, it is used in a different sense, as in "the Southern cause."

Causation has a long history. In its many forms it made sense when considering much of the history written in the twentieth century. If one constructed the past as consisting of events or actions at micro or macro scales, either a singular action at the micro end or a grand event at the other (the French Revolution, the First World War), it made sense to define necessary and sufficient conditions, to weigh these conditions, and to label them as causes (or perhaps "origins"). The problem of causation took on a new life in reactions to, and away from, positivism. In the 1940s, the German philosopher Carl Hempel provoked on-going debates with his "covering law" model, which held that to explain any event by reference to other events required assuming a general law or proposition to connect

---

[126] Ivana Markova, "Method and Explanation in History and in Social Representations," *Integrative Psychological and Behavioral Science*, 46 (2012), 463.
[127] Emmanuel Le Roy Ladurie, *The Peasants of Languedoc*, trans. John Day (Urbana: University of Illinois Press, 1974).

initial conditions to an outcome.[128] His famous example was that of the cracked radiator in a car during a cold night. The initial conditions were a radiator of iron that was filled with water, a lid screwed on tight, and a temperature falling to 25 degrees Fahrenheit. The causal chain required a law about the expansion of water as it turns to ice. The "covering law" idea was intellectual dynamite. It set off a long debate that was still continuing in the 1990s. Insofar as the discipline of history was involved, the debate still assumed that history was about events and causation.[129]

I recall introducing graduate students in the early 2000s to the problem of causation. Their reactions ranged from curious interest to puzzled indifference. I was introducing them, at best, to challenging thought experiments. But these experiments had no clear relevance either to the other histories that they were reading or to their own thinking and writing. Today, in the third decade of the twenty-first century, the old debates over causation seem rather archaic, important as they were at the time. Their connection to most of the histories that we read today is unclear at best. Causation is not going away, of course; but it is evolving, its older forms losing prominence, as our ways of understanding change evolve.[130]

So far, we have encountered modes of reasoning that do not appear to be prominent in the historical work I have chosen, the book by Thavolia Glymph. So, what modes of reasoning can be discerned?

---

[128] Carl G. Hempel, "The Function of General Laws in History," *The Journal of Philosophy*, 39, 2 (January 1942), 35–48. A retrospective assessment is Fons Dewulf, "Revisiting Hempel's 1942 Contribution to the Philosophy of History," *Journal of the History of Ideas*, 79, 3 (July 2018), 385–406.

[129] At times in the debate, necessary and sufficient conditions were superseded by such concepts as colligation. An example is offered by Clayton Roberts, *The Logic of Historical Explanation* (University Park, PA: University of Pennsylvania Press, 1996). Roberts attempts to find some space for covering laws.

[130] "AHR Conversation: Explaining Historical Change; or, The Lost History of Causes," *American Historical Review*, 120, 4 (October 2015), 1369–1423.

6 Parts and Wholes

Who am I? The question is about my identity as an individual. Well, for a start, I am a university professor, a member of an institution dedicated to teaching and research, a small cog in a big wheel. Even when I was the "Chair" or administrative leader of my department, I was a very small cog in a wheel. Certainly, I did not have much power or influence. I organized things, moved paper or emails around, and tried to do what most of my colleagues wanted me to do.

But the answer depends very much on which part of my identity is chosen. I have many other identities: elderly white guy, father, spouse, golfer, member of a choir. In each of these identities, I am a cog in a different wheel. To put it another way, I am a part of many different wholes. Aren't we all?

So, what does this have to do with history?

I have often read that history is an idiographic discipline. That is, history deals with individuals and instances, and we find value in exploring the singular. By contrast, the natural and social sciences, which are nomothetic, deal with generalities or general laws. The distinction originates with the German philosopher Wilhelm Windelband (1848–1915); he argued that the idiographic disciplines sought to arrive at singular assertions that represent unique objects and individual beings. I struggle to make sense of the distinction between idiographic and nomothetic (can you make sense of it?).[131] Let us accept that history is not about a search for general laws. Nevertheless, the notion that history is about individuals or unique objects risks missing the obvious, that there is no such thing as an individual existing apart from the groups or collectivities in which they live. History is not about fictional Robinson Crusoes. It is always about people understood in their relations with others and within the contexts of their being.

Consider those writings of Natalie Zemon Davis that present individual persons from the past and put them in the foreground. In her *Trickster Travels*, the identity of Leo Africanus resides in his connections with others in space and time, in the liminal cultural spaces through which he moved and lived. Yes, Davis is

---

131 Frank Ankersmit says: "there is a kernel of truth in the distinction that cannot be denied." Nomothetic refers to an approach in which general principles or categories are adduced from a large number of individual cases. Idiographic refers to the identification of a unique historical phenomenon such as the Renaissance, which is a colligatory concept. Frank Ankersmit, "Being Realistic about Anti-Realism," *Journal of the Philosophy of History*, 18, 2 (June 2024), 140.

exploring an individual case. But we cannot draw a hard distinction here between individual and general; that would miss the core of Davis's history.[132]

What, then, are we to make of the historian's ubiquitous presentation of individual persons, small events, and seemingly unique actions? They cannot be *sui generis* offerings. They cannot appear in a historical work merely as "interesting in themselves." Are they, therefore, traces of the past to be treated as meaningless or inconsequential until the point at which the historian constructs them as evidence in support of a conclusion? Or are they instances or instantiations of larger events or larger conceptual entities? There is a distinction here between evidence and instantiation. In the former, evidence has an ontological status as an entity prior to conclusion; items of evidence, separately and together, exist in order to confirm a conclusive statement that follows. With instantiation, an event or action is a specific object within a larger conceptual whole; it is an instance of that whole. There are different reasoning processes in each of these cases. So what is the reasoning process in Glymph's argument?

Consider a moment at the beginning of the third chapter of *The Women's Fight*, on the subject of "Enslaved Women."

> When she [Caddie, a Mississippi slave] heard that Lee had surrendered, she "threw down her hoe, she marched herself up to the big house, then she looked around and found the mistress. She went over to the mistress, she flipped up her dress and told the white woman to do something. She said it mean and ugly. This is what she said: 'Kiss my ass.'"[133]

This anecdote follows immediately after a sentence that clearly refers to a larger condition: "the part enslaved women play in the destruction of slavery" and "the building and consolidation of the antislavery ground on which they stood." We may read the specific event – Caddie's action – as an instantiation of the larger condition. More precisely, we might read the action as a *part* of a larger *whole*, that whole being the roles enslaved women played in the building and consolidation of antislavery ground. Just as the hand is part of the body, Caddie's action is part of a specific whole and is to be understood as such. The close juxtaposition of micro-historical action and generalized condition invites this observation. But do we require close juxtaposition for the point to apply? What of the small events and actions and thoughts that follow through this chapter? Surely, they too can be seen as parts of the larger whole that the text is presenting to the reader.

---

[132] Natalie Zemon Davis, *Trickster Travels: A Sixteenth-Century Muslim Between Worlds* (New York: Farrar, Strauss and Giroux, 2006).
[133] Glymph, *Women's Fight*, 88.

Is historical reasoning about parts and wholes, the relationship of parts to wholes, wholes to parts, and parts to parts? If so, we have entered very deep waters, going back to Aristotle and his discussions of parts and wholes, and also to the Greek historian Polybius.[134] Today, the subject is called mereology – the theory of parthood relations. Mereology is a subject within logic, mathematics, and philosophy, and it has applications in other disciplines. I have yet to discover an investigation of history for its mereological methods or content. I am in no position to undertake a thorough investigation. I suggest, however, that historical thinking does involve parts and wholes.

First, can we say that in historical argumentation there is ever a "whole," in any sense? A whole is a thing that is complete in itself. In historical reasoning, as in visual art, it is a composition, a "putting together" of elements in order to form a completed whole. In Glymph's book, we may see each chapter as a whole having many parts, and the book as a completed composition of parts. The chapters are wholes but also parts in the larger, completed whole.

What, then, are the parts, and what is the process by which they are composed into a whole? Can we discern a logic, or if not that, a reasoning process? Let us take Chapter 4 of Glymph's book as our template. This is the only chapter the title of which contains a question: "Am I a Soldier of the Cross?" There is a subtitle: "Northern Women's Fight and the Legacy of Slavery." The title indicates the frame or boundaries within which parts will be selected: parts will relate to northern women, war ("fight"), slavery, and religion ("the Cross"). There are two more framing elements, stated explicitly in the Abstract to the chapter and the opening paragraphs: race, closely connected to slavery, of course; and class, in particular the distinction between elite and propertied women on the one hand, and poor or working-class women on the other.[135] The historian has selected these elements to go into the six-sided frame, but where have they come from? The Introduction to the book has already answered the question: they come from the author's assessments and analyses of the war written during and after the

---

134 Christian Pfeiffer, "Aristotle and the Thesis of Mereological Potentialism," *Philosophical Inquiry*, 42, 3–4 (2018), 28–66. The Greek historian Polybius (c.200-118 BCE) wrote about wholes and parts in history-writing. "For while it may be possible to get an impression of the whole from a part, it is impossible to gain knowledge and precise understanding . . . . [I]T is only by connecting and comparing all the parts with one another, by seeing their similarities and differences – it is only such an overview that puts one in a position to derive benefit and pleasure from history." Polybius, *The Histories*, 2 vols., trans. E.S. Shuckburgh, introduction by F.W. Walbank (Bloomington, IN: Indiana University Press, 1962), 1.5; cited in M. Hughes-Warrington, *Big and Little Histories*, 31.
135 Glymph, *Women's Fight*, 127–8.

war, and also from the "new body of scholarship" about the war and about women that has appeared in the previous thirty years.

The composition of a whole occurs within this six-sided frame. Every part to be included must take two or more of the stated elements in the frame and connect them. This "putting together" of two or more parts is an act of colligation. In grammar and linguistics, colligation refers to a grouping or linking of words given the way they operate in a syntactical structure. Philosophers of history have used the term to refer to a making of connections, a "going together [of parts] to constitute a single process, a whole of which they are all parts and in which they belong together in a specially intimate way."[136] During the last decades of the twentieth century, the term was often applied to narrative history and to causal explanation. Colligation was about "sequential explanation," or narrative explanation, or event-oriented cause and effect.[137] If we free colligation from such limits, the concept may be applied to history that is not merely about sequences or eventful causation.

Glymph's Chapter 4 begins by colligating two elements: northern women and slavery. A few northern women are observing a slave auction, and they react. Then, very quickly, the two-sided connection becomes three-sided as race enters: these are *white* women observing slaves. The next anecdotes connect three elements to a fourth: slavery is "sin" and women become "soldiers of the cross." Thus, the seeing of slavery by white northern women is colligated with religion. By the third page of the chapter, parts or instances are colligations among all six points of the frame, and the intersection of parts has become an immensely complex matrix. For all the complexity, the reader is able to discern meaning as the process unfolds and as parts conjoin and become an emergent whole. Women react emotionally and passionately to rhetorical portraits of slave suffering and to messianic calls to redemption; they hear about Toussaint L'Ouverture, the former slave who led the Haitian revolution, and some of the women seek "a usable revolution." And the actions of women that follow now make sense, historically:

---

[136] W.H. Walsh, *An Introduction to the Philosophy of History* (New York: Hutcheson University Library, 1958), 23; cited in Clayton Roberts, *The Logic of Historical Explanation* (University Park PA: University of Pennsylvania Press, 1996), 17. Aziever Tucker says: "Colligation is the explanation of known particular historical events by relating and synthesizing them into a single entity as parts into a directing whole that is greater than the sum of its parts." Tucker, *Our Knowledge of the Past*, 137.

[137] Clayton Roberts associates colligation with narrative explanation as used by authors as diverse as Louis Mink, William Dray and Arthur Danto: Roberts, *Logic of Historical Explanation*, 17.

we see them, and understand them, as they organize, create sewing circles, shelter fugitive slaves, and manufacture things in their homes.[138]

The colligation of parts does not bring forth a harmonious or homogeneous whole. Colligation of parts allows for juxtaposition of opposites and the derivation of meaning from objects in conflict. There can be a conjoining of opposites in historical composition, as there can be in visual arts. For instance, northern white women embrace the "holy flag" and the Union cause. But as these parts are connected to slavery, we observe disagreement and dissonance: some justify the war as leading to emancipation, while others reject emancipation as a war aim (and religion is still present in the matrix: "you cannot hurry God," one part says). Within an emergent whole, parts may collide. The colligation also permits irony and contradiction. Keep selecting parts where women, race, class and war are colligated, and eventually you arrive at a paradox. Northern "traffic" in slavery, the reaping of economic benefit from slavery, helps to fund the wartime work of pro-Union women. It is the act of colligation itself that makes the paradox visible.

We see women sending cash, food, clothing, medical supplies, and other goods to soldiers' hospitals and army camps, often through the U.S. Sanitary Commission (USSC). The anecdotal details are not idiographic offerings; they are not random or adventitious; they are parts of an expanding whole. In the section on the USSC and relief, class has come to the foreground but it is not a dominant element. Instead the framing elements serve to colligate parts so as to deliver meaning – "what it meant" to be "a soldier of the cross." And that meaning is not singular: there are tensions, different understandings, and even conflicts. In the whole that emerges there is no analytical priority given to class, race, gender, or politics; rather all of these are working simultaneously in the composition.

The last paragraph of the chapter is not a conclusion (at this point we may need to re-define or reject the term "conclusion"). It is not a synthetic statement derived from a body of evidence. It is a fugue – a dense concentration of parts and voices woven into a whole, the whole being at once composition and structure. The many voices are heard both separately and as a whole. The meaning lies in the composition of parts and whole.

Here, then, is historical thinking that is very powerful and, in the language of our technological era, widely portable. The historian observes the world, and sees phenomena as always and potentially parts of wholes, either completed or emergent, and parts related to other parts. No object within our vision is singular, idiographic, or unattached. All objects move in association with other objects, and within a frame of time.

---

138 Glymph, *Women's Fight*, 127–62.

7 Consilience

I spent a week in Bali in August, 1992. It is a fascinating but mysterious place. I was seduced by the gamelan music, and puzzled by the predominance of percussive instruments. Every Balinese person seems to practice an art or craft, and nowhere else had I observed such an abundance of artistic works in so many types and forms. I was aware that scholars from many disciplines and many places have studied Balinese society and culture. The challenges involved in such study, I thought, would be staggering.

Does this memory have anything to do with women in the American Civil War?

As I read *The Women's Fight*, I became immersed in a distant world. A world of cotton fields, refugee camps, battlefields, churches, hospitals, and kitchens. A world of the many individuals who moved through these spaces. I was taken into this world, and the strange became familiar, or so it seemed. Things distant and alien began to acquire a presence and even a meaning. And as I was reading, I began to hear an echo from my own past. A memory intruded, an irritating distraction, and it kept returning. A memory of Clifford Geertz, an anthropologist who worked in Bali, and something called "thick description."

What has triggered this memory? I have not found Geertz's name in the book. Is it something in the specific qualities of *The Women's Fight*? First, the breadth and richness of the local and micro-historical detail, which affords that sense of immersion in another world. Second, the synchrony: that is, the suspension of time in order to fix events and happenings, thereby to unravel and display their internal logics. Synchrony does not mean that the diachronic is lost altogether; in this historical text the synchronic and diachronic complement each other.[139] Having observed the moment, we return to its place in the movement of time. Third, the sense that historical thinking entails establishing empathy, listening to informants, hearing the voices speaking in texts, mapping locations, observing relations and interactions among people – in other words, doing ethnography.

Historians of my generation were attracted to Clifford Geertz and especially his "Thick Description: Towards an Interpretive Theory of Culture" (1973). The attraction went beyond those who were embarking on a "linguistic turn" and focus-

---

[139] I am indebted to the lucid appraisal in William H. Sewell Jr., "History, Synchrony, and Culture: Reflections on the Work of Clifford Geertz," Chapter 6 in Sewell, *Logics of History: Social Theory and Social Transformation* (Chicago: University of Chicago Press, 2005), 175–96.

ing on semiotics, the signs and symbols embedded in text and language. The entire intellectual framework within which social history arose predisposed us to hear that human beings are "suspended in webs of significance" that humans themselves have spun; that we can perceive "a multiplicity of complex conceptual structures" in the behavior of shepherds and discern meaning in that complexity; and that this ethnography is "like trying to read (in the sense of 'construct a reading of') a manuscript." In this reference to the manuscript, and in many other references – as for instance to social context and the "universe of human discourse" – Geertz was opening a door to historians who were predisposed to follow.[140]

Geertz was more often invoked than followed. There was much more to his theory of culture than many of us realized.[141] Squirrelly borrowers, we persisted with our references and summaries.[142] To speak of "influence" or "effect" may attribute too much to Geertz alone. We were witnessing the emergence of a mode of ethnographic history in which micro-history was the most obvious manifestation.[143] Almost half a century after Geertz's seminal essays, the ethnographic-historical mode is so deeply accepted as to be virtually unmarked. Yet here it is, in Glymph's opening paragraphs. We listen to previously unheard voices. The recorded voices are not thickly described but thickly observed. The speakers are reckoning with "laws and customs." Women have "roles" and they act these roles in "unaccustomed places." Roles support and also protest against "notions and assumptions" embedded in culture. In that culture, "gendered and racially gendered policies" sustain "notions of home." Women appear in their "relationship" to each

---

140 Clifford Geertz, "Thick Description: Toward an Interpretative Theory of Culture," in Geertz, *The Interpretation of Cultures: Selected Essays* (New York: Basic Books, 1973), 3–30.
141 Stuart Clark, "Thick Description, Thin History: Did Historians Always Understand Clifford Geertz?", in Jeffrey C. Alexander, Philip Smith, and Matthew Norton, eds., *Interpreting Clifford Geertz: Cultural Investigation in the Social Sciences* (New York: Palgrave Macmillan, 2011), 105–119.
142 Commenting on the broad shifts in historiography in the late twentieth century, as he saw them (he did not refer to gender in history), Eric Hobsbawm wrote: "Perhaps the best way to summarize the change is to say that the young historians after 1945 found their inspiration in Braudel's *Mediterranean* (1949), the young historians after 1968 in the anthropologist Clifford Geertz's brilliant tour de force of 'thick description,' 'Deep Play: Notes on the Balinese Cockfight' (1973)." Hobsbawm, *Interesting Times: A Twentieth-Century Life* (London: Allen Lane, 2002), 294. The related developments of anthropological history and historical anthropology have prompted many writings. See Peter Burke, *The Historical Anthropology of Early Modern Italy* (Cambridge: Cambridge University Press, 2005); William G. Pooley, "Native to the Past: History, Anthropology, and Folklore in *Past & Present*," *Past & Present*, 239 (May 2018).
143 On the history of historical ethnography, see Bronwen Douglas and Dario Di Rosa, "Ethnohistory and Historical Ethnography," in John Jackson, ed., *Oxford Bibliographies in Anthropology* (New York: Oxford University Press, 2020), n.p.

other and also to "ideas." And all of this is more than the word "description" implies, because out of the assembly of the microscopic parts comes "meaning."[144]

Of course the historian cannot be a participant-observer. We cannot go back to the 1860s and meet American women and ask them questions about what they are doing and thinking. The difference exists, but it should not be exaggerated. The ethnographer must collect and assemble testimony and observation, piece by piece, interacting with individuals over time. But even a team of ethnographers working together in a single location over many years would not be able to collect the immense volume of testimony and observation available to Thavolia Glymph after her decades of immersion in the sources. The historian, as Glymph demonstrates, may frame a question and put that question before the surviving universe of testimony by and about American women in the 1860s. Then the historian may massage the question in many ways and receive a chorus of voices in response.

The rise of anthropological history, or history in the ethnographic mode, raises questions about historical thinking and logic that remain to be answered. We are not observing new types of deductive or inductive logic, or even a transmuted logic of causation. There may be abductive reasoning at work here (more on this later), but the fit is not yet clear. A search for guidance from the methods, rules, and logic of ethnography yields little, and that is no surprise – we are seeking to understand an ethnographically inflected history, not ethnography. There must be rules or tests that we can apply to this historical thinking. What form of truth appears in this history? What reasoning lies behind the truth claims? *The Women's Fight* certainly offers important and original truths. But *how* does it do so? And how does it do so in ways that are so thoroughly persuasive?

These observations lead me to bigger questions that arise in our era of digitization. There is an immense volume of testimony and detail in Glymph's book, but what of the hyperabundance of text and data that digitization has given us? Technology has transformed the way historians – and not just the more digitally aware historians – do their research.[145] The changes have happened so rapidly that an understanding of the implications lags behind the changes in methods. What is happening when the historian's sources include corpora of texts that are so large that they will never be read by individuals, and will be read only by machines? What is happening to the relationship between historians and sources

---

144 Glymph, *Women's Fight*, 1–2.
145 A recent summary is Ian Milligan, "The Transformation of Historical Research in the Digital Age" (published online by Cambridge University Press, 2022): https://www.cambridge.org/core/elements/transformation-of-historical-research-in-the-digital-age/30DFBEAA3B753370946B7A98045CFEF4. Jo Guldi raises questions of meaning in her book *The Dangerous Art of Text Mining: A Methodology for Digital History* (Cambridge: Cambridge University Press, 2023).

when we no longer observe fragments from an original (paper texts, printed objects), but entire archives mediated and re-presented through digitization? What, indeed, is a "topic" or "subject" when the target of our scrutiny is provided by a topic-modeling algorithm?

We have begun to pose the questions, and our understanding of both the potential and pitfalls of digitization is deepening. It may be, as some have suggested, that digitization has led to a history that is obsessed with tools and methods rather than results, and that the written histories using such tools tend to be descriptions of findings more often than original interpretations or arguments.[146] Such reservations may miss the point: since the tools and methods contribute to framing the questions and answers, it is likely that we are observing not just new tools and methods, but also questions and answers of a new type and form.

Consider the language of the user of the digitized text corpus. We read of "patterns" and pattern recognition – the uncovering of "patterns through correlation, resemblance, or proximity."[147] Together with "patterns" come "categories" – the uncovering of categories latent in text, but unlikely to be observed without machine-reading. We hear also the language of "spatialization" and "visualization": places, events, and individuals are made visible, not as discrete entities, but as conjoined and interactive agents. We read of "relational ways of understanding space and place" as we track sex trade workers moving through the streets of sixteenth-century Florence.[148] The terms "model" and "modeling" reappear in new contexts, as historians build detailed replicas of cities, or generate conceptual models and topic models induced from massive text corpora.

I could cite more examples of the language that accompanies digital history. Instead, I hasten to an observation, or perhaps it is a speculation. Digitization has not displaced older notions of "argument" or "interpretation" so much as it has expanded their meaning. Even those who identify as digitally oriented historians deploy arguments of a form that has long existed: sources are culled for what historians present as "evidence"; the evidence is used in support of conclusions. Causation has not disappeared, and narrative remains one of history's modes. Never-

---

[146] Stephen Robertson and Lincoln A. Mullen ask, "why have digital historians not made arguments?" in their "Arguing with Digital History: Patterns of Historical Interpretation," *Journal of Social History*, 54, 4 (2021), 1005–22; also in *Models of Argument-Driven Digital History*: https://model-articles.rrchnm.org/articles/introduction/#fn:1.

[147] Stephen Robertson and Lincoln A. Mullen, "Arguing with Digital History: Patterns of Historical Interpretation," *Journal of Social History*, 54, 4 (2021), 1005–22.

[148] Nicholas Terpstra, "Locating the Sex Trade in the Early Modern City: Space, Sense and Regulation in Sixteenth-Century Florence," in Nicholas Terpstra and Colin Rose, eds., *Mapping Space, Sense, and Movement in Florence* (London: Routledge, 2016), 122.

theless, such older forms of argument are accompanied by new forms and understandings of argument. The synchronic has a new priority, while not displacing diachronic temporality. Deep and extended personal and even subjective immersion in sources is assumed. The discovery of pattern is itself an argument: the individual from the past may be observed, in his or her behavior, speech, and even emotions; and with others, observed within social and semantic contexts at varying scales. These are among the characteristics of ethnography; and the universe of digital history is tending to reinforce the ethnographic turn in historiography.

I return now to earlier questions. In this expanding ethnographically inflected history, what form of truth claim are we observing? What reasoning lies behind the truth claims and the meanings? I have no clear answer because we have arrived at a limit beyond which those who think about historical meaning and practice have not yet gone. I have instead a suggestion, based on my observations about digital history, and also on the vast assembly of actions, testimony, and detail in Glymph's book. The array of pointillist detail, as in Glymph's book, is not arbitrary or unordered. There is an order, if not exactly a logic, that serves in the creation of a whole. The analogy with a great work of visual art is apt: the work is a composition in which each element has a place. One might say that there is a coherence in the composition. But I prefer another word, a word that is more appropriate to historical composition: consilience.

The term consilience was used by the nineteenth-century philosopher William Whewell to refer to a "convergence" of evidence or convergence of inductions. Well-established theories in science, he said, are those supported by multiple inductions; they exist because inductions from different classes of fact have "jumped together." There is another, perhaps more common meaning, associated especially with a book by Edward O. Wilson, titled *Consilience: The Unity of Knowledge*; consilience refers to the convergence of knowledge, as for instance in the coming together of sciences and humanities.[149] I prefer to adapt the first meaning of consilience. This meaning appears most often in the sciences. An example is climate science. Why is there a consensus on anthropogenic global warming, despite differences among scientists on specific issues? Because of consilience: there are multiple bodies of evidence pointing in the same direction (including pollen, tree rings, ice cores, corals, ice melts, carbon dioxide measurements, temperature measurements) and virtually none pointing in any other

---

[149] Edward O. Wilson, *Consilience: The Unity of Knowledge* (New York: Knopf, 1998).

direction. In history, consilience has been used in the confrontation with Holocaust denial.[150]

Consilience exists when multiple observations from different sources and locations contribute to the same conclusive motif or holistic depiction. I use motif in the sense of a distinctive idea or dominant theme in an artistic or literary composition; and at this point, I am replacing "conclusion" with "motif." Each microhistorical element may contain particular characteristics and even ambiguities, but some characteristic within it converges upon the leitmotif – the guiding or dominant motif. If the consilience is sustained, then the leitmotif precludes the acceptance of an alternative, and a truth claim is made.[151]

To demonstrate what I mean by consilience, I turn to another remarkable book: Allison Margaret Bigelow's *Mining Language: Racial Thinking, Indigenous Knowledge, and Colonial Metallurgy in the Early Modern Iberian World* (2020). I do not begin by summarizing the "argument" or "conclusions" of the book. I begin instead by pointing to specific terminology used by the author when referring to the reasoning process. This book stands within and even beyond the ethnographic turn. We do not encounter the language of cause and effect, or words commonly found in a narrative mode. We do encounter the metaphor of light. "Viewing" in a specific way allows us to see "in a new light;" the book "sheds light"; specific sources articulate "visions"; "clarification" serves to remedy "confusion" and absence.[152] Related to vision is the analogy to painting, as in the language of framing and reframing: the book approaches archives so as to "reframe

---

[150] Michael Shermer, *Holocaust Denial: Who Says the Holocaust Never Happened and Why Do They Say It?* (University of California Press, 2000); Michael Shermer, "Consilience and Consensus," *Scientific American*, 313 issue 6 (December 2015); Illka Niiniluoto, "Unification and Confirmation," *Theoria*, 31, 1 (2016), 107–23.

[151] Consider Chapter 6 in *The Women's Fight*: "Under the Restless Wings of an Army." The first sentence of the Abstract gestures toward consilience in asserting that "Confederate women converged the stories of the home front and battlefront" (Glymph, *The Women's Fight*, 199). The convergence is toward specific motifs: women frequently blamed men for the war they experienced; Confederate women rarely experienced deliberate violence from the Union army; enslaved women and black women refugees did suffer deliberate harm. These motifs are part of a leitmotif: women were not occasional or secondary participants in the war; they were fully engaged participants. The motifs are inflected by the frames of gender, class, and race. The consilience of micro-historical observations in sustaining the motifs is basic to the persuasiveness of the work. No matter how distant any variation may seem, it still contains the motif. The convergence of observations is such that an alternative motif – an alternative meaning – is precluded.

[152] Allison Margaret Bigelow, *Mining Language: Racial Thinking, Indigenous Knowledge, and Colonial Metallurgy in the Early Modern Iberian World* (Chapel Hill: University of North Carolina Press, 2020), 1, 9, 19.

their historical silences;" it "brings to the fore" and "throws into sharp relief" that which has previously stood in the background or been hidden from sight.[153]

The goal is not a new body of knowledge, in the sense of an assembly of data or evidence about specific objects or actions in the past (although the volume of observation in the book is immense). Instead, the reader is invited to share an "understanding": a key word that appears twenty-two times in the short Introduction. Understanding, if I read the text correctly, refers to the apprehension of meaning through reading of text; it may also refer to the integration of objects and actions into a whole. This understanding is not the same as an accumulation of fact or data; it is possible to "know" in the latter sense without having an understanding of the objects in view. *Mining Language* suggests that there can be more than one understanding. There is, for instance, "an older understanding;" the book is offering "a new understanding" and even "a deeper understanding." I infer that the concept of understanding in this book is consistent with the concept that I discussed in Chapter 2.

Bigelow does not give us a lengthy discussion of methodology. She does refer throughout to multiple points of view or perspectives, and to the disciplinary positions that guide her understanding. Hers is a "literary approach" to sixteenth- and seventeenth-century works on metals. It is that and much more, because the avenues of approach are numerous and overlapping. In the analysis of texts, there is no "hard line at the border between anthropology and history."[154] Indeed, there seem to be no hard lines at all between history, anthropology, archeology, linguistics, geography, economics and semiotics. One might describe the approach as multidisciplinary; a better term might be codisciplinary.

In reading texts and visual artifacts, Bigelow refers to the "necessary series of contrapuntal readings of objects and words" and to "contrapuntal criticism."[155] Counterpoint originates in music: it refers to a composition in which two or more lines or voices occur simultaneously but independently of each other. In the interpretation of texts, the concept derives from Edward Said (1935–2003), the eminent postcolonial theorist who knew a lot about counterpoint, since he was also a gifted musician.[156] A contrapuntal reading means hearing the simultaneous presence of distinct voices, including silent ones. Said wrote: "We must therefore read the great canonical texts with an effort to draw out, extend, give emphasis to what is silent or marginally present or ideologically represented in such works.

---

[153] Bigelow, *Mining Language*, 9, 19.
[154] Bigelow, *Mining Language*, 323.
[155] Bigelow, *Mining Language* 10, 326.
[156] Edward W. Said, *Musical Elaborations* (New York: Columbia University Press, 1991). Said is the author of the influential *Orientalism* (New York: Pantheon Books, 1978).

The contrapuntal reading must take account of both processes – that of imperialism and that of resistance to it, which can be done by extending our reading of the texts to include what was once forcibly excluded."[157] This way of reading allows *Mining Language* to display "awkward pairings," silences, conjoined understandings and misunderstandings, and "entangled histories."

There is an obvious *double entendre* in the title of Bigelow's book: it is about the lexicons of metal and mining in the early modern period, and about the scholar's mining of text and language. From this double meaning, and also from the absence of the word "history" in the title, one should not infer that historical temporality is understated, nor even that synchronicity is always in the foreground. On the contrary, there is a deep sensitivity to the diachronic, to shifts of vocabulary and meaning across short and long spans of time. Indigenous techniques and words are incorporated very quickly into the colonizers' lexicon; some words and ideas can be embedded in colonial mining vocabularies across long spans of time. If the historian asks whether this is microhistory or macrohistory, the answer, I suggest, is that it is both. We can observe, on the same page, ancient Roman technologies beside the very local extractive techniques of sixteenth-century miners, including the "minute actions" of turning their wrists and shifting their balance on wet rocks.[158] The analysis is multi-scalar, and the gaze moves from macroscope to microscope.

There may be many different readings of so complex a work, and different lessons drawn. My point is that we rest on under-examined hermeneutical ground. What is the "history" embedded in such a work? How does it sustain the "understanding" that it proposes? I can do no more than try to justify my argument about the presence of consilience. There is a leitmotif – a dominant or recurrent motif – in the book: "the substantial contributions of subaltern knowledge makers to the science and technologies of global Iberian empires." The Spanish empire was "dynamic, locally defined, and contextual." In the "entangled history" of colonization, there was no "linear march toward scientific modernity in which European imperialism is imposed from above."[159]

Today, our consensus on the general direction of anthropogenic climate change rests on the consilience of evidence from many distinct sources and scientific domains. The truth of Bigelow's leitmotif rests on the consilience and convergence of readings across a wide range of domains. Among these are the mechanical arts of mining; the techniques to wash gold; the gender-inflected labor relations systems

---

[157] Edward W. Said, *Culture and Imperialism* (New York: Vintage Books, 1994), 66.
[158] Bigelow, *Mining Language*, 44.
[159] Bigelow, *Mining Language*, 9, 330.

in mining; the understandings of metal as commodity, symbolic object, and spiritual entity; the many spaces of gold mining, including the houses (*bohios*) in which refining occurred; the Spanish mapping and re-mapping of Indigenous spaces; patterns and customs of marriage and household formation; the design of towns; the incorporation of Indigenous words for topographies and techniques into colonial lexicons; and the language of metallurgy relating to four metals – gold, silver, iron, and copper. Across these and other domains, and in several regions of the Iberian empire, the leitmotif is sustained.

Sustaining the consilience requires that alternative non-Indigenous roots of mining knowledge, such as alchemical thinking in early modern Spain, be anticipated and given lesser priority.[160] Of course, there were contradictions and differences, silences and ambiguities, and shifting meanings. Even silence sustains the consilience: imperial reports and writers fashioned a narrative in which Indigenous peoples were absent. But across all of these domains, the presence of the subaltern – especially Indigenous and African women and men – was necessary to the construction of meaning, to the art and technology of mining, and to scientific knowledge and practice.

A skeptic might say that we are observing no more here than a sufficiency of evidence assembled in support of a particular conclusion. Yes, but you would be ignoring the language and the mode of argumentation present in the book itself. The book does not present "evidence" in support of a "conclusion." It offers contrapuntal readings and literary "modes of analysis" in support of an understanding. In doing so, it denies and displaces alternative and older understandings. Among these is the older understanding that colonial mining vocabularies and knowledge were primitive and even nonsensical, and the older understanding of a linear march toward scientific modernity. More deeply, faced with the consilience of Bigelow's domains of observation, an older understanding of the Spanish empire is displaced by a new understanding: "the Spanish empire was less of a monolithic imposition from above and more like the protean, contingent human, plant, and metallic matter that composed it – dynamic, locally defined and contextual." And this new understanding is achieved without denying, but by incorporating "the unbalanced doctrinal, epistemological, political, and socioeconomic powers of imperial Spanish agents."[161]

Multitudinous observations converge upon specific dominant or recurring themes. This consilience does not imply a singularity of meaning, or a self-contained unity of thought, such as the word "conclusion" suggests. The point about consil-

---

[160] Bigelow, *Mining Language*, 94–5.
[161] Bigelow, *Mining Language*, 6, 12.

ience and motifs is that these concepts allow a plurality of themes and framing devices within a reasoning process, and they allow room for us to re-consider the objects that we historians summon forth from the past and seek to understand. Perhaps we are *obligated* to re-think those objects. Many years ago, as a young historian, I was too inclined to think of past objects as stable entities. A sailing ship might show change in its technological components, and its uses might change, but a barque was always a barque.

As I read what Bigelow says about iron "in dialogue," I am persuaded to re-think and de-essentialize iron (to cite merely one example from many that I could choose from the book). What is iron? A malleable and ductile metal having a variety of shapes and uses. It is that, to be sure. But change the time and location: iron becomes a repository of certain spiritual principles and beliefs; or it becomes a symbol of the relationship between earth and sky; or it becomes a source of healing medicine; or it becomes a mirror giving access to the supernatural.[162] Iron has no singular or stable identity; it moves and discloses its meanings through time and space. Its meaning lies in this historicity. The same point applies to the categories that we create and deploy as historians. As Bigelow tells us, Indigenous, African, Iberian – these and other categories are not stable singularities, but contested and internally diverse conceptual entities.[163] Consilience, as Bigelow's book so clearly demonstrates, does not bear with it the risk of essentializing.

Consilience is an element in the historian's arsenal of reasoning. It sets a standard for credibility. Multiple observations within the field of vision contribute to the same motif; no observations support an alternative motif. The validity of an argument rests not simply on an abundance of evidence, but on the coherence of observations in the historian's act of consilient composition.

---

[162] Bigelow, *Mining Language*, 105–12, 114.
[163] Bigelow, *Mining Language*, 106. I would make the same point about Glymph's categories. Consider, for instance, the last paragraph of Chapter 6 in *The Women's Fight*. The leitmotif is restated: "Women knew that the home front was a critical component of the machinery of war" (p. 219). That women's *knowing* is now in our history, as never before. But that is not the final thought here, because the author will not let "women" stand as a singularity. Thus: "it mattered whether they were black, white, or Native American, rich or poor, free or enslaved" (p. 220).

8 Perspectives

"What is perspective anyway?"
"Do you mean perspective in art?"
"Yes."
"Probably you are thinking of linear perspective."
"I guess so. But what is it exactly?"
"It's a technique for creating the illusion of depth and space in a flat surface. The artist uses parallel lines and a vanishing point. And the relative size of objects. Objects that are closer to the viewer appear larger."
"Okay. So when did linear perspective appear?"
"Well, the ancient Greeks had versions of it. But we usually think it begins in fifteenth-century Florence, with the architect Brunelleschi."
"Before Machiavelli then . . . . But *why* would it appear then?"
"You're the historian. You tell me! But it must have something to do with the science of optics, and ways of seeing, don't you think?"
"And also with spirituality."
"Now you're getting somewhere. So linear perspective can't *just* be a set of techniques, can it? It's also part of a way of understanding. You can't separate seeing from understanding. One argument is that linear perspective was part of the ending of the medieval Christian view of the world. Linear perspective was totally part of a secularized understanding of space that was part of the scientific revolution. Or so goes the argument."[164]

"I see," say I, in response to what she (the artist with whom I live) has just said. And by that, I mean "I get it" or "I understand." Or perhaps I mean: "I know." But are these – seeing, knowing, and understanding – the same things, even in everyday speech? How often do we speak of "knowing" or "understanding" in the language of sight: "insight," "vision," "the mind's eye." Historians do this too: we offer insights, we make seeing easier by shedding light, by illuminating, by clarifying. But is "seeing" merely another term for knowing or understanding?

I suggest that we cannot leave our "seeing" unexamined. To assume that seeing, knowing, and understanding refer to the same mental activities leaves unanswered questions. Seeing is only the beginning of knowing objects in the real world, albeit an essential beginning. I see a red apple, and my seeing tells me it is red. But when I was a few months old, my seeing did not tell me that the apple

---

[164] Samuel Y. Edgerton, *The Mirror, the Window, and the Telescope: How Renaissance Linear Perspective Changed Our Vision of the Universe* (Ithaca, NY: Cornell University Press, 2009).

was red, or even that it was an apple. My knowing came later, from somewhere outside my seeing.

Can we really assume that seeing is merely a synonym for knowing? Not always. Consider *Seeing and Knowing: Women and Learning in Medieval Europe, 1200–1550*, edited by Anneke Mulder-Bakker (2004). Seeing is intimately related to knowing, but the categories are separable. The "seeing" here refers to mechanisms of visibility, means of communication, and techniques for the transmission of knowledge. Understanding this "seeing" is a prerequisite to the historical understanding of women's knowledge. But it is not the same as the knowledge.

These reflections are prompted by my reading of Glymph's *The Women's Fight*. One cannot go far in this book without encountering the language of sight. At one level, the book is about things seen and things not seen, in both past and present. "See," "saw," "visible," "capacity to see," "perceptions," "insight," "witnessed" – the vocabulary of seeing is extensive. To this, we should add the terms of non-seeing: "to obscure," "erasure," "invisible." And to this, we might add the objects that must be seen to be known, even partially – distances, landscapes, maps, spaces, and much more. And who does the seeing? Those who see include past agents, the reader, the author, and previous historians. More than that: past objects and entities have the capacity to shed light, to make it easier to see: "the Civil War highlighted," the war "illuminated," the war "exposes," the war "laid bare," the war "magnified," and so on. I could go on – so far I have noted only what appears in the short Introduction to the book.[165] The language is telling us that ways of seeing are basic to ways of knowing. Another word, also in the Introduction, merges seeing and knowing: "perspective." Perspective means a way of seeing, thinking, and knowing, from a position or location – a point of view. Perspective tells us that all knowing occurs in the position or location of the viewer. Perspective, therefore, is at the heart of our acceptance of subjectivity.

History is about visibility: making apparent to sight and mind that which has previously been unseen, or apparent only partially or dimly. Even our word "evidence" is rooted in seeing: it comes from the Latin "evidentem" (perceptible, apparent) and "videre" (to see); evidence is a thing seen. There may be more to this visibility than the reader wants to hear, but please bear with me. Since "visible" means "capable of being seen," the question immediately arises as to what "seeing" is, and what is the relation between sight, a human sensory faculty, and other activities of mind, such as knowing. And another question: how does knowing, or knowledge, relate to truth? Once again, the words we use inevitably rest upon foundations and assumptions that we rarely question or even perceive. Seeing and knowing: we are

---

165 Glymph, *Women's Fight*, 3–13.

in Plato's allegory of the cave, and in his other dialogues about knowledge. Sight also takes us to phenomenology, with its focus on lived experiences and what we get from the senses, and specifically the phenomenology of perception.[166]

More familiar to most historians is the way visibility relates to power. Michel Foucault's book *The Birth of the Clinic* begins as follows: "This book is about space, about language, and about death; it is about the act of seeing, the gaze."[167] Note also the subtitle of the book: *An Archaeology of Medical Perception*. The medical gaze comprises both the act of seeing as well as the body of knowledge that enables the perception. In the prison the criminal body is made visible in the act of seeing – surveillance. The hospital, for Foucault, is an apparatus of visibility. The gaze is a strategy of power, a disciplining of bodies. Visibility is a recurring theme in Foucault's histories and his conceptualization of power. We need not follow Foucault to all of his theoretical destinations in order to learn from his discussions of optics and power.

Elsewhere, we find other, very different approaches to gaze, power, and empowerment. Gaze and gender: in *Ways of Seeing*, the art critic John Berger (1926–2017) wrote about how men and women see and are seen, as men look at women and women watch themselves being looked at.[168] The idea of the male gaze was followed by the idea of the female gaze, and debates around both concepts. In another area, the idea of the imperial gaze was followed by the postcolonial gaze. From all of this, we may take many things, but above all, the idea that seeing and visibility are ways of apprehending and discussing power, disempowerment, and empowerment.

We are confronted with many terms related to seeing and many philosophical orientations, not all of which are compatible with each other. How do we extract from all of this something meaningful about historical thinking? I suggest that we examine the concept already mentioned above: perspective. We understand that two observers standing at different vantage points will have different views of an object and so will "see" it differently. As a term used by historians, we take perspective to mean that both seeing and knowing are bound within the contingent subject-positions of the viewer. This applies, we assume, to all human beings: language, beliefs, values, interests, experiences, and emotions guide and

---

[166] Michael Ayers writes about the phenomenology of perception and the "perspicuity of knowledge" in *Knowing and Seeing: Groundwork for a New Empiricism* (Oxford: Oxford University Press, 2019). See also Barry Stroud, *Seeing, Understanding, Knowing: Philosophical Essays* (Oxford: Oxford University Press, 2018).

[167] Michel Foucault, *The Birth of the Clinic: An Archaeology of Medical Perception*, trans. A.M. Sheridan (London: Routledge, 2003 [1973]), ix.

[168] John Berger, *Ways of Seeing* (New York: Penguin, 1990).

control the way we see and know the world. There is no such thing as a view from nowhere. There is, therefore, no absolute objectivity – a seeing or knowing independent of perspective. Notice the implications of these assumptions. First, seeing and knowing are no longer separable. Both are contingent outcomes, even components of perspective. Second, if a non-perspectival knowing of reality does not exist, is all knowledge relative to each knower? Does perspectivism lead to relativism? And what is the relationship between knowledge and truth? If all truth is perspectival, how can we evaluate differing claims to truth? Such questions are, I think, even more pressing today when we read about representations of the past in virtual reality, where perspective becomes highly fluid, "interactive," and "participatory."[169]

All modern discussions of these questions begin with the "perspectivism" of the German philosopher Friedrich Nietzsche (1844–1900). "Let us guard ourselves from the tentacles of such contradictory ideas as 'pure reason,' 'absolute spirituality,' 'knowledge in itself' . . . . There is only a seeing from a perspective, only a 'knowing' from a perspective . . . ."[170] This "perspective" is not merely a metaphor for seeing. It is a condition of living and knowing: Nietzsche refers to perspective as "the basic condition of all life," and claims that "there would be no life at all if not on the basis of perspective estimates and appearances."[171] This perspectivism is part of Nietzsche's denial of absolute objectivity, his denial of the Platonic idea that it is possible to penetrate beyond all subjective appearances to reveal the way things really are. His perspectivism is also related to his doctrine of "will to power": where there is no certain truth, there is only perspective and interpretation, and a necessary contestation among differing interpretations and truth claims.

This understanding of perspective does not make Nietzsche a relativist. He believed that perspectives can be deployed in the service of knowledge and the avoidance of metaphysical error. The more perspectives we have, the better: "the *more* emotions we express over a thing, the *more* eyes, different eyes, we train on the same thing, the more complete will be our 'idea' of that thing, our 'objectivity'."[172] The quotes around "objectivity" are presumably meant to rule out the idea of absolute objectivity. A specific and different objectivity is being referenced: the "object"

---

[169] Ruta Kazlauskalté, "Knowing Is Seeing: Distance and Proximity in Affective Virtual Reality History," *Rethinking History*, 26, 1 (2022), 67.
[170] Friedrich Nietzsche, *The Genealogy of Morals*, trans. Horace B. Samuel (New York: The Modern Library, 1918), 124.
[171] Nietzsche, *Beyond Good and Evil*, trans. W. Kaufmann (New York: Vintage Books, 1966), 11, 34; quoted in Christoph Cox, "The 'Subject' of Nietzsche's Perspectivism," *Journal of the History of Philosophy*, 35, 2 (April 1997), 271.
[172] Nietzsche, *Genealogy of Morals*, 124.

remains perspectival, but the more perspectives we deploy, the more "complete" will be the object in our knowledge (this reasoning is sometimes said to be "asymptotic": see the footnote).[173] Disinterested knowledge, in this view, remains impossible, and no knowledge can ever be definitively complete. Nevertheless – and what follows has been the subject of much discussion – some interpretations are better than others, and there is a future "objectivity," to be understood as a capacity to have power over differing perspectives, a capacity to overcome the limitations of some perspectives, and the capacity "to make precisely the *difference* in perspectives and interpretations useful for knowledge."[174]

There may be more questions than answers in Nietzsche's formulation of perspective. But we may draw a lesson: the metaphor of perspective as a "point of view" is inadequate. There is much more to perspective than "viewpoint." Perspective is the form that observers, having different interests and values, impart to groups of objects, endowing them with coherence and meaning. In historical thinking, this perspective is never singular; meaning is endowed from a plurality of perspectives that are conjoined and juxtaposed.[175] Historical thinking is, among other things, this conjoining and juxtaposing of multiple perspectives.

It is the winter of 1863. We, the readers of *The Women's Fight*, observe a family of twenty people who are seeing, looking, and searching. We are asked to share their perspective in this moment, as they seek work and freedom from enslavement. Then the moment shifts, and they see destitution, persecution, and death. In this perspective, they falter, hesitate, change their minds, and then they return to slavery.[176] But these sentences distill only part of the "interpretation," because perspectives are always multiple and conjoined. There are the perspectives of other observers looking at this suffering family; we hear what a Northern woman sees

---

[173] Asymptotic is a mathematical term related to limiting behavior, or the behavior of functions as they approach some limit. An example of an asymptote is a line that approaches but never meets a curve. Outside its context in mathematics and statistics, the term may refer to an explanation that accounts for a behavior or state of affairs at its limit.

[174] Nietzsche, *On the Genealogy of Morality* (1998 edition), 12, quoted in R. Lanier Andersen, "Friedrich Nietzsche," *Stanford Encyclopedia of Philosophy*, 6.2 (2017). See Brian Leiter, "Perspectivism in Nietzsche's Genealogy of Morals," in Richard Schacht, ed., *Nietzsche, Genealogy, Morality: Essays on Nietzsche's Genealogy of Morals* (Berkeley: University of California Press, 1994), 334–57; Mark E. Jonas and Yoshiaki M. Nakazawa, "Finding Truth in 'Lies': Nietzsche's Perspectivism and Its Relation to Education," *Journal of the Philosophy of Education*, 42, 2 (2008), 269–85; Christoph Cox, "The 'Subject' of Nietzsche's Perspectivism," *Journal of the History of Philosophy*, 35, 2 (April 1997), 269–91.

[175] I am following, and in part paraphrasing, Javier Paricio, "Perspective as a Threshhold Concept for Learning History," *History Education Research Journal*, 18, 1 (2021), 116.

[176] Glymph, *Women's Fight*, 221–2.

and what a chaplain sees. Without these perspectives, the decisions of the family would make less sense – the history of the moment would be incomplete. There is another observer, introduced explicitly into the "interpretation": it is you and me – the reader. "It is difficult to imagine the decision of these people . . . ."[177] But we are challenged to imagine, in *our* perspective, on the basis of what "we know" and what *we* see "when freedom in the making looked so much like slavery." Our looking conjoins with their looking, and in that conjoining, a meaning arises.

The conjoining of perspectives is carefully articulated, moving from one to the other, and one within the other. The conjoining is so seamless and subtle as to be scarcely apparent; yet it is always there. Our view is directed throughout by another observer, always present but unobtrusive, standing in a perspective that is distant and sometimes panoptic, but never detached: "Across the Mississippi Valley and the larger slave south, enslaved women acted on the belief that the war was about slavery and that their freedom lay in the balance."[178] This observer is the author, Thavolia Glymph, the weaver of multiple perspectives including her own.

In the historical text, perspectives conjoin: one enters the other. Multiple perspectives brought from the past enter the perspective of the author in an act of imaginative composition. The historian is the impresario of perspectival shifts as these move in space and time. The conjoining requires a plurality of perspectives, and plurality allows an approach, not to absolute objectivity, but to a provisional truth. Alternative perspectives or "interpretations" are rendered implausible in the face of the emerging provisional truth. The older ways of seeing, in which women's contributions were "lost," have come to hold little truth and little value. In the new perspectival dispensation, "we are more inclined to see" women's contributions to the war "in the work of women who knit and sewed for the soldiers like the Woolsey sisters."[179] In the historian's collage of perspectives comes this new truth claim: "men's business was women's business."[180] And this as well: "With the defeat of the Confederate South's bid for independence, slavery was destroyed, but the meaning of freedom, nation and home remained contested."[181] Bearing directly upon that truth, the book concludes in a concise conjoining of perspectives from "scholars," "memoirs," "reminiscences," "narratives," and "testimony."

Perspective is deeply ingrained in the historian's thinking. Perspectival thinking means transporting ourselves into the locations and positions of the "other,"

---

[177] Glymph, *Women's Fight*, 221.
[178] Glymph, *Women's Fight*, 222.
[179] Glymph, *Women's Fight*, 253.
[180] Glymph, *Women's Fight*, 256.
[181] Glymph, *Women's Fight*, 260.

whether that other is in our past or our present. It sustains our claim to imaginative empathy without risking moral relativism.[182] It sustains our claim to a holistic, multi-dimensional interrogation and understanding of past and present. It has even been suggested that "perspective" may include writing from the position of a non-human other, such as a natural environment.[183] Perspective tells us something important about history as a way of understanding. It tells us that a correspondence theory of truth must be discarded. History is not a faithful or exact representation of the past; it does not give us unmediated or authentic access to the past. It is, rather, a way of seeing and thinking that imparts order and meaning. In the words of historians, events, actions, and objects that are otherwise chaotic and meaningless acquire form and meaning. In this way of thinking, we see our way in the world.

---

[182] Empathy receives comprehensive consideration in Tyson Retz's, *Empathy and History: Understanding in Re-enactment, Hermeneutics, and Education* (New York: Berghahn Books, 2018).
[183] Douglas Booth, "Experiments in History: The Voice of Bondi," *Rethinking History*, 27, 1 (2023), 124–43.

9 Analogy

I have had the good fortune to attend performances of operas in a few cities in Germany. The productions were of the highest quality. I have not been to Munich, and I am considering going there on my next trip to Europe. I infer that the quality of productions at the Bavarian State Opera will be very high. Do you think that my inference is plausible? I should, of course, do further research and read reviews. But note something: I have already begun the decision-making process by making a logical inference. I have drawn an analogy: put simply, I have said that a characteristic (high quality) evident in one or more objects (opera productions in different cities in one country) is likely to be possessed by another object in that country. The analogy is a type of comparison, and it is based on experience or memory of events in the past. It is also, in this instance, predictive: it predicts a condition based on characteristics known to exist in similar cases.

Analogical thinking is ubiquitous in everyday life. It is so commonplace that we are usually unaware of its presence. We begin to make use of analogy in childhood, don't we? Our first school provides a model of school; when we change schools, we meet an analog of school, with similarities and differences that must be perceived and negotiated. Analogy is most apparent to us when similarities are made explicit, or when the similarities are unexpected or the points of comparison difficult to see ("life is like a box of chocolates"). A metaphor is a type of analogy: one thing is said to be analogous to another with respect to one or more elements. There are times when analogy appears in our attempts to define history as a form of knowledge: "the past is a foreign country."[184] Mark S. Phillips draws an analogy between historical time and "a city street, where the traffic changes its rhythms with the flow of everyday life."[185] Two centuries ago, Wilhelm von Humboldt suggested an analogy between historical insight and the perception of the shape of clouds, which can only be seen from a distance.[186]

Analogies take many forms and often do not appear as formal arguments. Analogical reasoning has a long history, going back to Aristotle, who set out to explain under what conditions an analogical argument can be valid. Analogical reasoning takes many forms in many disciplines.[187] In the form of an analogical

---

[184] "The past is a foreign country; they do things differently there." The first sentence of L.P. Hartley's 1953 novel *The Go-Between*.
[185] Mark S. Phillips, *On Historical Distance* (New Haven: Yale University Press, 2013), 4.
[186] Wilhelm von Humboldt, *The Task of the Historian*, 1821, cited in Javier Fernandez-Sebastian, *Key Metaphors for History: Mirrors of Time* (London: Routledge, 2024), 111.
[187] For a discussion of analogy in early Greek thought, see G.E.R. Lloyd, *Polarity and Analogy* (Cambridge: Cambridge University Press, 1966). The first example may be that of Thales of Mile-

argument, there are premises and a conclusion. Premise 1 may be that object A has characteristics a, b, and c; Premise 2 is that object B also has a, b, and c. Premise 3 is that object A possesses d. The conclusion is that object B will also possess d. An analogical argument of this form is predictive, and this kind of argument is often used in problem-solving. Presented in this way, it might seem that an analogical argument is a form of inductive reasoning. But it should be apparent in what follows that an analogical argument is not always deductive or inductive.[188]

What has this to do with historical thinking? I have already given you clues. I have invoked experience, memory, and prediction in this simple account of reasoning by analogy; affinities with history should be obvious. Perhaps a connection is more clearly indicated – and here comes an argument by analogy! – if I refer to the prominence of analogy in law, and especially criminal law.[189] The affinities between law and history are well known: in criminal law cases, a known outcome is connected to specific causal conditions in the past, and the connection is probabilistic (the legal standard of proof is "beyond reasonable doubt"). In juridical practice, the rationale for a judgment is based on precedents: the present case is related by analogy to a previous decision or decisions. A judge will apply the reasoning in a previous case to the present one, and in doing so must weigh any apparent differences between the two cases. This is practical analogical reasoning, reasoning in which the conclusion has a present application. It is also a form of historical reasoning, although unlike what historians do in many respects. In criminal justice, "fact" from the past is assessed when deployed as evidence in support of conclusions. Evidence and principle from the past are used to support an ultimate conclusion (and that conclusion may itself be tentative, if it is appealed).

Perhaps even closer to history is archeology, a field in which analogical reasoning is frequently used and much debated. In ethnographic analogy, for instance, analogy means using customs and patterns apparent in ethnographic sources as a way of informing or supporting inferences in cases where only archeological evidence exists. A very simple example might be: in most pastoral societies, men

---

tus in the sixth century BCE. Thales is said to have measured the height of pyramids by observing the length of the shadow of the pyramids at the moment when a person's shadow is equal to the height of that person.

188 Paul Bartha offers a useful introduction to analogical reasoning, including a summary of its relationship to deduction and induction, in his article "Analogy and Analogical Reasoning," *Stanford Encyclopedia of Philosophy* (revised 25 January 2019).

189 Gadamer points to the analogy between the tasks of the historian and the judge: Hans-Georg Gadamer, *Truth and Method* (London: Continuum, 2004), 334.

rather than women are herders of large animals; in a pastoral society where only archaeological evidence exists, and where little direct evidence of herding survives, one might infer by analogy that men rather than women were herders. Debates often focus on what analogy provides: for some, it cannot provide answers or solid confirmation; it can only generate hypotheses or questions. For others, analogy, when carefully used, can provide support for a tentative conclusion. Historians have something to learn from the debates among anthropologists: critiques of analogous reasoning will be similar in both disciplines.[190] Historians might learn from the rules suggested for acceptable ethnographic analogy. These include ensuring the strength of relevant data in both the analog and the target case; assessing the regularity and frequency of patterns observed in the analogous cases; trying to minimize temporal and cultural distance between analogues and the target case.[191]

Analogy exists within and far beyond our scholarly disciplines. Wherever it appears, analogy is often a means, either overt or covert, of imparting new meanings. Compelling examples are offered in Stefan Helmreich's sweeping study of the metaphors and analogies of "waves." His *Book of Waves* embraces many fields of knowledge, including history. Helmreich argues that the notion of a wave as a form that can move through a social or cultural body arrives in the nineteenth century, at the same time as the idea emerged that the past could be studied scientifically, as a natural process.[192] The wave image appeared prominently in English studies of disease trends. In the first of these studies, according to Helmreich, "the wave image was primarily metaphorical, a heuristic way of talking about patterns in data." By the twentieth century, scientists had new ways of presenting epidemic "waves," including mathematical models of propagation. "With

---

190 Here I am adapting a point made by Adrian Currie: "the archaeologist answers the same charges as the biologist." Adrian Currie, "Ethnographic Analogy, the Comparative Method, and Archaeological Special Pleading," *Studies in History and Philosophy of Science Part A*, vol.55 (February 2016), 88.

191 Adrian Currie presents a few rules for robust analogical inference in his very cautious defense of analogical reasoning: Currie, "Ethnographic Analogy," 84–94. Among other works of general interest: Cameron Shelley, "Multiple Analogies in Archaeology," *Philosophy of Science*, 66, 4 (December 1999), 579–606; Paul Roscoe, "On the 'Pacification' of the European Neolithic: Ethnographic Analogy and the Neglect of History," *World Archaeology*, 41, 4 (December 2009), 578–88; "More About Ethnographic Analogy," University of California at San Diego (2022) at https://pages.ucsd.edu/~dkjordan/cgi-bin/moreabout.pl?tyimuh=ethnographicanalogy; A.S. Dias, "Analogy in Archaeological Theory," in C. Smith, ed., *Encyclopedia of Global Archaeology* (New York: Spring, 2014); R. Nyrup, *Three Uses of Analogy: A Philosophical View of the Archaeologist's Toolbox* (University of Cambridge: University of Cambridge Repository, 2020), https://doi.org/10.17863/CAM.36216.

192 Stefan Helmreich, *A Book of Waves* (Durham, NC: Duke University Press, 2023), 259.

such models the wave gradually became more than a metaphor and a mere graphical accompaniment to statistical representation; it was now a naturalistic and technical object, one whose causal basis might be discovered and understood."[193]

As both metaphor and analogy, wave forms and flows have a strong presence in economics and economic history. Kondratieff waves, for instance, are cyclical waves: expansion, stagnation, and recession are represented as wave images, up and down undulations along a horizontal axis that represents time. Kondratieff's idea that economic change was characterized by wave cycles of roughly forty to sixty years found strong support among economic historians.[194] But analogy goes much further in economics and economic history because neo-classical economics uses models as basic analytical tools. A model is a hypothesized construct purporting to represent economic processes; a real-world situation or process can be compared to the model in order to isolate similarities and differences. Understood in this way, economic models are analogies, a form of "case-based" analogical reasoning.[195]

If courses on historical logic were standard fare in History curricula, we might learn a great deal about analogical reasoning in multi-disciplinary contexts. We might also be more aware of the lineage of analogy in our own discipline. As Michael Carignan has argued, analogical reasoning has an important place in Victorian historical epistemology.[196] The emerging objectivist and empiricist tendencies in Victorian historiography encountered skepticism among those who insisted that available evidence was always inadequate to the task of representation. That inadequacy meant that there would always be a role for imagination in history, and a role for analogy. The case was put most succinctly by the great English novelist George Eliot:

---

[193] Helmreich, *A Book of Waves*, 266.

[194] The model endures: A.E. Tyulin et al., "The Development of Kondratieff's Theory of Long Waves: The Place of the AI Economic Humanization in the 'Competencies-innovations-market' Model," *Humanities and Social Sciences Communications*, 10, 54 (2023): https://www.nature.com/articles/s41599-022-01434-8. Joseph Schumpeter adapted Kondratieff's model. See, for instance, Alfred Kleinknecht, "Are There Schumpeterian Waves of Innovations?" *Cambridge Journal of Economics*, 14, 1 (March 1990), 81–92.

[195] Itzak Gilboa, Andrew Postlethwaite, Larry Samuelson and David Schmeidler, "Economic Models as Analogies," *The Economic Journal*, 124 (August 2014), 513–33. See also Nicolas T.O. Mouton, "Metaphor and Economic Thought: A Historical Perspective," in Honesto Herrera and Michael White, eds., *Metaphor and Mills: Figurative Language in Business and Economics* (Boston: De Gruyter, 2012), 49–76.

[196] Michael Carignan, "Analogical Reasoning in Victorian Historical Epistemology," *Journal of the History of Ideas* 64, 3 (July 2003), 445–64.

> The exercise of a veracious imagination in historical picturing seems to be capable of a development that might help the judgment greatly with regard to present and future events. By veracious imagination, I mean the working out in detail of the various steps by which a political or social change was reached, using all extant evidence and supplying deficiencies by careful analogical creation.[197]

Eliot attempted to realize her principles of "veracious imagination" and "analogical creation." *Middlemarch* (1871–72), most obviously, is a work of fiction and of history. In that work, Eliot was filling gaps in the evidential record with inferences from her present, and the temporal distance between her present and the imagined past was small (a mere forty years).

A century and a half after Eliot's reflections on history, analogy still has a fragile status in our formal thinking. Even where courses on historical methods exist, analogical reasoning is unlikely to be given much, if any, priority. Probably many would accept the negative view of the Oxford English Dictionary that "analogy is not proof but illustration," or John Stuart Mill's view that analogy amounts to incomplete induction.[198] To stop there, however, would be to ignore Mill's view that analogical reasoning may be very powerful, and to miss the fact that analogy can be far more than illustration. Analogy, either as formal argument or deeply-informed intuition, is clearly present in many domains of history, serving purposes that need to be examined.

Consider, for instance, the history of revolutions, or of any specific revolution. The historian will already have in mind a model of revolution, derived from specific cases of revolution. The model becomes a comparative guide: this or that revolution is similar to, or different from, the model in specific respects. There is another level at which analogy operates and may be discerned by the historian: historical actors may deploy a previous revolution as an analogy to, or model of, their present revolutionary project. In his *Age of Revolution* (1962), Eric Hobsbawm says: "the most formidable legacy of the French Revolution itself was the set of models and patterns of political upheaval which it established for the general use of rebels everywhere." The models that informed political thought and action serve as the framework in which Hobsbawm perceives similarity, difference, and the ways in which discontent acquired "a specific object."[199]

---

[197] George Eliot, "Historic Imagination," *Essays of George Eliot*, ed., Thomas Pinney (New York, 1963), cited in Carignan, "Analogical Reasoning," 445.
[198] J.S. Mill, "Of Analogy," Chapter XX in *A System of Logic*, eighth edition (New York: Harper, 1882), 393.
[199] Eric Hobsbawm, *The Age of Revolution 1789–1848* [1962] (New York: Vintage Books, 1996), 112.

The explicit use of analogy in the study of revolutions goes back a long way. Widely read and admired in the twentieth century was Crane Brinton's *Anatomy of Revolution*, first published in 1938 and reprinted several times. Brinton uses analogical reasoning in his identification of similarities, differences, and uniformities among four revolutions (English, American, French, Russian). His reasoning shows how analogy in historical argument serves to bestow meaning in a conceptual whole. The main analogy is revolution as a specific kind of illness. Brinton says: "We shall regard revolutions as a kind of fever." The illness proceeds in stages, from preliminary signs to full disclosure of symptoms to a crisis ("frequently accompanied by delirium"), to "a period of convalescence," and then to a recovery ("the patient is himself again, perhaps in some respects actually strengthened").[200] When the stages or "cycle" of the disease are observed in each of the four revolutions, similarity, difference, and uniformity become apparent.

This reasoning process endows a particular meaning upon its history. Most obviously, a disease is a negative thing, something to be feared and avoided; a fever is a departure from some previous condition of health. The pre-revolutionary condition becomes prodromal (early signs of illness). One may well ask: do such images apply to pre-1789 France (or to the pre-revolutionary context of any of these four revolutions)? Brinton's analogy assumes that in the pre-illness condition political economies are in equilibrium, and that is a dubious assumption at best. One could point to other meanings imparted by the analogy. It is enough here to point out that options were and are available. An analogy to weather or climate change would impart a very different meaning. So would an analogy to waves – the surge, motion, and dissipation of wave energy.[201]

Analogy is easily perceived as a metaphorical or heuristic device; it may be less apparent as an analytical tool or framework. Is "industrial revolution" a metaphor? Yes, it is: the metaphor of rotation or overturning is obvious. But are we also aware of the fact that the word-pair began and survived as an analogical argument? Arnold Toynbee's *Lectures on the Industrial Revolution* were published posthumously in 1884 and reprinted many times; they were the first sustained

---

[200] Crane Brinton, *Anatomy of Revolution* (New York: Vintage Books, 1965), 16–18.
[201] Later works on the theory of revolution tend to avoid analogical frameworks. George Lawson uses spatial metaphors in his study of revolutions as "contextually-specific event complexes": actions are "embedded within fields" and "fields of action," for instance. But such metaphors are not placed within an overarching analogical frame of the kind used by Brinton. George Lawson, *Anatomies of Revolution* (Cambridge: Cambridge University Press, 2019), 58. While insisting upon "a *modified*, carefully nuanced structuralism" (p.489) [his italics], the historian of France, Bailey Stone, avoids analogy in his *Anatomy of Revolution Revisited: A Comparative Analysis of England, France, and Russia* (Cambridge: Cambridge University Press, 2014).

use of the term "industrial revolution." Central to his historical vision was "machine" or "mechanism": he was narrating the transformative impact of machines. As Daniel C.S. Wilson has pointed out, machinery "took on a double aspect in his writing: on the one hand as the phenomenon under explanation and on the other as a figure of speech for describing change itself." The machine "emerges with a temporal quality as both the cause and effect of change."[202] Those who studied machines, said Toynbee, should "turn away a little from the dead mechanism of the factory to the contemplation of the living mechanism of the social system."[203] Toynbee was seeing society historically, and seeing it as a mechanism – a giant social machine with motive forces and interacting parts. The analogy was basic to his vision as a Victorian-era social reformer: a machine is something that can be repaired and made to serve humanity. The analogy of the machine endured well into the next century, in both studies of industrialization and in social analysis.[204]

I could continue to list examples of analogy, but to do so would risk narrowing the gaze to those examples and to miss the range of analogy and analogizing in rhetoric and thought. Analogy may be, as Douglas Hofstadter and Emmanuel Sander have argued, basic to cognition – the "fuel and fire of thinking." "Each concept in our mind owes its existence to a long succession of analogies made unconsciously over many years," and "our concepts are selectively triggered by analogies."[205] Perhaps, says another author, "analogy is mother to creativity."[206] Whether or not we accept such sweeping claims, historians must acknowledge the ubiquity of analogy in our work and proceed to examine the kind of understandings that it affirms. Analogy inspires, imparts meaning, and prompts critical repudiation. Even where it meets rejection, it is contributing positively to our understanding.

In perhaps no other domains of historical inquiry are these reflections more pertinent than in the fields of gender, feminist history, and feminist theory. These

---

202 Daniel C.S. Wilson, "Arnold Toynbee and the Industrial Revolution: The Science of History, Political Economy and the Machine Past," *History and Memory*, 26, 2 (Fall/Winter 2014), 135.
203 Arnold Toynbee, "The Industrial Future of England," cited in Albert Mansbridge, *Arnold Toynbee* (London: Daniel, 1905), 11; see Wilson, "Arnold Toynbee and the Industrial Revolution," 133.
204 See, for instance, Alan Scott, "Modernity's Machine Metaphor," *British Journal of Sociology*, 48, 4 (December 1997), 561–75. A study of the machine analogy that ranges well beyond Canada is Cynthia Comacchio, "Mechanomorphosis: Science, Management, and 'Human Machinery' in Industrial Canada, 1900–45," *Labour/Le Travail*, 41 (Spring 1998), 35–67.
205 Douglas Hofstadter and Emmanuel Sander, *Surfaces and Essences: Analogy as the Fuel and Fire of Thinking* (New York: Basic Books, 2013), Prologue (n.p.).
206 Bruce Hannon, "The Use of Analogy in Biology and Economics: From Biology to Economics and Back," *Structural Change and Economic Dynamics*, 8, 4 (October 1997), 471–88, Abstract.

fields contain profuse bodies of analogy and analogous reasoning. Here, if anywhere, analogy is fuel and fire. In her *Vindication of the Rights of Woman* (1792), Mary Wollstonecraft said, and repeated: "I argue by analogy."[207] She used analogy as a rhetorical device in condemning the treatment of women. She also used analogical reasoning to define the condition of woman: as is the condition of these other beings, so is the condition of woman. In the nineteenth century, the analogical references proliferated and included those of children, mules, oxen, other animals, and plants.[208] The creative use of analogy led to such inventions as the Mock Parliament, especially popular in Canadian first-wave feminism: in these parodies, women politicians debated the pros and cons of granting men the right to vote.[209]

The most sustained analogy was to slaves, and Mary Wollstonecraft was not the first to deploy this analogy. For women who entered the abolitionist movement, the analogy was direct and personal. "We have good cause to be grateful to the Slave," said Abby Kelley. "In striving to strike *his* irons off, we found, most surely, that we were manacled *ourselves*."[210] The slavery analogy endured and so did the woman/Black analogy. In 1981, bell hooks wrote: "no other group in America has used black people as metaphors as extensively as white women involved in the women's movement."[211] When Simone de Beauvoir came to write *The Second Sex*, she drew upon available writings, especially those of Gunnar Myrdal and Richard Wright, to place the race/sex analogy within her systems of oppression. The American philosopher Kathryn Sophia Belle suggests that de Beauvoir "sets up competing frameworks of oppression, privileging gender difference in ways that suggest that women's subordination is a more significant and constitutive form of oppression than racism, antisemitism, class oppression, slavery, and/

---

[207] Mary Wollstonecraft, *A Vindication of the Rights of Woman* [1792], ed. Sylvana Tomaselli (Cambridge: Cambridge University Press, 1995), 126, 285, cited in Penelope Deutscher, "Abolitionism, Antiracism, Feminism, and Rights by Analogy: From Mary Wollstonecraft to Anna Julia Cooper," in Lydia Morland and Alison Laura Stone, eds., *The Oxford Handbook of American and British Women Philosophers in the Nineteenth Century* (Oxford Academic online edition, February 2024), n.p.
[208] Deutscher, "Abolitionism, Antiracism, Feminism, and Rights by Analogy," n.p.
[209] Kim Byrd, *Redressing the Past: The Politics of English-Canadian Women's Drama, 1880–1920* (Montreal & Kingston: McGill-Queen's University Press,2004), 68–76, 86–91.
[210] "An Anti-Slavery Album, or Contributions from Friends of Freedom" (Western Anti-Slavery Society Collection, Library of Congress, 100), cited in Keith Melder, "Abby Kelley and the Process of Liberation," in Jean Fagan Yellin and John C. Van Horne, *The Abolitionist Sisterhood* (Ithaca: Cornell University Press, 2018), 244. See also bell hooks, *Ain't I a Woman: Black Women and Feminism* (Boston: South End Press, 1981), 126.
[211] bell hooks, *Ain't I a Woman*, 141.

or colonialism."[212] In the United States, the analogy had a particular resonance. Despite its obvious flaws, argues Lisa Maria Hogeland, "the sex/race analogy was nonetheless a founding rhetoric of second-wave feminism: it permeated every kind of Movement writing and analysis, from outlines for consciousness raising, to theoretical works, to literary criticism, to poetry and fiction."[213]

So pervasive was analogy in writing about race and gender that by 2005 one scholar asked "whether it is possible to theorize race and gender in any way other than analogically."[214] Likely, most scholars in the field would answer that it was possible, or that analogy and metaphor, understood either as rhetoric or reasoning, should be used only with extreme caution and with full attention to their limits and pitfalls. Postcolonial histories reinforced the caution: analogy risks imposing colonial epistemologies.[215] Most obviously, the development/underdevelopment dichotomy was based on an analogy with society as modern, industrial, or capitalist. As Mahmood Mandami argued, "Experiences summed up by analogy were not just considered historical latecomers on the scene, but were also ascribed a pre-destiny."[216] There have been experiments with potentially safer analogies, but these seem to have offered no enduring escape from analogy's problems.[217]

There may be more than one enduring outcome of these long debates about analogy. We can, I suggest, derive an outcome relevant to historical thinking: we may discern a catalog of fallacies and a set of rules of reasoning. An obvious fallacy is that of selection bias: by focusing on specific similarities and differences, analogy excludes or de-emphasizes similarities or differences that may be crucial. This fallacy arises with the gender/race analogy, or so it has been alleged, when the similarities of oppression de-emphasize the difference between property in

---

212 Edward O'Byrn, "Simone de Beauvoir, Analogy, Intersectionality, and Expanding Philosophy: An Interview with Kathryn Sophia Belle," *Hypatia*, 38, 1 (2023), 221–2.
213 Lisa Maria Hogeland, "*Invisible Man* and Invisible Women: The Sex/Race Analogy of the 1970s," *Women's History Review*, 5, 1 (1996), 32.
214 Malini Johar Schueller, "Analogy and (White) Feminist Theory: Thinking Race and the Color of the Cyborg Body," *Signs*, 31, 1 (Autumn 2005), 86.
215 See, for instance, Elizabeth Strakosch, "The Violence of Analogy: Abstraction, Neoliberalism and Settler Colonial Possession," *Postcolonial Studies*, 23, 4 (2020), 505–26.
216 Mahmood Mamdani, *Citizen and Subject: Contemporary Africa and the Legacy of Late Colonialism* (Princeton: Princeton University Press, 2018 edition [first published 1996]), 9.
217 In the feminist responses, see, for instance, Donna Haraway, "A Cyborg Manifesto: Science, Technology, and Socialist-Feminism in the Late Twentieth Century," in Haraway, *Simians, Cyborgs, and Socialist-Feminism in the Late Twentieth Century* (New York: Routledge, 1991), 149–81. See also Haraway, "Race: Universal Donors in a Vampire Culture," in Haraway, *Modest_Witness@Second_Millenium.FemaleMan_Meets_OncoMouse: Feminism and Technoscience* (New York: Routledge, 1997), 213–65.

humans (slavery) and the subordinate but highly variable statuses of women in public and private law. It is these differences that must be understood historically if the oppressions are to be perceived and understood. Another fallacy – not peculiar to analogy – is that of reduction: analogy lumps into similar oppression those who inhabit two domains. The oft-cited example is that of Black women, who inhabit both sides of the race/gender analogy. One does not escape this fallacy by "additive" argument – the oppression is dual or cumulative – because the condition of being Black and a woman is distinct and beyond the frame of the analogy. Related to reductionism is what Judith Butler refers to as "conflation": the tendentious merging of conditions from both sides of the proposed analogy. This occurs most obviously in Freud, where analogy conflates sexuality (or erotogenicity) with pathology. A related conflation occurred in the construction of male homosexuality as pathology.[218] Even where such conflation does not occur, analogy can commit the error of placing two things in parallel domains so as to obscure their intersection: race and gender, like race and class, are not separable conditions, but interdependent and interwoven conditions. The intersectionality is often of primary interest to the historian.

We have turned up an old topic: errors that occur in analogical reasoning. We can still learn from David Hackett Fischer's seven fallacies of analogy in his *Historians' Fallacies* (1970). His "fallacy of the insidious analogy," for instance, refers to the way in which a metaphor, once embedded in language, becomes "more powerfully experienced than perceived."[219] The philosopher Paul Bartha developed the point in his study of analogical reasoning in science: "an underlying metaphor can function, like a paradigm, as a constitutive element" and it can be "difficult to shake" (Bartha is referring explicitly to the famous discussion of "paradigm" by the historian of science Thomas Kuhn).[220] The "insidious analogy" is related to reductionism, which Fischer addressed most clearly in his "fallacy of the perfect analogy": "reasoning from a partial resemblance between two entities to an entire and exact correspondence."[221] This fallacy is present in some older writings deploying the race/gender analogy. And as we shall see, the fallacy of the perfect analogy is commonplace in present political uses (or abuses) of history.

---

218 Judith Butler, *Bodies That Matter: On the Discursive Limits of "Sex"* (London: Routledge, 1993), 34–5.
219 David Hackett Fischer, *Historians' Fallacies: Toward a Logic of Historical Thought* (New York: Harper, 1970), 244.
220 Paul F.A. Bartha, *By Parallel Reasoning: The Construction and Evaluation of Analogical Arguments* (Oxford: Oxford University Press, 2010), 11–12.
221 Fischer, *Historians' Fallacies*, 247.

Alas, Fischer did not follow up his superbly provocative book with a more fully developed logic of historical thought. More surprising, perhaps, is the fact that today, in the third decade of the twenty-first century, it is difficult to find even a short manual of rules or guidelines about acceptable analogical reasoning in history. Informal rules exist, however: they are part of the mental equipment of historians, and they allow us to detect error in our own work as well as in the language and argument of others who enter unwaringly into the historians' domain. Here are a few such "common sense" guidelines, adapted, with changes, from those of Paul Bartha (and we might ask, in passing: why does such a book on analogical reasoning exist for the sciences and not for history?)[222]

- The more similarities between the two domains in the analogy, the stronger the analogy.
- A great distance, spatial or temporal, between two domains is likely to weaken the analogy.
- There is no such thing as a perfect or complete analogy; conclusions, therefore, are always tentative.
- Analogies that bear upon causal relations are especially fragile; in such cases independent confirmation must be strong.
- All analogical arguments require attention to differences as well as to similarity.
- Analogy may be a suggestive or intuitive entry to an argument, or it may be an argument in itself; the distinction must be clear.
- Analogy is an instrument of persuasion, often within an ethical position, and its persuasive intent must be clear.

It is precisely because we historians think in such ways that we are well qualified to detect and to correct errors of analogy as they appear in the present. And such errors exist in abundance, especially when politicians seek to use the past for present political purposes. Let's begin with a big caveat: politicians use *the past* – they do not use *history* – and the distinction is not trivial. History is a form of reasoning that requires an educated use of evidence and training in that use. The politician capable of such reasoning is an extremely rare bird among his or her species of chatterer; yet many of that species make habitual use and abuse of seeds they gather from the past. The abuse is not mere error. It can be immensely harmful, especially when it takes on the specious authority of "history."[223]

---

[222] Bartha, *By Parallel Reasoning*, 19–20.
[223] On analogy for ideological purposes see Andrew Mumford, "Parallels, Prescience, and the Past: Analogical Reasoning and Contemporary International Politics," *International Politics* 52 (2015), 1 – 19: https://link.springer.com/article/10.1057/ip.2014.40. On analogy and economic policy:

One does not need to refer to Vladimir Putin to make the point. In my lifetime, one of the most consequential uses of analogy for present purposes was the repeated analogy between appeasement, or the 1938 Munich Agreement in particular, and the wars in Indochina, both French and American, between the 1950s and 1970s. The Munich analogy was basic to the American "domino" theory in the 1960s: if one country fell to communism, adjacent countries would also fall. The analogy violated every one of the suggested rules stated above. So compelling was the Munich analogy that it reappeared in subsequent decades, as a justification for the first Iraq war in 1991, in reactions to the failure to stop the genocide in Rwanda in 1995, and in justifications for military operations in Bosnia in 1995 and Kosovo in 1999. The Vietnam War of the 1960s and 1970s, constructed as an American "quagmire," became another analogy, deployed as a justification for avoiding over-reaching military operations.[224]

Some analogies seem to magnify for us the political, ethical, and even epistemological problems associated with analogical argument. The Holocaust, when deployed as an analogy, can be explosive, as in 2019 when an American politician used the analogy, whereupon the United States Holocaust Memorial Museum issued a statement rejecting "the efforts to create analogies between the Holocaust and other events, whether historical or contemporary." A public debate followed, involving politicians, scholars, and social media.[225] As the American historian

---

Itzhak Gilboa et al., "Economic Models as Analogies," *The Economic Journal*, 124 (August 2014), 513–33; Barry Eichengreen, "Economic History and Economic Policy," *Journal of Economic History*, 72, 2 (June 2012), 289–307; Bruce Hannon, "The Use of Analogy in Biology and Economics: From Biology to Economics and Back," *Structural Change and Economic Dynamics*, 8, 4 (October 1997), 471–88.

224 Robert D. Kaplan, "Foreign Policy: Munich versus Vietnam," *The Atlantic* (May 2007). There are scholarly treatments of the Munich analogy: see especially Yuen Fooh Khong, *Analogies at War: Korea, Munich, Dien Bien Phu, and the Vietnam Decisions of 1965* (Princeton: Princeton University Press, 1992); Jeffrey Record, *Making War, Thinking History: Munich, Vietnam, and Presidential Uses of Force from Korea to Kosovo* (Annapolis MD: Naval Institute Press, 2002). Taylor and Rourke argue that analogy was not a determining factor in decision-making so much as an ex post facto rationalization. I am not persuaded, in part because of their narrow focus on debates and votes in Congress during the 1991 Persian Gulf War. Andrew J. Taylor and John T. Rourke, "Historical Analogies in the Congressional Foreign Policy Process," *Journal of Politics*, 57, 2 (May 1995), 460–8.

225 On 1st July, 2019, a group of scholars published a letter criticizing the Museum's position: "An Open Letter to the Director of the US Holocaust Memorial Museum" at https://www-nybooks-com.ezproxy.library.uvic.ca/online/2019/07/01/an-open-letter-to-the-director-of-the-holocaust-memorial-museum/. See also Edna Friedberg, "Why Holocaust Analogies Are Dangerous" (12 December 2018): https://www.ushmm.org/information/press/press-releases/why-holocaust-analogies-are-dangerous.

Peter E. Gordon has argued, the debate raised the question of whether the Holocaust – or, indeed, other discrete events – are incommensurable: that is, lying outside any common standard of judgment, and hence beyond comparison. Gordon pointed to something that, however obvious, needs repeating: historians do not treat past events as always unique, separable, and incommensurable. If we did so, then we could not speak of similarities or differences at all, and comparisons would be impossible. As Gordon says, "the claim that discrete phenomena are unique in themselves and cannot be compared to anything else . . . leaves us with a picture of human society as shattered into discrete spheres of time and space, as if A belonged to one world and B to another."[226] When we historians say that "the past is a foreign country," we do not mean that the past is so alien as to be beyond all common elements of language or culture, and hence beyond comparison. The comparative impulse is part of our mental functioning, and we will not get rid of comparative analysis as a necessary part of historical thinking; it follows that we will not get rid of analogy. The Holocaust exists at the summit of human atrocities, and many would identify it as unique; such claims are inherently comparative and historical. The Holocaust analogy will endure; it is the task of history to put the use of that analogy to our tests of evidence and reasoning.

We cannot avoid analogy. We can only use it while knowing its potential and its pitfalls.[227] To deny analogy, or to speak only of its weaknesses and perils, would be to ignore its power to instruct and inspire. Analogy does not always mean reductionism or a denial of diversity. On the contrary, analogy denies univocality: it says that meaning lies in the apprehension of difference adjacent to similarity. It accepts that there is no single reality out there to which appeal can be made.[228]

The necessity of analogy is perhaps nowhere more evident in our time than in reactions to the COVID-19 pandemic of the early 2020s. There was no escaping comparison with previous epidemics; analogy itself became infectious. If historians wished for a public education in the need for history, we got our wish, and with it the need to be careful of what we had wished for. Difference, and the distinct paths of each epidemic, were so evident that one writer could ask whether

---

[226] Peter E. Gordon, "Why Historical Analogy Matters," *New York Review of Books*, 7 January 2020.
[227] There is an extensive discussion of analogy in the fields of public and applied history. See Sjoerd Keulen, "Historical Analogies: Functions, Limitations and the Correct Use of Historical Analogies in Applied History," *Journal of Applied History*, 5, 2 (September 2023), 111–31.
[228] G.E.R. Lloyd, *Analogical Investigations: Historical and Cross-Cultural Perspectives on Human Reasoning* (Cambridge: Cambridge University Press, 2019), 89, 109–10.

there were analogies at all, and whether history was of any use.[229] Analogies bearing upon the causes of pandemics were especially suspect, confirming the rule that in analogical reasoning, inferences about cause are especially fragile. As a saying among epidemiologists puts it, "when you've seen one pandemic, you've seen one pandemic."[230] This is not to endorse incommensurability, however: a pandemic is identified and its parameters are defined by comparison with analogues from the past. The 1918–19 influenza epidemic served as one template on which the specific clinical, epidemiological, transmission, and mitigation patterns of COVID-19 could be identified. The analogical identification of similarities and differences also raised the key question about persistence and re-emergence. Descendants of the 1918 influenza virus persisted: will descendants of SARS-CoV-2 persist, and if so, in what forms?[231]

Know something about past epidemics, and then reason by analogy: any current pandemic will exist in a historical, social, and economic context. And as for the 1918 influenza pandemic, so it is for COVID-19: morbidity and mortality are not spread equally; they are not "democratic;" economic inequality is itself a crucial vector and condition. Analogical reasoning in history tells us so.[232]

Analogy can be powerfully creative. It can inspire meaning. There may be no better example than a design for a prison drawn up by the English philosopher Jeremy Bentham in 1785: the panopticon. In Bentham's prison model, inmates were in cells and all could be observed from a central tower. From the tower, vision was panoptic: all-seeing. One obvious purpose was efficiency: a few guards could monitor all prisoners; more costly methods of control and discipline could be avoided. The panopticon became a metaphor and an analogy, most obviously in the thought of Michel Foucault and especially in his book *Discipline and Punish* (1975). Panopticon soon acquired a sweeping applicability. It became a model for the exercise of power and the understanding of power, an analog and template

---

[229] Gaetan Thomas and Guillaume Lachenal, "COVID-19: When History Has No Lessons," History News Network, 4/6/2020: https://historynewsnetwork.org/article/covid-19-when-history-has-no-lessons.
[230] Quoted in Stephen Colbrook, "Writing the History of Pandemics in the Age of COVID-19," *Journal of American Studies*, 57 (2023), 114.
[231] David M. Morens, Jeffery K. Taubenberger, and Anthony S. Fauci, "A Centenary Tale of Two Pandemics: The 1918 Influenza Pandemic and COVID-19 Part I," *American Journal of Public Health*, 111, 6 (June 2021), 1086–94.
[232] To refer only to the 1918 analogy: Patricia J. Fanning, *Influenza and Inequality: One Town's Tragic Response to the Great Epidemic of 1918* (Amherst: University of Massachusetts Press, 2012); Esyllt Jones, "Surviving Influenza: Lived Experiences of Health Inequity and Pandemic Disease in Canada," *CMAJ* [Canadian Medical Association Journal], vol. 192, issue 25 (22 June 2020): https://www.cmaj.ca/content/192/25/E688.

for modern society and its "carceral culture." The panopticon entered scholarly discourse where mechanisms of surveillance were deployed, and even where overt surveillance was not apparent. The analogy has a new life in the world of social media and "surveillance capitalism."[233]

Foucault's formulation arrived at a moment when older conceptions of power were widely seen to be inadequate, and our understanding of power was ripe for paradigmatic change. In liberal thought, the sovereign, self-governing, utility-maximizing individual was being shunted into anachronistic neo-liberal corners. Power, understood as a top-down imposition of force, was losing credibility. The panoptic power of "visibility" answered a need: it was basic to a new conception of the individual and of power. Panoptic visibility meant self-surveillance; individuals became the bearers of power. Those who are watched do not need to know they are being watched at any moment; they need only to know that they *can* be watched. As Foucault put it, the effect of the panopticon is "to induce in the inmate a state of conscious and permanent visibility that assures the automatic functioning of power. So to arrange things that the surveillance is permanent in its effects, even if it is discontinuous in its action; that the perfection of power should tend to render its actual exercise unnecessary; that this architectural apparatus should be a machine for creating and sustaining a power relation independent of the person who exercises it; in short, that the inmates should be caught up in a power situation of which they are themselves the bearers . . . ."[234] Foucault then said that the panopticon is "polyvalent in its applications," and he extended the application to a wide range of individuals and subjects in modern societies.[235]

The panopticon did not need to be an actual prison. It began as a model and endured as such. The similarities between the model and its analogues overwhelmed any superficial differences between actual prison inmates and modern workers or citizens. The original panopticon of the 1780s may have been distant, but as a model, the panopticon collapsed the distance with later analogues. The potential fragility of analogy in causal reasoning was avoided since the analogy existed largely outside causal argument. The analogy was suggestive, intuitive, and its persuasive intent within Foucault's dyadic conception "power/knowledge" was clear.

There is no such thing as a perfect analogy. In Foucault's panopticism, and the understandings of power and knowledge in which it appeared, scholars

---

[233] Shoshana Zuboff, *The Age of Surveillance Capitalism: The Fight for a Human Future at the New Frontier of Power* (New York: Hachette Book Group, 2019), 470–1.
[234] Michel Foucault, *Discipline and Punish: The Birth of the Prison,* trans. Alan Sheridan (New York: Vintage Books, 1995) [first published 1975; in English 1977], 201.
[235] Foucault, *Discipline and Punish,* 205.

began to detect imperfections, erasures, and even suppressions. Here too we can see something of the quality of analogy in historical thinking: it inspires the effort to see what lies outside the frame of the analogy. When historians looked at Foucault's work, many found "she" – and beyond that, any perception of gender – to be missing. Yes, the oppression of women could no longer be associated simply with men's possession of power. But was Foucault's conceptualization of power compatible with feminist theory? The idea that power is constitutive of that on which it acts was both problematic and stimulating. If "the individual is not the vis-à-vis of power" but "one of its prime effects," then the female subject, Judith Butler suggested in 1990, is "formed, defined, and reproduced" in accordance with the power relations in which she exists. Butler added: "the category of 'women,' the subject of feminism, is produced and restrained by the very structures of power through which emancipation is sought."[236] Such ideas were explosive, and there followed an immensely tangled debate – impossible to summarize briefly – running through a large body of writings.[237]

Analogy brings into view similarities and differences that might not be perceived at all outside its frame. It also prompts questions about what the frame cannot contain. Where it succeeds, analogy serves to identify symmetry and difference. To borrow from Paul Bartha's study of analogical arguments, analogy bears the "potential for generalization," meaning "finding a common pattern between the source and target domains."[238] That also means finding difference or asymmetry: source and target domains in which symmetry does not exist. To generalize is to make connections between objects that would otherwise be unconnected. And that is what history does. It follows that analogical reasoning, including its cautionary rules, is fundamental to historical thinking.

---

[236] Judith Butler, *Gender Trouble: Feminism and the Subversion of Identity* (New York: Routledge, 1990), 2.
[237] For the literature up to 2002, see the bibliography in Margaret A. McLaren, *Feminism, Foucault, and Embodied Subjectivity* (Albany: State University of New York Press, 2002).
[238] Bartha, *By Parallel Reasoning*, 105.

10 Quantification

Forty-eight years ago, for the first and only time in my life, I attended lectures in a course on statistics. How could this happen? Because I was about to use a mass of routinely-generated "data." I needed, therefore, a basic introduction to methods of quantitative analysis. I was a postdoctoral fellow in a large collaborative project called the Atlantic Canada Shipping Project. We would analyze the Agreements and Account of Crew, the paper records of voyages and sailors for all British ships from the 1860s to the mid-twentieth-century. These Crew Agreements are one of the largest collections of paper documents in the world. Where archivists are accustomed to measuring documentary records in centimeters or meters, the collection of Crew Agreements measures seven kilometers. We would select the Agreements for ships of Atlantic Canada, and with the assistance of computers, we would write articles and one or more books on a large nineteenth-century shipping industry.[239] The task would take several years. It would expand in many directions my intellectual horizons and the range of my methods. It was also the beginning of my career as a historian of Canada.

What is the point of this small fragment of memoir? The point is to introduce the presence of quantifiers – statements of quantity – in the thinking and writing of historians. So I ask you to read again the 188 words of that first paragraph. How many quantifiers do you detect? There are at least thirteen. Some logicians would also detect an implicit quantifier in the final sentence: "beginning" denotes an initiating phase; it also indicates a small quantity within a long span of years.

In the early decades of my career, between the 1960s and 1990s, quantification and quantitative methods found increasing acceptance among historians.[240] At the same time, the methods prompted rejections and some hostility. I do not propose to review the debates over quantitative methods.[241] I prefer instead to return to an observation of the American economic historian R.W. Fogel in 1975

---

[239] Eric W. Sager, *Seafaring Labour: The Merchant Marine of Atlantic Canada, 1820–1914* (Montreal & Kingston: McGill-Queen's University Press, 1989); Eric W. Sager with Gerald E. Panting, *Maritime Capital: The Shipping Industry in Atlantic Canada, 1820–1914* (Montreal & Kingston: McGill-Queen's University Press, 1990). Most of the Crew Agreements are held in the Maritime History Archive at Memorial University of Newfoundland.
[240] Steven Ruggles documents the expanded use of quantitative methods in the United States in Steven Ruggles, "The Revival of Quantification: Reflections on Old New Histories," *Social Science History*, 45, 1 (Spring 2021), 5–7.
[241] A useful review of the debates is in Ruggles, "The Revival of Quantification," 11–14. A well-known sample of the debate is R.W. Fogel and G.R. Elton, *Which Road to the Past? Two Views of History* (New Haven: Yale University Press, 1983).

https://doi.org/10.1515/9783111563800-010

when he noted "how ingrained and pervasive implicit quantification can be."[242] Fogel illustrated his observation by referring to a work of economic history – an example that easily lent itself to his purpose. One might well ask: how extensive would the implicit quantification be if he had chosen a work of cultural history? I would also ask: were all the quantifiers in Fogel's example really implicit? The word "many" is surely an explicit quantifier. It is sometimes difficult to distinguish between implicit and explicit quantifiers.

Quantification in speech and text is an enormously complex subject. The subject has a long history in both logic and linguistics; it was dominated for 2,000 years by Aristotle's seminal work on logic and quantification theory. One challenge today stems from our understanding that the surface semantics of a statement may convey more than we hear. As Ariel Cohen puts it in his study of the semantics of quantification, "there are phonologically null elements in surface structure." Cohen is referring to "cases where a sentence contains no overt quantifier, yet its interpretation is quantificational." Here is his example:
a. Dogs are barking outside right now.
b. Dogs are intelligent.

There is no explicit quantifier in either of these sentences. But our interpretation is quantificational. From the first sentence, we understand that some dogs, or a specific limited number of dogs, are barking. The second sentence is less clear, but we infer that a significant number of dogs, or perhaps even all dogs, are intelligent.[243]

From these observations, I draw two points: quantifiers are often difficult to detect, and they are more frequent and recurrent than our conscious minds may apprehend (and there is another quantification for you!). These conditions make it difficult to estimate the frequency and importance of quantifiers in the utterances of historians, and no less difficult to say anything about the role of quantification in historical thinking. Of course, the latter is directly related to the former. It would make little sense to argue that quantifiers are merely inconsequential semantics. The words register the thinking.

It is easy enough to count commonplace quantifiers in the writings of historians. Linguists focus on the simple quantifiers: many, each, some, all, few, most, al-

---

242 Robert William Fogel, "The Limits of Quantitative Methods in History," *American Historical Review*, 80, 2 (April 1975), 330. William O. Aydelotte argued that "all generalizations [in History] are implicitly quantitative, whether or not this is made clear in presenting them." Aydelotte, *Quantification in History* (Reading, Mass.: Addison-Wesley, 1971), 4.
243 Ariel Cohen, *Something Out of Nothing: Semantics and Pragmatics of Implicit Quantification* (Leiden: Brill, 2020), 1–2. For an introduction to the subject in linguistics and logic, see Stanley Peters and Dag Westerstahl, *Quantifiers in Language and Logic* (Oxford: Oxford University Press, 2008).

ways. These words recur throughout the book that you are now reading. Or take *Family Fortunes* by Leonore Davidoff and Catherine Hall. Word counts require caution, but here is an estimate: many (328), each (109), some (408), all (581), few (113), most (305), always (125).[244] Now consider another book in which the quantifiers are clearly fundamental to an argument about race: Bill Schwartz's *The White Man's World* (2011). In the first paragraph of Chapter 3 on "Remembering Race," the quantifiers are basic to the meaning: "signs of whiteness" assumed "a new prominence" in public speech; the "subjective power" of whiteness could "intensify"; occasions "multiplied"; colonial idioms "came to be amplified"; there was no "single language" of whiteness; identifications operated with "different degrees of gravity"; imaginings play out in "multiple historical times"; identifications are "diverse" and even "infinite"; the symbols of whiteness were "increasingly present." Here the observations of quantity are core to the argument.[245]

Let us proceed to cases where the quantification may be present in our reading of a text, even when it is more implicit. Consider the following, well-known words:

> We have been warned in recent years, by George Rudé and others, against the loose employment of the term 'mob'. I wish in this chapter to extend the warning to the term 'riot', especially where the food riot in eighteenth-century England is concerned.[246]

There is no explicit quantifier in these two sentences at the beginning of E.P. Thompson's influential article on "The Moral Economy of the English Crowd in the Eighteenth Century." But do we infer a quantity? Yes, we do. Because if there had been one or two instances of "loose employment" in the literature, Thompson's warning would not have been worth making. The presence of quantity is more explicit in the paragraphs that follow: it is precisely because "several" have committed themselves to the "spasmodic view" of popular history, and because "too many" resort to "economic reductionism," that an alternative interpretation is urgent and

---

[244] Leonore Davidoff and Catherine Hall, *Family Fortunes: Men and Women of the English Middle Class 1780–1850*, 3rd edition (London: Routledge, 2018). One has to search on spaceWORDspace in order to avoid including "teach" as "each," for instance. We must remember that the interpretive significance of the quantifier will vary enormously with each use. For assistance, I am indebted to Martin Holmes of the Humanities Computing and Media Centre at the University of Victoria.

[245] Bill Schwarz, *Memories of Empire vol. I: The White Man's World* (Oxford: Oxford University Press, 2011), 165–6.

[246] E.P. Thompson, "The Moral Economy of the English Crowd in the Eighteenth Century," in E.P. Thompson, *Customs in Common: Studies in Traditional Popular Culture* (New York: The New Press, 1993), 185. The article was first published in *Past & Present*, 50 (1971).

necessary. The argument that follows does not require quantitative methods, but it is replete with quantifiers.[247]

We accept the quantitative statements. Surely few readers will take particular notice of them, unless they set out deliberately to do so. But why do we accept them? Thompson says that "marketing procedures became less transparent" across the century, but he does not offer an index of transparency over time. He says that riots exhibit a "pattern of behaviour" that becomes "more, rather than less, sophisticated in the eighteenth century"; he does not give us an index of sophistication over time, and he does not need to. He says that "the elementary moral precepts of the 'reasonable price'" are "universal," and we accept that claim (at least I have accepted it).[248] On what grounds does our acceptance rest? There may be many answers to this question. I suggest that the quantifiers acquire plausibility from their seamless integration into the argument and their immersion in the historian's engaged listening to an immense array of voices and sources. The fatal weakness of the supporters of the "spasmodic view" is this: "They have reflected in only a cursory way upon the materials which they themselves disclose."[249] The quantifiers in Thompson's essay are persuasive and important precisely because they are subordinate and contingent elements in a thorough immersion in the sources behind the readily visible data on trade, markets, and riots.

Quantifiers have a way of sneaking back into a historian's text even when the analysis is said to be qualitative. I find an example in Keith Bradley's "The Slave Society of Rome," Chapter 2 in his important book *Slavery and Society at Rome* (1994). After noting the great variation in slaveholdings in ancient Rome, Bradley asks: "In what sense was Rome a slave society?" He then discusses three methods of determining the presence of a slave society. The first is a "demographic test" which is necessarily quantitative: slaves have a substantial role in production and are a large proportion of the total population.[250] The second test is "qualitative" and relates to the "location" of slaves and their roles. It turns out, however, that the qualitative includes implicit or even explicit quantification: slaves "dominated" large-scale production, provided "the bulk" of income from property, and enabled the extraction of "great revenue." The third test is "much broader" and requires placing slavery in a larger category of "unfree labour." This too turns out to involve quantifiers because "wealthy Romans drew most of

---

[247] Among the obvious ones: many, some, all, most.
[248] Thompson, "The Moral Economy," 205, 224, 257.
[249] Ibid., 185.
[250] Keith Bradley, *Slavery and Society at Rome* (Cambridge: Cambridge University Press, 1994), 12–13.

their incomes from exploiting unfree labour."[251] The argument then moves beyond the three tests to consider the place of slavery in law, culture, and social organization. Thus, the presence of a slave society is much more than a matter of numbers: it is about the cultural acceptance of slavery as a moral and social norm. But here too the quantifiers are not displaced; rather, they become enmeshed within the discussion of law and culture. Once slavery is approached as a "social institution," Bradley says, "it becomes possible to appreciate the vast amounts of time and space in which the Romans themselves were conscious of the presence of slavery among them and of the impact slavery made upon their culture." "The right to enslave" was taken as "axiomatic" in a milieu where "civic freedom was not looked upon as naturally available to all"; slavery was "at no time an incidental feature of Roman social organization and at no time an inconsequential element of Roman mentality." Owning slaves "always served to express potestas [power, authority]" and "Rome was always a slave society."[252] In this balanced and subtle analysis, the distinction between quantitative and qualitative has dissolved.

At this point, one might well ask: so what? It is surely obvious that there will be quantifiers, either explicit or implicit, in historical writing. They exist elsewhere, in both non-fiction and fiction, and indeed in all forms of communication. In historical writing, where scholars deploy large amounts of evidence from a range of sources, references to number, frequency, and quantity are bound to appear. Does the presence of quantifiers tell us anything worth knowing about historical thinking? I suggest that it does tell us a few things worth knowing. First, there is no simple dichotomy between quantifiers and non-quantifiers. All historians make quantitative statements. There is, however, enormous variation in the grounds, semantic and logical, underlying such statements. Second, history has no discipline-specific method or mode of quantifying; the quantifying, as either semantics or method, is always a trans-disciplinary borrowing. Third, quantifiers are an analytical semantics that historians apply to bodies of "evidence"; as such, they raise the broad question of what meaning is thereby derived.

A final and very important justification for a re-thinking of quantification is that the frontier of text analysis is forcing such re-thinking upon us. We live in a world where sources are read not only by humans but by machines. In this world, research involves keyword searches and much more: it involves extraction and concatenation in the production of meaning, and at some level, these involve quantification. As the sociologist Ana Macanovic puts it: using text mining to identify concepts in texts has "reignited" discussions on "whether the meaning expressed in

---

[251] Bradley, *Slavery and Society*, 13.
[252] Bradley, *Slavery and Society*, 16, 29–30.

text can be summarized into quantifiable categories that reflect ontologically real social entities."[253] From a different perspective, Steven Ruggles points to the immense challenges facing historians when "the next frontier is text": "virtually the entire contents of the world's archives and libraries are being transferred into machine-readable form. We do not yet really know how to capitalize on the computerization of the entire historical record, but it is certain to involve counting at some level." He adds a stern warning: "if historians do not get on board, we will become irrelevant."[254]

In entering this new world, it helps to know that quantity and quantifying are already elements in historical thinking. Historical thinking involves a sensitive detection of repetition, frequency, and quantity. I am aware of this quantifying tendency in my own work, even when I was examining the history of an idea and not using quantitative methods. In 2020, I published a book in which I argued that in the first flourishing of political economy in Canada, between the 1880s and 1920s, Canadian economists wrote relatively little about inequality or distributive justice.[255] On what grounds did that "relatively little" rest? It rested on an extensive comparative analysis, involving wide reading and keyword searching of Canadian, British, and American political economy. Where the British and American writing on inequality was rich, extensive, and innovative, the Canadian writing was meager, even given the much smaller size of the pool of economists in Canada. My argument was about both content and relative frequency.

It helps also to know that quantitative methods and displays go back a long way in our discipline. As Ruggles has pointed out, the first great wave of quantification in history in the United States occurred in the first half of the twentieth century.[256] The contexts were different in the 1970s and 1980s, and again in the 2010s, but those decades saw "revivals," not the appearance of something entirely new. Technological changes have reduced the barriers to quantitative methods and formal quantitative displays, but the cultural and historiographical condi-

---

253 Ana Macanovic, "Text Mining for Social Science – The State and the Future of Computational Text Analysis in Sociology," *Social Science Research*, 108 (November 2022), 9.
254 Steven Ruggles, "The Revival of Quantification," 21.
255 Eric W. Sager, *Inequality in Canada: The History and Politics of an Idea* (Montreal & Kingston: McGill-Queen's University Press, 2020), Chapters 1 (18–52) and 6 (184–218).
256 The percentage of articles in the *American Historical Review* that included a statistical table increased significantly in the 1910s and 1920s. Ruggles, "The Revival of Quantification," 2–6. See also Steven Ruggles and Diana L. Magnusson, "The History of Quantification in History: The JIH as a Case Study," *Journal of Interdisciplinary History*, 50, 3 (Winter 2020), 363–81. The revival of quantitative approaches in Canadian historical writing in the first decades of the twenty-first century is documented in Peter Baskerville and Kris Inwood, "The Return of Quantitative Approaches to Canadian History," *Canadian Historical Review*, 101, 4 (December 2020), 585–601.

tions that spawned the revivals are not well understood. With respect to the revival in the 2010s, Ruggles offers the hypothesis that political conditions and perceived crises – climate change, globalization, rising inequality, and surging right-wing nationalism – made obvious the need for measurement and caused the stigma against quantification to disappear.[257] The same hypothesis might apply to implicit and non-formal quantification, but the connections between wider contexts and historians' practices can only be a matter of speculation. We may observe much more than we can explain.

I observe, then, that historians are frequency detectors. Confronted with a particular notion, idea, or assertion in a text, we ask: does this expression stand alone? Will it be repeated elsewhere, either intact or in some altered form? If a repetition is not found, after extensive searching, do we then understand it as an anomaly or departure from a norm? This capacity for frequency detection is largely intuitive, but the intuition is informed and guided by long experience. In this capacity, we may find in embryo the impulse to quantify. Faced with a vast and complex collection of documents, I visualize these documents as containers of evidence or data, and I ask: how many such pieces of evidence are there, and how many of each category?

I could choose many examples of frequency detection. Here I choose one that is perhaps as remote from formal and explicit quantification as any in European historical writing. Richard Cobb (1917–1996) was an English historian with a deep understanding of France and its history. "A total rejection of sociology and quantification," says Cobb of his book *The Police and the People*.[258] The rejection of explicit counting is not total (there is numerical information on age, for instance), but it is almost complete.[259] Nevertheless, basic to Cobb's vast pointillist collage is an assiduous pursuit of frequency and repetition. The pursuit is clearly stated: "believing, as I do, that twenty-five examples to illustrate a point are better than fifteen, and that fifty are better still."[260] The book is about language, the meaning of words, and *mentalité*. The purpose is to "identify" and to "explain," and these tasks require the perception of frequency and variation: "The important fact is the sheer repetition of certain affirmations." "It is a matter of scale, of extent, as well as of content and repetition." "Our purpose has been to reassess the sans-culotte movement and to render it in its contemporary proportions." "Les filous, les voleurs, les assassins – categories that recur like a trinity." "The regional incidence of desertion offers a

---

257 Ibid., 21.
258 Richard Cobb, *The Police and the People: French Popular Protest, 1789–1820* (Oxford Clarendon Press, 1970), xv, note 1.
259 Cobb, *The Police and the People*, 168.
260 Cobb, *The Police and the People*, xxi.

valuable indication of the strength or weakness of surviving Jacobinism." "All the historian can do is to indicate, from a wide selection of case histories and from the long habit of these people, certain common traits, and at the same time to reiterate the endless variety of the species."[261] Cobb's book is a prodigious act of frequency and "incidence" detection, something that can emerge only from thirty years of living "inside, not outside, my subject." Here the perception of frequency, incidence, extent, proportion, and recurrence is necessary to the task of decomposition and an account that is "impressionistic rather than exhaustive."[262]

There is no way, of course, that Cobb's detection of frequency and repetition would lead to an embrace of formal quantification. It is precisely because of his distance from formal quantification that his work may indicate the presence of a way of thinking that may be discipline-wide. One can easily think of other examples where quantification is scarce and the interpretation stands independently of formal quantification. Take, for instance, the question: what is the meaning, or character, of the Renaissance in Italy? The answer, as in Jacob Burckhardt's *Civilisation of the Renaissance in Italy*, does not depend on quantifiers. The association of art with politics and modernity can be made in largely non-quantitative statements. At the same time, it is worth noting that quantifiers occur throughout Burckhardt's book.[263]

The question about the status of quantifiers remains extremely difficult to answer. I demonstrate the difficulty by pursuing a little further the example of Cobb's book. At one point, introducing his respectful dissent from Albert Soboul's "rather formalized account of the relations between classes," Cobb says of the sans-culotte (in the singular): "apart from the difficulties of an exact definition of this status . . . he exists at all only as a unit within a collectivity, which exists only in virtue of certain specific, unusual, and temporary institutions: once the institutions have been destroyed, or tamed, the sans-culotte too disappears; in his place, there is what there had been before – a shoemaker, a hatter, a tailor, a tanner, a wine merchant, a clerk, a carpenter, a cabinet-maker, an engraver, a miniaturist, a fan-maker, a fencing-master, a teacher . . . . The sans-culotte then is not a social

---

261 Cobb, *The Police and the People*, 38, 76, 97, 202, 204, 207.
262 Cobb, *The Police and the People*, xvi, xix.
263 Jacob Burckhardt, *The Civilisation of the Renaissance in Italy*, trans. S.G.C. Middlemore (London: George Allen and Unwin, 2nd ed., 1890). The quantifier "many," for instance, appears many times, and in most instances its import is of little consequence to the interpretation. The curious might, however, consider the uses of "many" on the following pages, where the word does have consequential import: 83, 103, 174, 222, 238, 240, 243, 244, 258, 273, 328, 332, 382, 396, 480, 490, 507, 531. In no way does this comment imply that Burckhardt's use of the quantifier was careless or ill-considered.

or economic being; he is a political accident."[264] The thirteen occupations listed indicate the singular and varied identities of people when perceived outside Soboul's "rigorous choreography" of class.[265] Cobb's portrait of sans-culottes does not require an estimate of the numbers of persons in each occupation. The portrait exists independently of any quantitative estimate.

But does it? Here is the problem: the sentences quoted above contain quantifiers ("a unit" is a quantifier; so also is the indefinite article "a"). Cobb has not said how many persons he has found in the archives who possess both each occupation and association with sans-culotterie. But we interpret a frequency, however imprecisely. We do not read the indefinite article "a" to mean that there is only one such individual. We understand that Cobb has found at least one, or perhaps more than a few, of each. Non-zero or "a few" are counts, and they are enough to confirm Cobb's point that the identity sans-culotte lies beyond reductionist categorization; the counts are also *necessary* confirmation of the point. And what, other than perceived repetition in the sources and frequency detection, led to this selection of thirteen occupations? The portrait of sans-culottes does not exist independently of quantification.

I have drawn two very different conclusions from the same evidence, and I find both conclusions plausible. If I have no clear way to choose between them, the point is this: the ontology of quantity and quantifiers in historical thinking remains unclear. The theoretical work has simply not been done, despite the attention given to quantitative methods for historians. Quantifiers often remain a silent presence, lurking in corners where we fail to see them. An example is the anomaly, the singular case that is the object of attention in microhistory. Carlo Ginzburg writes: "Anomalous cases are especially promising, since anomalies, as Kierkegaard once noted, are richer, from a cognitive point of view, than norms, insofar as the former invariably includes the latter – but not the other way round."[266] There is a false dichotomy here. The anomaly is a departure from a norm, and only once the historian identifies the norm can the anomaly be perceived. It is the presence of the norm that makes the anomaly visible. Thus both exist together, not as opposites. And the norm can be identified only as a pattern or recurring practice, custom, or value. Lurking behind the norm is the silent presence of frequency detection through which the norm is constructed.

---

264 Cobb, *The Police and the People*, 120.
265 Cobb, *The Police and the People*, 121.
266 Carlo Ginzburg, "Our Words, and Theirs: A Reflection on the Historian's Craft Today," in Susanna Fellman and Marjatta Rahikainen, eds., *Historical Knowledge: In Quest of Theory, Method and Evidence* (Newcastle Upon Tyne: Cambridge Scholars Publishing, 2012), 114.

Consider also temporality, a core element in historical thinking. What is time? Time has become a measurable abstraction, especially since the invention of clock time. How do we perceive this abstraction? In no small part as and through quantity. Braudel's temporalities existed as quantities of *durée*. Koselleck's "sediments of time" are "formations that differ in age and depth;" they are "multiple layers;" they involve "structures of repetition that are not exhausted in singularity."[267] Repetitions occur and accumulate, and some acquire greater volume or quantity, and in this accumulation of repetitions, we see the movement and even the acceleration of time. As Koselleck says: "The bourgeois world unfolded under the sign of acceleration. Ever more pianos – the mark of distinction of every bourgeois salon – were produced in ever-shorter periods of time."[268] So also with changes in transportation technology: with the arrival of railways, space shrank, its volume and extent collapsing, and in this shrinkage, an acceleration of time was perceived. Quantity, frequency, and recurrence are all present in our European-origin understandings of time.

I am aware that there are concepts here that should not be lumped together. Quantity, volume, frequency, recurrence – these are not all the same thing. But they are all scalars – quantities that have only magnitude and not direction. History is a multi-scalar optics, a way of seeing and understanding in which the apprehension of quantity is embedded. Historians deploy a language of quantity, and until somebody undertakes a thorough study of the semantics of history, our understanding of that language will remain incomplete.

Quantity is present in our thinking, and it is pressing further upon us with the expansion of big data, text mining, and humanities computing. At stake for cultural history, as Richard Jean So says in his recent study of "data history and racial inequality," is "how we think about the relationship between data and cultural history and the relationships between numbers and reading."[269] Quantity presses upon us when historians move from reading a small number of texts to interpreting the reading done by algorithms applied to gigantic corpora of texts. There is no longer a choice; one cannot be for or against quantifiers when we have to begin by reporting the number of texts or semantic units "read" by our machines. The problem is how to use quantities and quantifiers, as semantics and as method. We may lose something, as So says, because thinking with numbers risks "reduction and

---

267 Reinhart Koselleck, *Sediments of Time: On Possible Histories* (Stanford: Stanford University Press, 2018), 3, 5.
268 Koselleck, *Sediments of Time*, 88.
269 Richard Jean So, *Redlining Culture: A Data History of Racial Inequality and Postwar Fiction* (New York: Columbia University Press, 2021), 6.

reification."²⁷⁰ We may also gain much, as our capacity for reading and analysis expands as never before.²⁷¹ Texts of any kind are immensely complex. They do not present to us readily-visible patterns and transparent meanings. Our rapidly-changing technologies construct patterns, categories, and concatenations and present these to us in specifiable quantities. What historians see, therefore, is constructed and contingent – and quantified – in ways that we must seek to decompose.

In North America, we live in a media universe saturated with numbers, data, and what we refer to, in everyday speech, as statistics.²⁷² It is precisely because quantifiers are so ubiquitous that we hear so much today about the need for better numeracy and statistical literacy. Two centuries ago, large proportions of the population did not know numbers that we take for granted: one's own age, the time of day, the day of the month. Numbers were restricted more directly to work and means of living. In our culture, quantities and quantifiers inhabit our weather, our politics, our entertainment, our sports, and much more. We accept quantifiers, even if we do not always understand them or contextualize them carefully. We learn to expect them.

We may think of quantifiers – and even of statistics – as a form of language that is particularly extensive in our culture. Language, after all, is a body of signs or symbols that we use to communicate meaning. Perhaps statistics is one of our many languages? This idea might help to resolve a problem that attentive readers may have detected, a problem that may have arisen from my observations in this chapter. Earlier, I invoked a hermeneutic approach to understanding. This approach stands opposed to ideas of detached or disembodied truth that can be discovered by appropriate methods or impersonal modes of reasoning. Some would cite the German philosopher Hans-Georg Gadamer, who said that "the problem of hermeneutics goes beyond the limits of the concept of method as set by modern science."²⁷³ It might seem, then, that a hermeneutic approach is inconsistent with

---

270 So, *Redlining Culture*, 6.
271 The risks and the gains are neatly summarized in Claire Lemercier and Claire Zalc, "History by Numbers," *Aeon* (September 2022), at https://aeon.co/essays/historical-data-is-not-a-kitten-its-a-sabre-toothed-tiger. See also the final chapters in Jo Guldi, *The Dangerous Art of Text Mining: A Methodology for Digital History* (Cambridge: Cambridge University Press, 2023), 407–53.
272 For what it is worth, do a Google NGrams search and consider the increase in recent decades of the following terms: data, statistic, quantitative, quantify, numeracy. Of course, the counts are substantially affected by the sample of texts being read, however large; and so the counts must be taken as fragile suggestions at best.
273 Hans-Georg Gadamer, *Truth and Method*, 2nd revised edition, trans. Joel Weinsheimer and Donald G. Marshall (New York: Continuum, 2006), xx. In his Foreword to the second edition, Gadamer clarified his position on method and insisted that "I did not remotely intend to deny the necessity of methodical work within the human sciences" (p. xxvi).

quantification and especially formal methods of quantitative analysis; or, at least, that a hermeneutic approach is especially resistant to any reification of numbers (numbers presented as images of a past reality). Certainly, hermeneutic approaches have been widely deployed in support of "qualitative" methods and non-quantitative interpretation of texts.

Let me recall a personal anecdote that may help to resolve this problem. Many years ago, a distinguished intellectual historian, who knew little of statistics, insisted that in my writing, which relied in part on statistical methods I was returning to an antiquated acceptance of facts in a vain pursuit of objectivity.[274] Nothing could budge him from that conviction. We might have seen beyond the mutual incomprehension if we had started with a few definitions. My colleague was equating "statistics" with numerical displays. But the term has another meaning: it refers to a very large body of procedures and methods in applied mathematics; the numerical displays come from those procedures. The researcher must have data: traces from the past that are put into service as evidence. The data are deployed within specific procedures, which then yield summary measures – perhaps a chi square, a Beta coefficient, or a p value. All of this lies within the domain of statistics. And what then has become of "fact" and "objectivity"? A p value is not a "fact" and not a representation of a past reality. It is a very specific probability measure in null-hypothesis significance testing, and it is often necessary when observing a potential association between variables in a model. The model is an analogy – a figurative construct. The numerical things are, therefore, highly subjective – the products of carefully specified perspectival orientations.[275] The results – the tentative conclusions – emerge from the methods and procedures as much as from the data. That is why so much debate in social science revolves not just around data, but around the methods and procedures appropriate to any specific problem. And that was why my colleague's conviction that I was dealing in "facts" made no sense to me. He could not see subjectivity where it was transparently present.

I do not deny that in numerical displays the subjectivity is often unacknowledged. But I suggest that the illusory realism may also be a construct of the reader's perception: the reader infers or imputes the realism. Instead, let us read statistics as language, whether statistics refer to numerical displays or to techniques

---

[274] "Great is the temptation to believe that a statistic would be more 'scientific' than an article from the archive or a logical argument," writes Ivan Jablonka. "Figures have a mathematical aspect giving the illusion of a scientific fact." Ivan Jablonka, *History Is a Contemporary Literature*, 146.
[275] So persistent is the objective/subjective dichotomy that some scholars seek to replace those terms with broader conceptions: Andrew Gelman and Christian Hennig, "Beyond Objective and Subjective in Statistics," *Journal of the Royal Statistical Society Series A*, 180, 4 (2017), 967–1033.

of analysis. Read the statistics as language, a syntax of signs and symbols deeply embedded in our culture and our historical beings, and the numerical displays lose their putative objectivity. Read this language as suggestive and evocative. Statistical series presenting measures of change over time, for instance, are always approximate, and they are products of their assumptions as much as of the data. There is no longer a detached, disengaged observer representing a past reality as "fact." There is instead a widely shared language, even if some do not speak it fluently. And it is a language that we are conditioned to hear and to expect.

Start reading the Introduction in Eric Nelson's provocative and original study, *The Royalist Revolution: Monarchy and the American Founding* (2014). We hear voices, and then the voice of the historian as he makes a startling claim: "The American Revolution ... was ... a revolution against a legislature, not against a king. It was, indeed, a rebellion in favour of royal power." Should we accept this claim? The historian who is reading will expect a further elaboration and a deep grounding of the argument in a range of sources. The historian also awaits the inescapable quantifier. We are already asking: who? And how many? We do not wait long for Nelson's answer: "a great many."[276] That quantifier, and those that follow in Nelson's book, are not inconsequential discursions. They are prominent elements in historical argumentation.

There are no clear rules of quantification in historical reasoning, other than those that apply when quantitative methods are borrowed from outside our discipline. There are standards that historians accept, however, although these remain under-developed. We know when numbers claim too much and when they may tend to a specious precision. We know when a quantitative measure is necessary but missing. We know "the fallacy of statistical impressionism," as David Hackett Fischer describes it: when a few numbers purport to sustain a generalization whose weight they will not bear.[277] Our sensitivity to nuances of meaning persuades us to interrogate the semantics of number and quantity. We know that an honest caution must apply when we use semantic quantifiers: many, some, all, most, few. We know when a number, cited without context, requires a comparative measure before it makes sense. These are a few of the standards of reasoning that we already know. They are an embryonic introduction to an element of historical thinking that would acquire greater refinement if logic and method held appropriate status in the education of historians.

---

[276] Eric Nelson, *The Royalist Revolution: Monarchy and the American Founding* (Cambridge, Mass.: Belknap Press of Harvard University Press, 2014), 1–2.
[277] Fischer, *Historians' Fallacies*, 113–6.

11 Abductive Reasoning

One day recently, I came home to find a painting newly mounted on the living room wall. I was astonished. I had never seen this painting before. In recent years this kind of surprise has happened quite often. The consequence, perhaps, of living with a brilliantly spontaneous artist. There was a mystery here. Where had this painting come from? I love such mysteries.

Rather than wait for an explanation to be provided by somebody else, I started to think. It was possible that my wife had suddenly decided to buy this painting. It was also possible that she had received it as a gift from a fellow artist. It was also possible that she had painted the work herself and decided to mount it. I could think of no other possible explanation. The first of these three explanations required a few assumptions: that my wife would have spent a considerable sum of money (it was a very good painting) without consulting me in advance, and that she had found a way to transport a canvas of this size from its point of sale into our house. The second explanation required the assumption that she had been visiting an artist friend that day and had received the gift (although it might have been a loan, of course). The third explanation also required an assumption: that she had been working on this painting in our basement and I had never noticed it. There was also a piece of evidence in support of the third explanation: the painting, an acrylic of leaves and petals, light blues and greens with dashes of pink, was in a minimalist style favored by my wife in recent months. I had my explanation, and I was prepared to say that my third explanation was correct, to a high degree of probability. Why was the third explanation the best one? Because I had evidence in its support. And second, the third explanation required the fewest assumptions, and the key assumption was easy to accept (well known to be unobservant, I had not noticed the painting in progress).

We do this kind of reasoning all the time, especially when we encounter something unexpected or surprising and seek an explanation.[278] It is called abductive reasoning. Abductive reasoning is a type of inferential reasoning: an inference is drawn from a set of data, and that inference is taken as an explanation (it may also

---

[278] In his pioneering discussions of abduction, Charles Peirce said that abduction begins with surprise or a "curious circumstance"; abduction is the process that makes sense of the surprise. Douglas N. Walton, *Abductive Reasoning* (Tuscaloosa: University of Alabama Press, 2004), 4; J.R. Wible, "C.S. Peirce's Theory of Abductive Expectations," *European Journal of the History of Economic Thought*, 27, 1 (2020), 26. Jan van der Dussen argues that Collingwood's conception of inference corresponds closely to Charles Peirce's theory of abductive reasoning: Van der Dussen, "Collingwood's Claim that History is a Science," in Van der Dussen, *Studies on Collingwood, History and Civilization* (Cham: Springer, 2016), 137–52.

https://doi.org/10.1515/9783111563800-011

be a provisional explanation in the form of a hypothesis). The textbook definition is: given a specific set of data D, explanation E is the explanation, from alternatives available, that best explains or accounts for D. Thus, abduction is often referred to as "inference to the best explanation."[279] There are problems and unanswered questions here. If E is only one among many possible explanations, then where did the possible explanations come from? What makes any explanation a "candidate" explanation? Also, what is the meaning of "best"? What are the criteria by which one explanation can be "best," or better than others? If nothing else, such questions point to key differences between abduction on the one hand, and deductive and inductive reasoning on the other. Abductive reasoning has a ubiquity and plasticity not shared by the other forms of reasoning. It cannot easily be deployed, for instance, in syllogisms.[280] It does not allow certainty, as does deductive logic. Inductive reasoning involves inference from premises, but the premises are usually taken as true; in abductive reasoning, premises are only probable and the inference or explanation is always probable. Abduction does not have strict logical formality, and the "truth" it yields is said to be probable or approximate.

So I ask my long-suffering reader to stop and think. Have you had a real surprise in your life recently? And have you tried to explain what happened? Very likely, then, you were using abductive reasoning, whether you knew it or not. And surprise, by the way, is a common trigger and incentive to historical inquiry. We seize upon the unexpected and we seek to explain it. "History is merely a list of surprises," said the American novelist Kurt Vonnegut. "It can only prepare us to be surprised yet again."[281] In history, we seek to contain surprise within reason.

Abductive reasoning is commonplace in the sciences (it also appears in fields as diverse as artificial intelligence, psychology, nursing, archeology, and music). It is most obviously present in medical diagnostics, where inferences are made to find the best explanation for a set of observed conditions. It is also present in law,

---

279 The conflation of abduction with inference to the best explanation begins with Gilbert H. Harman, "The Inference to the Best Explanation," *Philosophical Review*, 74, 1 (1965), 88–95. There has been debate ever since about whether the conflation is appropriate. Philosophers of science often separate abduction from inference to the best explanation: for instance, Adolfas Mackonas, "Inference to the Best Explanation, Coherence, and other Explanatory Virtues," *Synthese*, 190, 6 (April 2013), 975–95.

280 Nevertheless, as long ago as 1903, Charles Peirce proposed a syllogistic form for abductive reasoning:

"The surprising fact, C, is observed;
But if A were true, C would be a matter of course.
Hence, there is reason to suspect that A is true." Cited in Wible, "C.S. Peirce's Theory," 30.

281 Kurt Vonnegut, *Slapstick! Or Lonesome No More* (New York: Delacorte Press, 1976), 255.

when a hypothesis is drawn from a set of evidence. It was present, according to the historian Ben Novak, in the surprising political reasoning of Adolf Hitler, and may help us to understand Hitler's appeal. Novak himself uses abductive reasoning in his analysis, and rarely is abduction cited so explicitly in historical work.[282] Whatever one thinks of Novak's argument, I suggest that abduction is an extensive characteristic of historical thinking. Historians are specialists in abduction. We push this form of reasoning to its limits, and we experiment with ways of doing it effectively.

Even if we take abductive reasoning to be prominent in historical thinking, the question remains: how prominent? In my view, such reasoning is commonplace. It is readily apparent in works that are framed around questions about "what happened?" or "was it the case that?" A classic instance is Natalie Zemon Davis's *The Return of Martin Guerre* (1983). The book deals with a few specific questions: what happened when a man claiming to be Martin Guerre appeared in the village of Artigat in 1556? And what did Bertrande de Rols know about this pretender, Arnauld du Tilh, when they lived together as husband and wife? In answer to these questions, Davis offers not logical inferences from unproblematic evidence, but "conjectural knowledge and possible truth" based on a wide range of circumstantial and contextual evidence.[283] Another well-known example is offered by the writings that address the questions "did Thomas Jefferson father children with the slave Sally Hemings?" and "what did the neighbours know about Thomas Jefferson and Sally Hemings?" The reasoning in answer to that question, as Allan Megill argues, is abductive, yielding answers only to a degree of probability.[284]

Abductive reasoning is most clearly apparent in historical causation. And even if we would no longer agree with E.H. Carr that "the study of history is the study of causes," nevertheless, questions of cause arise frequently, and not only when we discuss the origins of wars. Where there is a specific outcome, or where there is a set of outcomes, there will be more than one possible "explanation." But what an explanation consists of, and what a "best" explanation might be, are difficult questions, and the form that abduction takes will vary.

As a starting point, let us turn to E.H. Carr's thought experiment about a car accident. Jones's car collides with Robinson, who is crossing the road to buy cigarettes. Robinson is killed, and the "candidate" causes of his death include alcohol

---

[282] Ben Novak, *Hitler and Abductive Logic: The Strategy of a Tyrant* (Plymouth UK: Lexington Books, 2014).
[283] Natalie Zemon Davis, "On the Lame," *American Historical Review*, 93, 3 (June 1988), 574. The book is *The Return of Martin Guerre* (Cambridge Mass.: Harvard University Press, 1983).
[284] Allan Megill, *Historical Knowledge, Historical Error: A Contemporary Guide to Practice* (Chicago: University of Chicago Press, 2007), 125–50.

consumption by Jones, faulty brakes, and a blind corner where visibility is poor (Robinson's desire for cigarettes is easily excluded from the list). The example is neatly designed to demonstrate that value judgment is part of the evaluation of causes, and hence part of the reasoning process. The problem is that the story, for a number of reasons, is a poor example of historical causation, even as a thought experiment. For one thing, the outcome is a singular and independent event. In historical analysis, outcomes rarely, if ever, take this form. One gets a bit closer to history if one re-writes the story to include two people crossing the road at the same moment; one is killed and the other is not; and the behavior of one influences the behavior of the other. Furthermore, in Carr's story, there are no interactions among the proposed causal factors. Thus, there is no connection between faulty brakes and the blind corner; the corner did not affect the condition of the brakes, and the brakes did not affect the corner. But in the world of the past, among candidate explanations or conditions proposed by historians, such interactions are almost invariably present; at least their presence must be considered. In the historian's world, there are no isolated, independent variables or conditions.

When applied to historical causation, abductive reasoning differs from abduction in other domains in its treatment of the explanandum – the thing to be explained. It is commonplace in law to begin by taking as given the outcome: a murder has been committed, as is shown by the presence of a deceased person with a bullet in the skull. In medicine, if a specific pain is located somewhere in the human body, the pain is assumed to exist in some form, and abductive reasoning is applied to generate a hypothesis as to etiology. In historical causation, the thing to be explained is never taken as given, and it is never so simple as a deceased person or different outcomes for two people crossing a road. The outcome is never a found object. The outcome itself must be created and given plausible status as an event or meaningful entity. Similarly, the conditions to be offered as explanatory are not found objects, and they are neither simple nor independent. They are also likely to be numerous. They interact with each other, and the interactions may carry significant weight.

The reasoning process is still abductive because inferences are being made about relationships between an outcome and other prior or concurrent conditions, and the relationships are presented in the form of explanatory hypotheses. But the reasoning process quickly becomes immensely complex. One might be able to depict the process visually, in an argumentation map, but the result would be horribly congested. We may have entered a domain of reasoning sometimes referred to as "creative abduction." In creative abduction, the reasoning does not assume sets of simple and independent objects and a selection of such objects presented as "data." Rather, the observations and hypotheses are constructions and the process is theory-generating; in science, for instance, new theoretical terms appear, such as "atom," "electron," or "quark."[285] So far as I know, there has been no sustained attempt to define creative abduction as it may appear in historical thinking.[286]

I am suggesting that in history there is a reasoning process within which the historical truth claim is made. Where the truth claim is causal, the reasoning is abductive, and it exists as a mode of cognition prior to its application to any observed past.

I offer as an example a well-known problem in history in recent decades: the alleged "divergence" of economic development between Europe and certain Asian countries in the modern period. I will refer to Kenneth Pomeranz's book *The Great Divergence* (2000), a book very well known to historians of colonization and world history.[287] Pomeranz does not begin his book with an argumentation map. He does, however, make explicit a complex abductive process in which his meaning as "explanation" is embedded.[288] Some might argue that his problem is not a causal one at all: he does not refer to "causes" or to "causation." Nevertheless, he is clearly trying to answer a "why" question with an "explanation" (his word) for an outcome or explanandum. Divergence means the differing economic paths of "Europe" and certain "other parts of the world" in the modern period.[289] This divergence demands, and receives, further specification. Of what does the different economic path of "Europe" consist? As a start, it consists of earlier and more rapid development of "large-scale mechanized industry" that enabled very

---

[285] Charles S. Peirce insisted that abductive reasoning was idea-generating. Deductive reasoning, by contrast, "cannot provide new insights that are not already present in the premises," says Matus Halas, "In Error We Trust: An Apology of Abductive Inference," *Cambridge Review of International Affairs*, 28, 4 (2015), 705.

[286] Among others: Helmut Prendinger and Mitsuru Ishizuka, "A Creative Abduction Approach to Scientific and Knowledge Discovery," *Knowledge-Based Systems*, 18, 7 (November 2005), 321–6; Paul Thagard and Caeron Shelley, "Abductive Reasoning: Logic, Visual Thinking, and Coherence" (1997), cogsci.uwaterloo.ca/Articles/Pages/%7Abductive.html; Mario Veen, "Creative Leaps in Theory: The Might of Abduction," *Advances in Health Sciences Education*, 26 (2021), 1173–83; Lorenzo Magnani, "The Abductive Structure of Scientific Creativity: An Essay on the Ecology of Cognition," *Transactions of the Charles S. Peirce Society*, 56, 3 (Summer 2020), 456–65; Stefan Timmermans and Iddo Tavory, "Theory Construction in Qualitative Research: From Grounded Theory to Abductive Analysis," *Sociological Theory*, 30, 3 (September 2012), 167–86.

[287] Kenneth Pomeranz, *The Great Divergence: China, Europe, and the Making of the Modern World Economy* (Princeton: Princeton University Press, 2000). A summary of the first ten years of debate on Pomeranz's book is in Gregory Blue, "Chinese History in World History," in Michael Szonyi, ed., *A Companion to Chinese History* (Chichester: John Wiley, 2017), 80–3.

[288] See especially the section on "Comparisons, Connections, and the Structure of the Argument," *Great Divergence*, 24–5.

[289] See "A Note on Geographic Coverage," *Great Divergence*, 25–7.

rapid per capita economic growth.[290] Other problematic parts of the outcome also need refining: what is meant by "Europe"? What are "other parts of the world"? It is also essential that the temporal dimension of the outcome be defined: the explanandum is a contrast between time-specific trends in two generalized spaces. Hence, the explanandum is not a singular event but two or more complex temporal conditions. Note what is happening here: the process of inferential or abductive reasoning requires that the outcome – the thing to be "explained" – must be defined and located, spatially and temporally. It is not a found object.

Note that the outcome is not singular – it is, at the outset, dual – and the dual conditions are likely to interact with each other over time. Furthermore, the interactions within the *outcome* may themselves be explanatory. Thus, for instance, the early development path in Europe may interact with conditions in other parts of the world in such a way as to accelerate the divergence. At this point, any simple dichotomy between causal condition and outcome dissolves. This complexity is acknowledged in what Pomeranz calls a "comparative and integrative approach."[291] The analysis is comparative because change in one spatial location is compared to change in another location. But the approach cannot be "purely" comparative because of the interactions; hence, it must also be integrative, recognizing a "polycentric world" containing "global conjunctures" – interactions or conjunctures in a global context. The conjunctures may have worked to the "advantage" of one side, but not necessarily because that side "imposed" them. Something may have occurred independently in China, for instance, which then interacted with prior conditions in Europe.[292]

The global context is a polycentric world: the result is a multi-dimensional matrix of interactions that would be difficult to represent in an argumentation diagram. The third paragraph of the Introduction acknowledges that spatial location in the outcome – "Europe" or "other parts of the world" – is not always a duality, and that some explanatory "factors" do not fit firmly into either category. Some factors may operate, for instance, only in parts of Europe, or only in parts of China. Thus, any "explanation" must allow for inclusion and weighting of factors that operate sub-regionally. The reasoning process is explicit: "Thus the book combines comparative analysis, some purely local contingency, and an integrative or global approach." Even in the Introduction, the reasoning process has already produced at least one theoretical or epistemic conclusion: pre-1800 global conjunctures cannot be understood as "a European-centred world system."[293]

---

290 Pomeranz, *Great Divergence*, 3–4.
291 Pomeranz, *Great Divergence*, 4.
292 Pomeranz, *Great Divergence*, 5.
293 Pomeranz, *Great Divergence*, 3–4.

11 Abductive Reasoning

Abductive reasoning moves from outcome to explanation. But what is explanation in history? It may be impossible to specify a single form of explanation when the intellectual endeavor of history has so many forms. So let us focus on history that seeks to answer a "why" question, as in the history of the great divergence. Even here, any definition will be controversial. I suggest that explanation means the specification, or inference, of those conditions that are both necessary and sufficient to the presence of the defined outcome. The statement of such conditions is probabilistic, and so the statement or statements are hypotheses.[294]

There are likely to be three types of inference. The first is the inference of a condition that is too weak to be included in the explanation. Often, the weak inference is one previously proposed by others in previous writing on the subject, and which the current reasoning process finds to be neither necessary nor sufficient. A second type is the necessary condition: a condition which does not by itself lead to the outcome, but without which the outcome could not have occurred. The third type is the sufficient condition: one which, in the presence of the necessary conditions, does produce the outcome.

In broad outline, this is the reasoning process – the "structure" of "argument" (his words) – that is evident in Pomeranz's book. He is working explicitly with necessary and sufficient conditions, as, for instance, when he refers to technological invention: "Technological inventiveness was necessary for the Industrial Revolution, but it was not sufficient, or uniquely European."[295] As this sentence indicates, the comparative method is part of the inferential process. Part One of the book is about "general statements" that have previously been included in "explanations," but which, in his view, will not qualify as necessary or sufficient in the current explanation. One such statement is that Europeans were uniquely wealthy prior to industrialization; that their capital stock was unusually large and growing steadily prior to industrialization, and that this "advantage" was a

---

[294] Douglas Walton states that "an account of what explanation is has to be a vitally important first step of any analysis of abductive reasoning," and he devotes a chapter to "A Dialogue Model of Explanation" (Walton, *Abductive Reasoning*, 51 – 96). The nature and meaning of explanation have produced a vast literature and are inextricably connected to the epistemological status of history. The question turns also to "the claim of scientificity of historical thinking," as Jörn Rüsen notes (*Evidence and Meaning*, 115). The question also takes us back to the literature on narrative, where explanation is assumed to be an account of temporal change through narrative. In his book on abduction, Walton gives little attention to the discipline of history, but he does argue that in history "empathetic" explanation is common: "one person tries to explain the actions of another person by attributing goals, motives, beliefs, or other kinds of internal states to the other person" (52). This takes us very close to Collingwood, and much of the present book is my attempt to shift attention to historical thinking rather than to the schematic minefield of "explanation" and its meaning.
[295] Pomeranz, *Great Divergence*, 17.

condition of the great divergence. To downgrade this hypothesis requires deployment of a range of evidence related to agriculture, livestock, transport, human population, and much more, and historians may differ over whether the evidence presented is adequate to the purpose. But the reasoning process is not in question, and it proceeds to the consideration of the European demographic regime, the relative productivity of labor, the alleged technological advantage of Europe, and the alleged advantage of a "scientific culture," especially in England. Related to technology is the labor-replacement argument, which has had considerable support among historians. Pomeranz deploys both evidence and logic in downgrading the hypothesis that Europeans, and especially the English, were impelled by high wages to economize on labor through labor-saving innovations.

There is an integral connection between the three types of inference: weak, necessary, and sufficient conditions. The process of eliminating or downgrading certain hypothesized conditions (usually explanations from past accounts) affects the viability of other hypotheses. As more and more are eliminated, the probability that the remaining ones will survive rises. There is a similarity here to abductive reasoning in law: to confirm a specific allegation of causal responsibility "beyond reasonable doubt" requires that other causal chains be cast in doubt.

Comparative analysis is an integral part of reasoning. As Pomeranz says at the end of the book, the "long journey through interregional comparisons has brought us to at least some resolution of the methodological question with which we began" (that question being how to understand the role of pre-existing connections and conjunctures in creating the differences that became "divergence" after 1800).[296] At the risk of over-simplifying a complex argument, the comparative reasoning can be summarized as follows. Take two spatial entities (in fact, there are many more in the book, of course). Each has incentives to save on local wood supply; each has a highly commercialized economy; each has advanced technology by the standards of the time; each has a market system and capital available for investment; each has water transport systems; each has other roughly similar conditions. But one experiences a transition to mechanized industrial production and consequent growth, and the other does not. So what conditions does the one place have that the other does not? Those differences become explanatory. They include a huge supply of coal and the location of this coal close to pools of specific artisanal techniques and skills and close to specific handicraft production sites. They include colonies and the import of vast New World resources that solve a "blockage" in the form of a "land constraint," especially in Britain. In the presence of specific necessary conditions, these conditions become "deci-

---

[296] Pomeranz, *Great Divergence*, 297.

sive."[297] The sufficient conditions have been identified. The complex chain of inference has concluded, and the reasoning process, applied to an immense range of evidence, has created a best (or, if not that, a better) explanation.

In the reasoning process, specific problems of inference force larger theoretical issues into view. At one point, during the discussion of New World resources, Pomeranz asks, "what do the numbers mean?" The question has arisen because abductive reasoning requires that we assign weight, or relative significance, to conditions that may qualify as explanatory. So how do we infer that a condition is significant, or consequential, even if its measured importance relative to other conditions is small? Pomeranz points out that in an "equilibrium-seeking model," small differences "should not create large *and lasting* divergences" [his italics]. There is indeed an "awkward marriage" here between history and economics – "at least those schools of economics that posit a single equilibrium as the destination toward which a given system tends." As Pomeranz points out, this question is important "for conceptualizing historical processes more generally."[298] In historical reasoning, the measurably smaller condition may be relatively consequential. There are situations where a small increment in something may make a substantial difference. That "substantial" difference becomes apparent only through the logic of abduction and its process of elimination and weighting of conditions. In no small part the substantial difference is related to interactions, or spin-off effects that result when one change intersects with another. Consider, for instance, the incremental effects of increasing consumption of tobacco, sugar, coffee, and tea on habits, diet, and labor productivity. The interactive and consequential significances are greater than might be indicated by any measured weighting.

A focus on the reasoning process raises other issues relating to the conceptualization of historical processes. Where and how do value judgments enter the reasoning process? "Inference to the best explanation" cannot mean a detached, value-neutral procedure of drawing hypotheses out of evidence. The array of inferences in Pomeranz's comparative and integrative reasoning does not refer to impersonal, agent-less structural forces (although his references to "fortuitous global conjunctures," "crucial accidents," and "geographic good luck" have prompted doubts on this score). I would argue that abductive reasoning pushes ethical and political values into the foreground, for at least two reasons. First, to infer and to give weight to a condition of change necessarily raises counter-factual possibilities (and this happens throughout Pomeranz's book).[299] In historical abduction, there is always

---

297 Pomeranz, *Great Divergence*, 279.
298 Pomeranz, *Great Divergence*, 279–80.
299 Much of the argument about overseas coercion and its effects is a "thought experiment" (*Great Divergence*, 188). Why? Because of the presence of implied alternatives or counter-

an implied alternative to the condition being observed. Europeans seized vast coercive-intensive opportunities in the New World and deployed slave labor; this alternative was not the inevitable outcome of markets and a price structure. China, by contrast, did not have its Americas. No inferential process will stop at that observation. The absence of vast Chinese peripheries is connected to political economy, the Chinese state, and culture. And we are immediately back to the ethics and politics of paths taken and not taken.

The second reason why the reasoning process pushes ethical and political values into the foreground is that abductive reasoning is always probabilistic. The "evidence" used in the reasoning is always selected, not merely found. An inference is always a proposed or conjectural connection. The conditions identified as necessary to an explanation follow not simply from neutral evidence but from a choice among value-laden alternatives. This is fully evident in Pomeranz's reasoning, when he distances himself from both the market fundamentalism of neo-liberal economics and much of postmodern scholarship. To deploy the logic of inference is to acknowledge the necessity of choice, in the past and in the historian's present. Abductive reasoning in history is always a marriage of logic and value.[300]

How far can the abductive process that I detect in *The Great Divergence* be found in other historical works? Obviously, there can be no single model of abduc-

---

factuals. In historical abduction, there is always an implied alternative to any observed condition. We accept that Europeans seized vast coercion-intensive opportunities in the New World. To say that the seizing of vast coercion-intensive opportunities in the Americas diverted the British from opportunities at home is to make a counter-factual assumption: that in the absence of overseas opportunities, they would have drained more swamps at home.

[300] I anticipate an objection of the following kind: surely the truth claims in *The Great Divergence* rest upon the assembly of relevant evidence in support of an argument; the reasoning process is not a prior or independent mode of cognition. To put it more bluntly: history rests on the tests of evidence, not of logic (although of course we have a duty to avoid obvious fallacies). There is more than one answer to this hypothetical objection. One answer is to refer to Pomeranz's repeated references to his reasoning process. Another answer refers to the reactions of Pomeranz's readers. Critics directed attention to what they saw as problems of evidence. They also discussed, and often questioned, his reasoning. One scholar (Zhao Yifeng) refers aptly to "the dual quandary of evidence and logic." (Zhao Yifeng, "Great Divergence or Great Convergence? A Civilizational View of the Historical Trend in Ming-Qing China," *Chinese Studies in History*, 45, 1 (Fall 2011), 71). Yes, we may accept that "inferences" are being made; but what is the meaning of "comparison"? From two different locations the historian extracts "evidence" to infer the presence or absence of something: to do so requires a criterion or category – in this case, the category "economic" in a specific sense. It follows that the comparative method gives categorical and historical priority to certain conditions (economic growth, economic system, measured wealth) as opposed to others (political structure, culture) (Zhao Yifeng, "Great Divergence," 75). The issue for debate arises from both evidence and the reasoning process.

tive reasoning; there are only recurring elements or patterns, and in history, these will be different from what we may discern in science, law, or artificial intelligence. In Pomeranz's book and in many other works on the great divergence, comparative analysis is necessarily present: it follows from the "why" question being asked. Is some form of comparative analysis always present in historical abduction? I would suggest that comparison is more often present than we may realize. I observe it now in most of what I have written in the past. The entire abductive process in my *Inequality in Canada* (2020) involves a comparative framework: the idea of inequality, as it appeared in Canada, cannot be observed without first seeing the idea as it appeared elsewhere, or so my argument goes. And another of my subjects: the rise and decline of a shipping industry in Atlantic Canada has to be seen in specific temporal and spatial settings, settings or contexts that are distinct from others. My history of seafaring labor is a juxtaposition of patterns and processes that are distinctly different across time periods, technologies, and modes of production. Inferences and explanation involve comparison at every stage of the reasoning.

Please allow me to return briefly to a very personal iteration of abductive reasoning. Time moves quickly for me. My future is much shorter than my past. I have personal expectations for the future, but increasingly these are transferred to my children and grandchildren. Hopes and fears collide. Some things I can guess. From what I see of them now, I can guess at what the grandchildren are likely to do or become. Specific talents, either athletic or musical, have already appeared, and their ability to read and write, in either English or French, is far greater than mine was at their ages. It is very likely that they will complete high school and some postsecondary education, and enter a profession. Whatever profession they choose, it is unlikely that they will stay in the same job, with the same employer, for all of their employment careers. Whatever their personal and family lives will look like, the chances of what we call "job satisfaction" are very good.

Do you see what I have just done? I have given you another example of abductive reasoning. The reasoning may be sketchy and incomplete; it is abductive reasoning nonetheless. I have inferred specific outcomes following, with a high degree of probability, from a specific selection of evidence. I have defined the outcomes. I have not been very precise about the selection process or the weighting of conditions and interactions bearing on the outcomes. Nevertheless, the selection process is there. The evidence comes not merely from close observation of two children, but from bodies of research relating to social and economic mobility. These include, for instance, research on income, occupation, and educational attainment across generations; evidence on the quality of schooling available to my grandchildren; and evidence on postsecondary participation rates. The reasoning process is explicitly about change over time and about probability, as "likely" and "unlikely" clearly indicate. "Expectations" also refers to probability:

it is not about certainty but about prospects, or the belief that something may or may not happen after an interval of time. The abductive reasoning here is forward-looking: inferences are made about future outcomes. But it is still abductive reasoning, and it is about change over time.

There is nothing original here. The connection of abduction to expectation and an omnipresent future goes back to the pragmatist philosopher Charles Peirce (1839–1914) over a century ago.[301] For Peirce, all human thought is at some level influenced by the future, or our "being *in futuro*." Expectations may be valid or not valid, and abduction is a test of validity; the reasoning always points toward "a corrected formulation of the proposition."[302] It makes no difference that in history the outcomes are known, in a way that future outcomes are not. The future is indeterminate; so also was any outcome in the past before its arrival. To think historically is to accept the indeterminacy of past events or outcomes. The reasoning process by which we "explain" is the same for both past and future.

Historical thinking exists, to some degree, whatever the temporal frame to which it is applied. The thinking may be disciplined and seasoned by long experience, or it may be superficial. If it is disciplined by long practice, it will exhibit the explanatory virtues in abductive reasoning. The reasoner will accept the need to define the explanandum as a created and constructed entity rather than a found object. More than that, the reasoner will try to identify the assumptions that underpin that definition. Inferences will be stated as hypotheses, not facts, because the inference that links condition to explanandum is a testable conjecture subject to correction. And that means accepting the possibility – even the ubiquity – of error. "Truth will sooner come out from error than from confusion" (Francis Bacon, *Novum Organum*, 1620) is surely the historian's motto: we know that truth claims and error are inseparable companions, the former built on confronting the latter. Inference links conditions to the thing to be explained – and the reasoning always accepts the plurality and intersectionality of conditions.

No condition of existence stands alone, as a singularity. Thus, the interactions in lived experience are a primary focus in abduction's microscope. The thinking is always value-laden: the self-reflecting thinker acknowledges and investigates the assumptions and values that guide the presentation of interactions and of evidence. I think my way into a past; in doing so, I think a future into being.

---

301 Peirce developed his ideas on abduction between the 1880s and early 1900s, but his ideas were not widely known until the third quarter of the twentieth century. The first major work on the subject was K.T. Fann, *Peirce's Theory of Abduction* (The Hague: Martinus Nijhoff, 1970).
302 James R. Wible, "C.S. Peirce's Theory of Abductive Expectations," *The European Journal of the History of Economic Thought*, 27, 1 (2020), 28.

12 Reason and Imagination

Have you ever been asked about the "use" or "value" of History as a subject? If you are a student, perhaps you have been put in a position where you need to explain why you are taking History courses. I recall a true story told by a colleague about her son, then in the final year of high school. The young man was skiing and found himself seated on a chairlift next to a well-known politician who asked what he intended to do after graduation. The young man said he might get a job for a year and then go to university to do a degree in history. The politician responded by telling the young man not to waste his time. A history degree was useless. Why not study something that would help him get a job? I do not react to this story by saying that some politicians are ignorant. Not at all! We all need to have a better and more respectful answer. What would your answer be?

I have spent much time thinking about an answer. At many times during my career, I have written or spoken about the value of history and of a university degree in history. I have joined with others in lamenting the decline in History courses in both high school and university curriculums. In doing so, I admit that I have often emphasized the "transferable skills" that history teaches. To be sure, these skills do exist. But is that all? I suggest that if we stop there, we mislead our listeners and any public that we address. History cannot be reduced to skills, any more than it can be reduced to specific bodies of knowledge. History is a mode of thinking and reasoning. Either the thinking is present to a high degree or it is not. Where it is absent, we flounder not so much in error as in confusion.

Of course, history as knowledge is indispensable. We can all think of examples of the absence of historical knowledge and the costs of such absence. For much of my lifetime, the Vietnam War of the 1960s and 1970s was an obvious case: American decision-makers knew perilously little of the country in which they became entangled. More recently, we have the war in Afghanistan. In the early 2000s, the United States and several other countries invaded Afghanistan, equipped with weapons and a truly staggering ignorance of the history of that country. Once again, however, we must not reduce this absent "history" to a specific body of knowledge about that country. What was missing was the capacity to think historically: to apply the historian's abductive reasoning and perspectival knowing to a complex temporal and spatial conjuncture.

We live in a world of reductionisms, misinformation, lies, conspiracy theories, and social media-induced delusions. We suffer, some claim, from a collective Empathy Deficit Disorder. We suffer from an ahistorical amnesia about class, as theory and as social materiality. In the name of freedom, hyper-wealthy individuals have the power of gods, the power to determine what is and what is not ac-

https://doi.org/10.1515/9783111563800-012

ceptable speech in our media. Are we to respond by pleading that we need more attention to facts? More attention to evidence-based knowledge? More attention to skills? Yes, let us try all that. But "more investment" in these necessary things is not enough.

We live within unprecedented time surges. Past and present collapse into an ever-nearing future. In the history of communications, no change since Gutenberg and the printing press has been so transformative as the changes we have lived with in recent years. The difference is that cultural adaptation to print occurred over generations and even centuries; our transformation in communications media has happened in a few decades. Our capacity to adapt and to submit the transformation to collective and social control falters in technology's wake. Who, in such a time, dares not think historically? What price will we pay for ahistoricity?

All that is solid melts; foundations crack. We could look at climate change and its relentless advance, but I will look at another temporal disruption: the recent and still advancing decline in political democracy as a form of collective governance. The decline is perceived by such observers as the Economist Intelligence Unit, the Varieties of Democracy Project (V-Dem) at the University of Gothenburg, and Freedom House, as well as a number of political scientists. The professional background of those who study this subject – whether they be political scientists or sociologists or journalists or historians – has no bearing on the claim I make here: the unfolding outcome being observed is a temporal disruption with spatial dimensions; it is, therefore, historical, and it can be understood only in and through historical thinking.

It does not matter that the outcome being observed exists in a recent temporal zone, in the present, and in the future. The necessity of historical thinking, including abductive reasoning, remains. The object being observed is at least as complex and multi-faceted as Pomeranz's great divergence; indeed, it *is* a temporal and spatial divergence. The reasoning process must begin with the outcome itself: what is it? What is meant by "decline"? And what is meant by "democracy"? Historical thinking is at home in this challenge of definition: the two terms, decline and democracy, are jointly contingent because the former term depends on the latter. By some definitions of democracy, there may be little or no decline. Already the reasoning is comparative, as it was for Pomeranz. Whatever definition of democracy one chooses, that definition comes from specific spatial locations. The elements constituting the explanandum vary in weight and form across spatial locations; the object is not a singularity. Quantification, of course, is unavoidable, as it is in any study of something identified as "decline."

There is still more to the specification of outcome because the discussion is already complicated by adjectival modifiers. All too often, especially in convenient media summaries, the word "democracy" is modified by "liberal." In historical thinking, with our hyper-sensitivity to terminological precision and the risk of semantic bias, we accept no such easy conflation of terms. We might begin instead with simplified categories, as does the Economist Intelligence Unit with its five "measures" of democracy: "electoral process and pluralism, the functioning of government, political participation, democratic political culture, and civil liberties." This is followed by four categories of regime type (full democracy, flawed democracy, hybrid regime, authoritarian regime).[303] The procedure makes sense when the goal is to construct an index together with meanings that can be understood by most readers, including the meaning of "decline." The historical thinker will note how the framing of the outcome frames the selection and weighting of inferred causal conditions. Outside this thinking lies confusion.

Inference to an explanation means, as a first step, specifying proximate conditions. One problem is that the number of candidate conditions is very long. Another problem is that of circularity: how does one avoid mixing up a condition with something that is part of the outcome itself? Historical thinking is acutely sensitive to this problem and careful to avoid it: to put it simply, we claim to know the difference between symptoms and causes. Consider, then, a short list of candidates. We might begin with the end of the Cold War and the much-acclaimed victory over communism. There followed, in the 1990s, a measured increase in the number of democracies. By the end of the decade, by some measures, the number of democratic states equaled the number of autocratic states. The result may have been a political and intellectual torpor and complacency among pro-democracy and other progressive forces that allowed non-democratic ideologies to percolate uncontested. At this point, since the emphasis is on political thought and ideology, conditions often held to be either supportive or corrosive of democracy enter the argument. The most obvious of the supports is liberalism (hence the conflation "liberal democracy"). The forces working against liberalism (itself requiring definition) must be identified. These include religion and nationalism: these took forms often opposed to liberalism, and their power was often not perceived or understood by liberals and other progressives.[304]

---

[303] Democracy Index 2021 at https://www.eiu.com/n/campaigns/democracy-index-2021/.
[304] I could cite a long list of published works, but from this list I choose a book by a Canadian that I find to be a perceptive and useful survey: Jonathan Manthorpe, *Restoring Democracy in an Age of Populists and Pestilence* (Toronto: Cormorant Books, 2020). There are many histories of liberalism. A recent historical work that seeks to sort out conceptual confusions is Helena Rosenblatt, *The Lost History of Liberalism: From Ancient Rome to the Twenty-First Century* (Princeton: Princeton University Press, 2018).

My argument is that the relationship between outcome and conditions is already so complex that only historical thinking is equipped to deal with it. But we have only begun to state the conditions that might be considered causal or explanatory. Every discussion of democracy and its decline gives some weight to economic inequality (referring to measured increases in inequality within nations). This is a temporal condition and hence it is a historian's work: the timing of inequality must be persuasively connected to the timing of the decline of democracy. And more than that: historical thinking tells us that correlation does not by itself confirm causation; plausible links must be established. This step takes us to the interactions between conditions and outcome, and between conditions themselves. How, for instance, does inequality relate to religion, or nationalism, or ethno-nationalism, or other forces that contribute to a weakening of either liberalism or democracy?

Historical thinking, undaunted by such complexity, takes yet another step: it accepts the necessity of comparative analysis in the abductive process. The outcome is not singular; it takes multiple forms and varies by spatial location. We can indeed assert a connection between rising inequality and the rise of forces damaging to either liberalism or democracy. But what is the status of this connection? Is inequality a necessary condition or a sufficient condition? Consider, for instance, a preliminary comparison between France and the United States. Both, according to the Economist Intelligence Unit, are "flawed democracies" that sit close to each other on the global democracy index. But inequality cannot have the same weight in each case: whatever measure one chooses, inequality is low in France and high in the United States. Go further with the comparisons and we find other cases: Algeria, Hungary, Iraq, Kazakhstan, Moldova – these countries are low on the democracy index, but all exhibit low inequality (relatively low Gini coefficients, for instance).

Historical thinking sets the standard of plausible explanation at a very high level. And it must be so. There can be no certainty; we seek a high degree of probability. Elsewhere lies confusion. The reasoning process identifies and crushes reductionisms. In doing so, it also exposes ideologically driven reductionisms and the values that are inherent in all explanation.

We are still not done. The search for conditions that may be explanatory also leads to the media revolution of our era, which includes surveillance media and social media. There is much more here than the capacity of anti-democratic and foreign powers to intervene in democratic elections and to sow confusion and division. Politics itself is transformed when political communities are created in electronic media, and when politicians and their agents have the power to identify and even select voters, and to grow political communities in this media world. Democracy, it may be argued, was historically connected in many ways to print communications and print capitalism. Our inferential reasoning requires that we seek to include in our explanation the transition to electronic communication and screen capitalism.

To think historically is to accept and even to embrace the complexity of this present historical question. This does not mean that historians will rush to write books about the decline of democracy. I mean that historians reason with problems of similar complexity and offer models of reasoning without which the question cannot be answered. I have framed the question about democracy's decline in such a way as to reveal the complexity of the question. I have also framed the question so as to introduce a paradox at the heart of historical thinking. The paradox is this: we seek to know an answer to a question; yet we cannot know an answer. Historians can live with this paradox because we have a particular understanding of knowledge and *knowing*. We may not all be followers of Kant's idealism, but we do accept that there is no such thing as knowledge of a thing in itself, knowledge of a thing independent of observation or sensory experience. This is what lies behind the historian's rejection of essentialism (the idea that things have intrinsic meaning or being). So what do we seek when we ask about democracy's decline? Our thinking tells us to seek only the attainable, which is a provisional, tentative, or probabilistic claim to belief. "I believe the following . . . . And if my belief is defeated, I will change or adjust the belief."

The knowledge that we claim, therefore, is not an absolute or definitive certainty, as a commonplace popular understanding of "knowledge" might hold. The knowing, rather, is an admission of uncertainty, of the possibility – even the likelihood – of error. To use another term, historical reasoning accepts the defeasibility of its claims: every claim to truth or knowledge is defeasible, or subject to defeat, revision, or rejection. This property of historical thinking is what makes it subversive – subversive of all reductionisms, all dogmatic claims to certain truth, all ideologically-driven simplicities, and all misinformation.

In these last two paragraphs, I have been describing something known to philosophers as epistemic humility. The term does not refer to a psychological condition or personality trait (although connections certainly exist); it refers to a property of knowledge or belief. Epistemic humility has even been referred to as an intellectual virtue. The philosopher of science Ian James Kidd says that epistemic humility "builds in, at the ground level, an acute sense of the fact that epistemic confidence is conditional, complex, contingent, and therefore *fragile*." It means actively regulating intellectual activity within a "complex economy of confidence."[305] If that

---

[305] Ian James Kidd, "Confidence, Humility, and Hubris in Victorian Scientific Naturalism," in Jeroen Van Dongen and Herman Paul, eds., *Epistemic Virtues in the Sciences and the Humanities*

"acute sense" exists anywhere, it exists in historical thinking. "Economy of confidence" is surely one of history's great strengths. It manifests itself in the specific skepticism that fuels debate among historians: "the evidence does not support that argument . . ."; "your statement is surely going too far . . ."; "surely you have missed the following alternative . . . ." Such are the dialectics of epistemic humility. Such is our critical and self-critical gaze upon the world.

We live with uncertainty. Uncertainty means living in the presence of alternatives. What if . . . ? The question is about alternatives. Historical thinking pursues and formalizes (puts into a reasoned form) the commonplace "what if?" question. We call it the asking of counter-factual questions. We all engage in such thinking: what if I had never met my spouse? What if I had not missed that bus? What if Donald Trump had not won the election in 2016? Such "what if" questions are history in embryo: they are saying that the past and the present are conditional, contingent, and emergent. As the French historians Quentin Deluermoz and Pierre Singaravélou say in their "history of what could have been": "Asking why the world is as it is and not otherwise sits at the heart of all critical thought."[306] This is one reason why history is not going away, however often its formal and scholarly iterations may be evaded or ignored. The impulse to "what if?" thinking – to imagining alternative pasts and possible futures – is too deeply rooted in our culture.

There are many what ifs. Think about it: are there "what ifs" in your own past? Not unlikely ones, but plausible ones. I think of the following: when I was a child, I experienced many sudden changes of location and schools. What if those disruptions had not occurred? But wait – how do I know, or believe, that they really were disruptions? I believe it to be so only because I imagine a choice not made, a path not taken, a path that offered relative constancy and stability. My belief rests upon a counter-factual path that exists in my mind's eye, my imagination. I create an alternative path, and in doing so, my imagined "disruption" turns into belief. And if you have responded to my prompt and thought of a "what if" in your past, then you too have used imagination.

(Cham: Springer International Publishing, 2017), 13, 15. The concept takes us back to Aristotle, who said that acquiring knowledge required intellectual virtues such as honesty, impartiality, and fairness; and to Plato's discussion of knowledge and wisdom in his *Apology*. I have also drawn on Sharon Ryan, "Epistemic Humility, Defeat, and a Defense of Moderate Skepticism" in Branden Fitelson, Rodrigo Borges, and Cherie Braden, eds., *Themes from Klein: Knowledge, Skepticism, and Justification* (Cham: Spring, 2019), 129–43; and James Van Cleve, "Epistemic Humility and Causal Structuralism," in Johannes Roessler, Hemdat Lerman, and Naomi Eilan, eds., *Perception, Causation, and Objectivity* (Oxford Scholarship Online, 2011), 82–91. For Kant and epistemic humility: Rae Langton, *Kantian Humility: Our Ignorance of Things in Themselves* (Oxford: Clarendon Press, 1998).
306 Quentin Deluermoz and Pierre Singaravélou, *A Past of Possibilities: A History of What Could Have Been*, trans. Stephen W. Sawyer (New Haven: Yale University Press, 2021), x.

This tiny autobiographical example forces into the foreground the thorny question of historical imagination. In some form, imagination is a necessary part of historical thinking. No real past – no past as a "thing in itself" – is available to us. We have only traces and fragments existing in the present, and out of these, we think a past into being. We do so in reasoned, heuristic propositions that offer plausible explanatory scenarios of what might have been. What *might* have been: at some level, imagination is involved, although not the same imagination as in the writing of fiction. What is this historical imagination? And what does it have to do with historical reasoning?

David J. Staley has explored historical imagination in a recent book. Imagination cannot be simply mimesis, he says – the forming of an image or copy of an object or situation – because we do not have access to the original object or situation. Something of mimesis is present nonetheless when we form images based on present fragments surviving from the past (our "evidence"). But there is more than mimesis in historical imagination. Staley asks: "what does it mean to perceive or visualize an entity we have never directly experienced before?"[307] It means forming images of non-real or inactual objects (or people, or beliefs, and so on) as though they were real or actual. This is creative imagination. It was often relegated, in the nineteenth century, to a status below that of reason. Such relegation of imagination fed into the long debates over whether history was art or science.

Staley's distinction between mimetic imagination and creative imagination may be useful, so long as we accept that historical thinking includes a "complex combination" of both.[308] While noting the presence of both, Staley observes varying degrees or amounts of each form of imagination in different historical works. In *The Return of Martin Guerre* by Natalie Zemon Davis, he suggests, there is more creative imagination than mimetic imagination because of the book's frequent modal constructions ("may," "must have," "possibly"). The modal constructions, in turn, reflect an absence of "direct evidence" bearing on a specific question; the historian therefore falls back on indirect evidence and reasoning by analogy and inference.[309] This way of understanding imagination may be fully persuasive for many readers. But there is a risk if we draw too firm a boundary between different types of imagination and if we conceive of forms of imagination that appear in different ratios or amounts. In *The Return of Martin Guerre*, the historian's statements are probabilistic, and the inferences are acknowledged to have no precise levels of

---

307 David J. Staley, *Historical Imagination* (London: Routledge, 2021), 4.
308 Staley, *Historical Imagination*, 135.
309 Staley, *Historical Imagination*, 61–72.

probability. But both direct and indirect evidence are present in abundance, and both Staley's types of imagination are present in the inferential reasoning.

There are other ways of understanding imagination.[310] Let us return briefly to my autobiographical example of "disruption." I am postulating sudden and consequential changes of location and context. Imagination is certainly present in my mental picture of events and their consequences: I am thinking into mind consequences that are non-real or inactual. But note that in doing so, I am *thinking my way*: I am thinking "what if?" and making inferences based on evidence I possess about where I was then, what schools I went to, what expectations a child might have had, what I know of child development, and so on. In other words, I am using inferential reasoning. In this small instance, it makes no sense to draw a firm line between reasoning and imagination.

If it makes no sense there, why does such separation make sense anywhere? Long ago, Charles Peirce collapsed the boundary between reason and imagination. Sara Barrena and others argue that Peirce's abduction "involves a creative use of the imagination": in abductive reasoning, we ask how things might be, we create hypotheses that draw connections and envisage possible worlds.[311] This was a radically new conception of imagination, very different from the Romantic idea of imagination as invention beyond rational comprehension. Imagination, with Peirce, had become an active force behind reasoning: "the power of distinctly picturing to ourselves intricate configurations."[312] That imagination includes the reasoning of the scientist who creates images of unseen entities and relationships. Imagination also includes the abductive and analogical reasoning of Carlo Ginzburg when he connected peasant ways of thinking to the speech and actions of a sixteenth-century miller in the Friuli region of Italy.[313]

We may accept, with David Staley, that "without imagination, there can be no discipline of history."[314] But that leaves many questions unanswered. What is that

---

[310] For instance, Claes G. Ryn, *Will, Imagination, and Reason: Babbitt, Croce and the Problem of Reality* (London: Routledge, 1997); Dennis L. Sepper, *Understanding Imagination: The Reason of Images* (New York: Springer, 2013); Patricia Roberts and Virginia P. Jones, "Imagining Reasons: The Role of Imagination in Argumentation," *JAC: A Journal of Composition Theory*, 15, 3 (1995), 527–41.

[311] Sara Barrena, "Reason and Imagination in Charles S. Peirce," *European Journal of Pragmatism and American Philosophy*, vol. 5, no. 1 [online] (2013), n.p.; Thomas M. Alexander, "Pragmatic Imagination," *Transactions of the Charles S. Peirce Society*, 26 (1990), 325–48.

[312] Barrena, "Reason and Imagination." The "pure reason" of Descartes may have included a "poetics": Andrea Gadberry, *Cartesian Poetics: The Art of Thinking* (Chicago: Chicago University Press, 2020).

[313] Carlo Ginzburg, *The Cheese and the Worms: The Cosmos of a Sixteenth-Century Miller*, trans. John and Anne Tedeschi (Baltimore: Johns Hopkins University Press, 1980).

[314] Staley, *Historical Imagination*, 137.

imagination? It is clearly different from the Romantic imagination. Its freedom is constrained: we do not put any two objects into a frame and draw a line connecting them. The imagination of the historian is disciplined in specific ways. But how so? One answer is that historical thinking is always bound by the necessity of evidence: our statements must be firmly connected to probative grounding in evidence drawn from sources. In this way, our creations differ from those of fiction. Evidence is the measure of plausible truth. But there is a problem here! Evidence is the creation of the historian; it does not exist as evidence until the historian puts it into an argument. In short, evidence is the product of imaginative reasoning. It makes little sense to say that imagination is limited or constrained by products of imagination.

We begin to make sense if we remember that imagination and reason are inseparable. Historical thinking takes form as a defeasible argument. It is not the evidence alone that constrains the imagination; it is the way that the evidence is used. A historical argument is defeasible, or capable of being revised, not by evidence alone but by the deployment of evidence and reasoning together. A work of fiction may contain many traces or fragments or memories from the past. But that work of fiction cannot be refuted or revised on the basis of its reasoning. A work of history may be questioned on that basis.

The many forms of reasoning that we observe in history – contextualization, consilience, perspective, abduction, and more – all carry with them procedural standards and even rules. Many are so internalized in our thinking that they seem obvious and hardly worth stating. Contextual reasoning sets a standard of probative relevance: we do not commit the error of omission, failing to include as evidence something in the sources that should have been included. Consilience sets a standard of consistency and coherence: we do not commit the error of excluding or diminishing something that is inconsistent with what we have included.

Abductive reasoning sets a range of standards. There is, for instance, a joint standard of sufficiency and relevance. The data cited as "evidence" to substantiate a claim must be both sufficient and relevant to the claim as stated. This is really a standard of inferential reasoning. The evidence cited functions as a premise, from which the claim or hypothetical statement follows as a conclusion. An error occurs when the conclusion does not follow from the premises. David Hackett Fischer names similar probative standards in his discussion of fallacies of verification and of significance.[315] The fallacy of reductionism is one of these: it means giving such weight to one condition as to reduce complexity to simplicity.

---

315 Fischer, *Historian's Fallacies*, Chapters II and III, 40–102.

The necessity of evidence and its selection imposes specific rules and tests. Historical thinking is primed to detect sampling error, and sensitivity to such error applies both within and beyond the use of statistical methods. It is a firm rule that the data cited as evidence must be representative of the population to which an inference or conclusion is applied. The fallacy of "instancing" follows: using one case or a few cases to draw an inappropriately strong conclusion about a group. The ecological fallacy moves in the other direction: it is a mistake to infer that a single case must bear a characteristic shown to be prevalent in the wider population from which the case is drawn.

We all know that correlation does not by itself prove causation. We may say that this is a mistake in the use of evidence, but the error is one of logic. Related to this error is the fallacy of *post hoc propter hoc*: the assumption that when one thing followed after another, it did so because of the prior thing. Sensitivity to this error is itself a stimulus to deeper thinking and further abduction: if indeed one thing has followed closely upon another, is it possible that there is a connection between the two?

Today's historians are very good at detecting ethnocentrism, just as we are sensitive to any speech or act that is discriminatory, partisan, prejudicial, or non-inclusive. It is worth remembering that ethnocentrism is a fallacy: it is the attribution of characteristics or values of one's own group to another group, or the attribution of missing values in another group based on the values of one's own group. A fundamental challenge of ethnohistory is to avoid this error: how does the scholar create an empathetic understanding of the other, while necessarily acknowledging one's own values and subject-position?

Many of our rules of informal logic may seem transparent and obvious. There are times, however, when the place of evidence within abduction, for instance, is very complex. Here is an example, which readers can pursue in the published literature. The history of family and household is a venerable subject that has inspired much research in many countries since the nineteenth century. At the risk of oversimplifying a complex and contested body of writing, I will refer to a specific interpretation of family history in northwest Europe. This interpretation, emerging in the 1960s and enduring for around four decades, held that in early modern times, if not before, a family "system" emerged in northwestern Europe, characterized by nuclear family structure and neolocal marriage (where it was normal for adult children to leave the parental home and establish new households when they married). Some scholars saw this system as supportive of capitalism and industrialization. The evidence produced in support of this interpretation was enormous. We were observing one of the great data-gathering enterprises in the discipline of history to that time.

Can you see the problem? The problem is not simply one of missing evidence. The problem lies in the reasoning. Put succinctly: what is the meaning – what is the ontological status – of "northwest Europe"? If the same family patterns existed in many non-European countries, then what does it mean to say that the system was "northern European"? In the "European system" interpretation lies an implied and at times explicit comparison between northwest Europe and either the rest of the world or other large parts of the world. But adequate comparisons had not been made. A key element in abductive reasoning was missing. In order to invest any meaning in "northwest Europe," comparisons were essential. To be fair, scholars in the field understood the problem. Large teams of researchers set out to repair the gap in the reasoning by offering, in the words of Steven Ruggles, a "comparative historical perspective." By the early 2000s, they were succeeding. By 2009, we were seeing results from comparisons of 37 countries around the world, and the massive infrastructure of population data was still growing. The paradigm of a distinctive northwest European family began to crumble.[316]

Another dimension in the logic of historical thinking lies, I would argue, in interactionist reasoning. Interaction theory appears in more than one discipline, most notably in psychology and sociology. I am thinking instead of interactions as they appear in statistics. Consider a situation in which two conditions ("independent variables") have an apparent effect on an outcome; an interaction occurs when a third condition interacts with the first two so as to affect the outcome. It is easy to see an affinity with historical analysis: historical reasoning is about multi-causal or multi-conditional situations, and the ways in which one condition interacts with another in a non-linear and non-additive way. Such reasoning is part of our sensitivity to context and complexity. Wherever we posit a "disruption" or sudden change in the past, interaction reasoning will be present. An example might be a sudden increase in the incidence of drug addiction and drug-related deaths in a particular location. There may be a clear correlation between an increase in the market supply of drugs and fatalities from specific opioids. But that would be merely the beginning of serious analysis. A number of other conditions will be proposed as interacting with the sale and purchase of drugs, or with the social and psychological conditions of the drug users. The conclusions as to cause and possible solutions will rest critically upon the nature of those interactions and the weight assigned to them.

Sensitivity to connections and interactions is a basic property of historical thinking, and that sensitivity sets up an informal but rigorous rule: to ignore or under-estimate a potential interaction between two conditions is an error in the

---

[316] Steven Ruggles, "Reconsidering the Northwest European Family System: Living Arrangements of the Aged in Comparative Historical Perspective," *Population and Development Review*, 35, 2 (June 2009), 249–73.

use of evidence and an error of reasoning. David Hackett Fischer refers to this error as "the fallacy of the mechanistic cause," and he quotes the eminent sociologist and political scientist Robert M. MacIver (1882–1970). This fallacy "treats the various components of a social situation, or of any organized system, as though they were detachable, isolable, homogeneous, independently operative, and therefore susceptible of being added to or subtracted from the causal complex."[317] Among the examples that Fischer cites is an argument of J.B. Bury in his *History of the Later Roman Empire* (1923). Bury downgraded the roles of depopulation, Christian religion, and the fiscal system as causes of the dismemberment of the Empire. Bury wrote: "If these or any of them were responsible for the dismemberment by the barbarians in the West, it may be asked how it was that in the East, where the same causes operated, the Empire survived much longer intact and united."[318] Fischer says: "The three causal elements which Bury rejects may have interacted with each other, and with still other elements, in such a way as to produce very different results in the West than in the East."[319]

Interactions can become multiple, tangled, and very difficult to isolate. From many possibilities I choose the example of nation-state formation after the fall of empires in Eastern Europe in the wake of the First World War. The subject inspired a new interest in nationalism, and nationalism in Eastern Europe remains a subject of historical interest and political urgency in our own times. In a pioneering, oft-reprinted study of the "national idea" in 1944, Hans Kohn (1891–1971) detected a difference between nationalisms in Eastern and Western Europe. Nationalism in Western Europe, he suggested, was based on a "rational and universal concept of political liberty and the rights of man," whereas nationalism in the East was based on the weakness or absence of such principles.[320] It may be that Kohn's attention to the secular state and the distinction between civic and ethnic nationalism left insufficient room for the multiple interactions of religion with political culture and the state in imperial times. Historians have recently confronted the immense challenge of the interactions of religion, culture, politics, and nationalism in Eastern Europe.[321] And

---

317 R.M. MacIver, *Social Causation*, revised edition (New York: Harper, 1964), 94, cited in Fischer, *Historians' Fallacies*, 178.
318 J.B. Bury, *History of the Later Roman Empire* (New York: Dover Publications, 1958), vol. 1, 308–9; cited in Fischer, *Historians' Fallacies*, 179.
319 Fischer, *Historians' Fallacies*, 179.
320 Hans Kohn, *The Idea of Nationalism* (London: Routledge, 2005) [1944], 457, 560–1, 574; cited in Yoko Aoshima, "Introduction," in Aoshima, ed., *Entangled Interactions between Religion and National Consciousness in Central and Eastern Europe* (Boston: Academic Studies Press, 2020), viii.
321 The essays in Aoshima, *Entangled Interactions*, deal variously with religion in Eastern Europe, including Russia. An earlier revisionist survey is Ina Merdjanova, "In Search of Identity: Nationalism and Religion in Eastern Europe," *Religion, State & Society*, 28, 3 (Sept. 2000), 233–62. See also Eric

elsewhere, in many areas of social, cultural, and political history, historians in recent decades have responded to their awareness that religion and its interactions have been too often misunderstood or unexplored. They are responding, I argue, not only to a deficiency of evidence but also to a deficiency in historical reasoning.

Readers will be able to cite their own examples of missing interactions and of MacIver's fallacy of mechanistic reduction. In my lifetime, one obvious and still controversial example is the long history of the interaction of race and class in American labor history. At times, this history seemed to reflect a version of American exceptionalism: why was there no enduring socialist or social democratic party in the United States, as there was elsewhere? Or, why in the course of the twentieth century did an organized labor movement become comparatively weak? By the 1980s we were hearing from David Roediger and others the suggestion that the new labor history was ignoring or downplaying the interactive force of race and racism with the working class, organized labor, and labor politics. Those interactions could be found in many locations at many levels, macro-historical and micro-historical. The search for interactions led to renewed attention to comparative dimensions, including the diverging paths of Canada and the United States.[322] Here is one obvious instance of a search for synergistic interactions that resonated deeply with current political issues.

In each of these examples, it makes no sense to draw a line between imagination and reason. Historical thinking is imaginative thinking; it is also a reasoning process with definable elements. It also makes little sense to draw lines between reason or logic and specific forms of historical writing. Long ago, I might have argued that reason was marginally involved in historical narrative, for instance, since narrative was a form describing how an event was experienced, its meaning resided in intuitive and esthetic properties rather than reason. Such an argument can no longer survive our understanding of the rational practices and organizing principles that narrative contains.[323] To find understandings of pastness or of temporality that do not contain reason, one must look outside Western historicism. The integration of imagination with specific reasoning processes defines

---

Hobsbawm, *Nations and Nationalism Since 1780: Programme, Myth, Reality* (Cambridge: Cambridge University Press, 1990).

[322] The literature is now very extensive. The field exploded with David Roediger, *The Wages of Whiteness: Race and the Making of the American Working Class History* (London: Verso, 1991). A summary up to 2006 is Eric Arnesen, "Passion and Politics: Race and the Writing of Working-Class History," *Journal of the Historical Society*, 6, 3 (September 2006), 323–56. On Canada and the United States a recent work is Barry Eidlin, *Labor and the Class Idea in the United States and Canada* (Cambridge: Cambridge University Press, 2018).

[323] Mariana Imaz-Sheinbaum, "Principles of Narrative Reason," *History and Theory*, 60, 2 (June 2021), 249–70.

historical thinking. We might even refer to history as disciplined imagination or imaginative reasoning in the search for understanding.

Ivan Jablonka has preceded me in arguing for history as a way of imaginative reasoning. He goes much further than I do: Jablonka's mission is to collapse the boundaries that have been erected between history (and the social sciences more broadly) and literature. "Literary creation and the work of the social sciences are compatible because reasoning is already embedded in the heart of literature."[324] He insists that history is different from fiction, while arguing that in the act of writing, historians are necessarily producing literature. The only question is what kind of literature is produced. Historians need not limit themselves to sterile, bloodless, third-person modes inherited from nineteenth-century realism. In his own writing, Jablonka has found a freedom from those limits.[325]

History, Jablonka argues, conveys truth claims in texts that implement lines of reasoning. Jablonka's reasoning processes include distanciation: "researchers step back from the object of their analysis to put it in perspective." Investigating is another process: in the asking of a question, the historian turns traces from an archive into sources. Comparison is a reasoning process that fits the individual case into contexts and eliminates the illusion of the unique. Weighing evidence is "the essential heart of historical reasoning."[326] There is more, and a brief summary cannot do justice to Jablonka's creative and original discussion of "approaches to veridiction." I am left, however, with a sense of incompleteness. Is there not more to be found within distanciation, investigation, or the weighing of evidence? For all that Jablonka's discussion of reasoning procedures is subtle and thoroughly illustrated, I suggest that historical reasoning is more complex and substantive than his "approaches to veridiction" allow.[327]

---

[324] Jablonka, *History is a Contemporary Literature*, 9.
[325] Jablonka's books include *A History of the Grandparents I Never Had*, trans. Jane Kuntz (Stanford: Stanford University Press, 2016); *Laëtitia: Ou la Fin des Hommes* (Paris: Éditions du Seuil, 2016); *A History of Masculinity: From Patriarchy to Gender Justice*, trans. Nathan Bracher (London: Allen Lane, 2022). Why was the popular, award-winning *Laëtitia* not translated into English?
[326] Jablonka, *History Is a Contemporary Literature*, 9, 132, 137, 141–2, 143, 145. Jablonka also refers to argumentation: "argumentation transforms the archive gathered over the course of the investigation into evidence" (p. 145).
[327] I am puzzled by Jablonka's preoccupation with narrative, since a focus on narrative is not necessary for his argument. His perspective is that of a French historian, and student readers in North America may be perplexed by his association of history and social sciences, and his use of "science" and "scientific." It helps to remember the capacious meaning of *sciences* in French, which enables history to be one of the *sciences humaines*. Well worth reading is the extended review of Jablonka's book by Dominick LaCapra, "What Is History? What is Literature?" *History and Theory*, 56, 1 (March 2017), 98–113. I cannot say that I was inspired by Jablonka's *History Is a Contemporary*

The elements of historical thinking that I have proposed in this book are different from Jablonka's approaches, although not inconsistent with them. Rather than pursuing differences between us, I point to an important agreement: the reasoning process – the process of investing history with logic, method, and rationality – is in no way opposed to the imaginative representation of possible worlds. On the contrary, as Jablonka says, these processes constrain the texts we produce and also amplify their power. A history that is reasoning and imaginative – and hence literary – is "a history more rigorous, transparent, reflexive, and honest with itself."[328] And this history is empowering and liberating. It is free to move beyond the academic world: "History is not first of all an academic discipline but rather a set of intellectual ways of proceeding that aim to understand what humans truly do. It follows that history (as a way of reasoning) is present in activities that have nothing 'historical' about them: reporting, journalism, judicial investigations, travel accounts, and life stories. The field of history far surpasses History. That is very good news."[329]

To think historically is to accept the limits and the scope of what can be known and said. This acceptance occurs whenever we seek to understand and explain something in and of the past. The past has gone, leaving only fragments of what was. We use those fragments to imagine and reason a past into being in the present. And in this understanding, as I argue in the next chapter, we are thinking the future into being.

Literature because the first draft of my book, including the chapters on "elements," was written before I encountered his work. The title of his book led me, mistakenly, to think that he was writing only about the history of the relationship between history and literature.
328 Jablonka, *History Is a Contemporary Literature,* 258.
329 Ivan Jablonka, *History Is a Contemporary Literature,* 104, 109.

13 The Future

When I was in my twenties, I did not spend much time thinking about the future. I had too many worries in the present, like finishing my doctoral thesis. Even after achieving that goal, I did not think much about the future, beyond the need to get a job. Today I spend much more time thinking about the future, especially the future beyond my existence. It's easy to see why. Present conditions provoke alarm, and I have grandchildren who may well see the end of the twenty-first century. And what will be the state of humanity by then?

So, what does any of this have to do with history?

Think about your daily activities. How many of them are in and of the present only? Yes, certain things are just for fun in the present. Other things, like school or work, are for benefit and improvement – work earns money that allows you to pay rent and buy food, and education will help get you a better job in the future. And there it is: future. Even activities far less significant than work may relate to an expectation of future benefit. Why do I go for a swim a few times a week, thrashing my way slowly up and down the lanes at the local pool? I swim because I expect a future benefit: it helps to keep me fit so I may be alive ten years from now. And isn't this what *future* means? It is not just the time after the present. It refers to things that we anticipate or hope for in that time after the present. It refers to expectations.

Take the mundane example of swimming a bit further. Is there a connection here between past, present, and future? Yes, there is! The past – that is, accumulated understandings from the past about the relationships among physical exercise, fitness, and life expectancy – exists in the present. Those understandings persuade me to swim in anticipation of a future outcome. In many of our daily activities, the future in this sense is actively present. I wouldn't say that my swimming is an example of historical thinking. But I hope you will agree: we must think about how often the *future* is actively present in our historical thinking. And *how* it is present.

I suggest that, to some degree at least, historical research and writing require optimism, or if not that, then a tendency to be hopeful. Why would we spend so much time and effort on our discipline if we did not hope to get something of benefit from it, for ourselves and for the future? Hope, of course, is another venerable and much-debated subject in philosophy. I suggest that history's recent turn toward a "practical past" must reflect a renewed search for hope.[330] Certainly, that search will be apparent in this book, and some may suggest that I veer toward utopian dreaming. Who but a privileged dreamer could imagine that hard historical thinking offers hope for the future?

We study the past while remembering the future: have you heard this old saying? It seems a feeble nostrum to me. Yes, I know that we cannot use the past to predict the future. Our deep awareness of contingency prevents any such folly. But that is neither an end nor a beginning to our discussion of history and the future. Other disciplines speak of "past and future" or "history and future" – in the sciences (most obviously climate science), in medicine, in education, and elsewhere. The past is culled, if not for predictions, then for cautionary tales, potentials, and possible scenarios. Futurology is another field in which past and future are explored together. And governments engage in a geopolitics of prevision, a field in which state agents imagine possible social and political futures, from ideological perspectives and within what has been called "a mystique of clairvoyance."[331] We historians remain cautious and skeptical, for all our insistence on the necessity of history.

We enter the field nonetheless. At this point we must return, albeit briefly, to the thought of Reinhart Koselleck. In his *Futures Past*, Koselleck explored past, future and time, and told us that experience and expectation are wrapped up in each other: "No expectation without experience, no experience without expectation." And expectation is "the future made present."[332] A sense of time is embed-

---

[330] A recent example of practical historical reasoning bearing on hope is Samuel Cohn's, *All Societies Die: How to Keep Hope Alive* (Ithaca, NY: Cornell University Press, 2021). The journal *History and Anthropology* has a special issue on hope, time and future: vol. 27, no. 4 (2016).

[331] Matthew Connelly et al., "'General, I Have Fought Just as Many Nuclear Wars as You Have': Forecasts, Future Scenarios, and the Politics of Armageddon," *American Historical Review*, 117, 5 (December 2012), 1459. See also David C. Engerman, "Introduction: Histories of the Future and the Futures of History," *American Historical Review*, 117, 5 (December 2012), 1402–10, and other articles in this AHR Forum.

[332] Reinhart Koselleck, *Futures Past*, 270, 272. There are many analyses of Koselleck's work on time, including John Zammito, "Koselleck's Philosophy of Historical Times and the Practice of History," *History and Theory*, 43, 1 (February 2004), 124–35; Helge Jordheim, "Against Periodization: Koselleck's Theory of Multiple Temporalities," *History and Theory*, 51, 2 (May, 2012), 151–71; Juhan Hellerma, "Koselleck on Modernity, *Historik*, and Layers of Time," *History and Theory*, 59, 2 (June 2020), 188–209. See also Niklas Olsen, *History in the Plural: An Introduction to the Work of Reinhart Koselleck* (New York: Berghahn Books, 2012). In a different context, Jörn Rüsen argues: "In its temporal orientation, historical consciousness ties the past to the present in a manner that bestows on present actuality a future perspective." Rüsen, "Historical Consciousness: Narrative Structure, Moral Function, and Ontogenetic Development," in Peter Seixas, ed., *Theorizing Historical Consciousness* (Toronto: University of Toronto Press, 2004), 67.

ded in the consciousness in which history is conceived. Time embraces past, present and future, and all of our experience and our understanding are bound within these temporal dimensions. Koselleck says: "The past has passed, irrevocably – and it has not: the past is present and contains future. It restrains and opens up future possibilities . . . ."[333]

A futurity lies within our experience and our temporal understanding. Time, in this understanding, may be both linear and circular because phenomena recur. The idea of recurrence is part of Koselleck's surmounting of the dichotomy between linear and circular time: both may be concurrently present. He problematizes *Zeitgeschichte* – literally, contemporary history, or history of the present – within his geological metaphor of sediments or layers of time.

> Everywhere one looks, there are phenomena of recurrence: time hurries and time heals, it brings new things and reclaims what can only be discerned from a distance. Our *Zeitgeschichte* contains structures that are characteristic of more than just our *Zeitgeschichte*. There are repeatable constellations, long-term effects, contemporary manifestations of archaic attitudes, regularities of sequences of events, and the contemporary historian can inform himself about their actuality from history . . . .[334]

The model of layers of time allows an understanding of history as open, diverse, temporally multifarious, and plural. It also rends asunder the simple antinomy of past and future. And now, in the third decade of the twenty-first century, we encounter new re-conceptions of layers of temporality, including "chronocenosis": "a way of theorizing not simply the multiplicity but also the conflict of temporal regimes operating in any given moment."[335]

Outside Koselleck's philosophical frame, we encounter other re-thinkings of past and future. Experience impels us to imagine patterns in traces of the past. The American historian William McNeill (1917–2016) says: "Pattern recognition of the sort historians engage in is the chef d'oeuvre of human intelligence. It is achieved

---

333 Koselleck, "Wozu noch Historie?" *Historische Zeitschrift*, 212 (1971) 13, cited in Olsen, *History in the Plural*, 231. On Koselleck and "the utopian imaginaries of political thinking," see Anna Friborg, "Venturing Beyond Koselleck's Erwartungshorizont: On The Category of the Utopian," *Rethinking History*, 25, 3 (2021), 263–80. For a critique of Koselleck's geological model, see Chris Lorenz, "Probing the Limits of a Metaphor: On the Stratigraphic Model in History and Geology," in Simon and Deile, *Historical Understanding*, 203–15.
334 Koselleck, *Sediments of Time*, 115–6.
335 Dan Edelstein, Stefanos Geroulanos, and Natasha Wheatley, eds., *Chronocenosis: How to Imagine the Multiplicity of Temporalities Without Losing the Emphasis on Power and Conflicts* (Chicago: Chicago University Press, 2020), 4. See the "Review Essay" on this book by Margrit Pernau, *History and Theory* (June 2023), 1–9. The recent attention to temporalities has led to a renewed interest in "chronopolitics": see note 86.

by paying selective attention to the total input of stimuli that swarm in upon our consciousness . . . . Pattern recognition is what natural scientists are up to; it is what historians have always done, whether they knew it or not."[336] Where patterns are embedded, they may endure into the future. Such reflections have prompted a few historians to consider the potential for histories of the future, framed by patterns and within evidence- and rule-bound scenarios of plausibility. David Staley concludes: "Historians are well qualified to write imaginative, disciplined, and realistic histories of the future."[337]

I go no further with Staley's conclusion, except to say that historians are far better equipped to engage in prevision and forecasting than many others who do so. The hazards of writing a future on the basis of past or present patterns are obvious enough. It is precisely because we know the risks and pitfalls that we should not cede historically-informed scenario-building to others.[338]

I offer instead the following provocation: perhaps historians are creating futures, even when not writing histories of the future. Historical thinking contains a consciousness of the future. Expectation and anticipation lie everywhere in our imaginative reasoning. Wherever there are values, there must be expectation, the expectation that those values can be defended and even realized. "Every salvation has its paradise," says the Lebanese-Australian theorist Ghassan Hage.[339] To which I add: every allegation of sin carries its vision of redemption. In every past

---

[336] William H. McNeill, "Mythistory," in *Mythistory and Other Essays* (Chicago: University of Chicago Press, 1986), 5.

[337] David J. Staley, "A History of the Future," *History and Theory*, 41 (December 2002), 89; see also the argument in Jerome Baschet, "Reopening the Future: Emerging Worlds and Novel Historical Futures," *History and Theory*, 61, 2 (June 2022), 183–208. See also Staley, "The Future as a Domain of Historical Inquiry," in Simon and Deile, *Historical Understanding*, 155–65; Cornelius Holtorf, "Periodization of the Future," in Simon and Deile, *Historical Understanding*, 167–77. For a recent argument about how "historical explanation generates a set of possible futures," see Veli Virmajoki, "Frameworks in Historiography: Explanation, Scenarios, and Futures," *Journal of the Philosophy of History*, 17, 2 (July 2023), 288–309. For a retrospective on the recent "Historical Futures Project," see Zoltán Boldiszár Simon and Marek Tamm, "The Opening of Historical Futures," *History and Theory*, online early view version, 19 June 2024.

[338] Even so cautious a historian as David Hackett Fischer argued that history is "useful" in its relationship to the future. Historians, he said, are not forecasters of the future, but "Maybe they should bear a hand, for they have acquired by long experience a kind of tacit temporal sophistication which other disciplines lack - a sophistication which is specially theirs to contribute." Fischer, *Historians' Fallacies*, 315. He goes on to plead for an expansion of public history as a "remedy," and for a much-expanded teaching of "how to think historically" (316).

[339] Ghassan Hage, "Questions Concerning a Future Politics," *History and Anthropology*, 27, 4 (2016), 466.

inequality, we see a future equality. Indeed, without that vision of equality, the inequality would not be visible at all.

Thus, our perspectival thinking occurs in more than one viewing location: the present, and also an anticipated future, realized or unrealized. Unrealized: we are not predictors but givers of salutary warnings. The past speaks to us of terrible loss, of costs, of safer paths not taken, and also of victories or the overcoming of barriers. In speaking so, history tells us that those things may be in a future as well as the past. Thus, history speaks from a perspective in the future. Realized: the past speaks to us of lives lived, struggles waged, victories won, and the resistance that proves other ways to be possible. Again, history is speaking of and from a future. Consider, for instance, the following questions. When were women placed in unprecedented contact across the divides of race, gender, class, and region? What is, or was, the meaning of home, freedom, citizenship, national belonging, and women's relationship to each other? What happens when women become refugees, and also targets of military law and military fire? How does society respond when women take on unaccustomed roles? Yes, these questions are about a past: they are a few of the questions posed at the beginning of Glymph's *The Women's Fight*. But are they not also questions from and about a future? They are not predictive. But they are certainly prospective and anticipatory. Answer these questions of the past, and we begin to answer them for the future. We see from the vantage of a future, and the invisible becomes visible.

Decolonization history, including the history of the "great divergence," is even more clearly about the future. One explicit future is stated in the prospective demand, often made by historians of decolonization, for new perspectives, new paradigms, and new theories. Another relates to a future in which Eurocentrisms are transcended. As Erik Grimmer-Solem says, a purpose of "renarrating South Asia's economic history" is "recovering the dignity and agency stolen by the colonial experience and then buried under a mountain of neo-Orientalist assumptions, European modernization frameworks, and Eurocentric mythmaking."[340] "Recovering" makes the future explicit: at the end of the recovery process, a future is realized.

Envisioning a future historically: the idea presses upon us more urgently in our Anthropocene era. As we have seen, scholars are re-thinking temporality, embracing geological time and even planetary time. Dipesh Chakrabarty seeks to collapse the old distinction between natural history and human history; in this collapse, we

---

[340] Erik Grimmer-Solem, "India, the Great Divergence, and the Wreckage of Modernity," *History and Theory*, 57, 3 (September 2018), 481. History and futures are explicitly connected in the essays in Andrew W.M. Smith and Chris Jeppeson, eds., *Britain, France, and the Decolonization of Africa: Future Imperfect?* (London: UCL Press, 2017).

see a multiplicity of temporal rhythms, speeds, and durations.[341] Others too are rethinking the disciplines, seeing a multidisciplinarity that puts geology, anthropology, and history beside each other in a "Historical Futures" project. The "geological turn" claims a new way of "decentering" the human subject, and a path by which a future overcomes "the material limitations of the now," whether these limitations be biological, institutional, or technological.[342]

In these recent changes in historical understanding, we may see something of the perdurability of historical consciousness and historical thinking. Disruptions, including future cataclysms in the Anthropocene, are historicized: their identity lies in their history. And history itself evolves, its temporality and its scope expanding far beyond previous boundaries. History embraces posthumanism, "transhuman futures," and (according to Marek Tamm) "a new idea of subjectivity, a transversal alliance involving both human and non-human agents."[343] As Rosi Braidotti says in *Posthuman Knowledge*: "This means that the posthuman subject relates at the same time to the Earth – land, water, plants, animals, bacteria – and to technological agents – plastic, wires, cells, codes, algorithms."[344] Faced with such an expansion of scope, my younger self – the historian I was decades ago – might have asked: with what sources, and by what methods, are we to study these new subjects? Today, that simply will not do. Of course, we will ask about sources and methods. But we must also ask: in what forms of imaginative reasoning may these agents be comprehended? In what perspectival knowing may we see animals, or an algorithm? As Zoltán Boldiszár Simon says: "new future means new history."[345]

---

[341] Dipesh Chakrabarty, "The Climate of History: Four Theses," *Critical Inquiry*, 35, 2 (2009), 201.

[342] Lifetimes Research Collective, "Fossilization, or the Matter of Historical Futures," *History and Theory*, 61, 1 (March 2022), 5. See also Dipesh Chakrabarty, "Anthropocene Time," *History and Theory*, 57, 1 (2018), 5–32; Zoltán Boldizsár Simon and Marek Tamm, "Historical Futures," *History and Theory*, 60, 1 (March 2021), 3–22; Julia Adeney Thomas, Mark Williams and Jan Zalasiewicz, *The Anthropocene: A Multidisciplinary Approach* (Cambridge: Polity Press, 2020).

[343] On transhuman futures: Apolline Taillandier, "'Staring into the Singularity' and Other Posthuman Tales: Transhumanist Stories of Future Change," *History and Theory*, 60, 2 (June 2021), 215–33. Marek Tamm, "Future-Oriented History," in Zoltán Boldizsar Simon and Lars Deile, *Historical Understanding: Past, Present, and Future* (London: Bloomsbury, 2022), 134.

[344] Rosi Braidotti, *Posthuman Knowledge* (Cambridge: Polity Press, 2019), 46. Tamm and Simon point to "the deeply rooted illusion of humans as the sole actors on the stage of history." Marek Tamm and Zoltán Boldiszár Simon, "More-Than-Human History: Philosophy of History at the Time of the Anthropocene," in J.M. Kuukkanen, ed., *Philosophy of History: Twenty-First Century Perspectives* (London: Bloomsbury, 2020), 205.

[345] Zoltán Boldiszár Simon, "History Begins in the Future: On Historical Sensibility in the Age of Technology," in Stefan Helgesson and Jayne Svenungsson, eds., *The Ethos of History: Time and Responsibility* (New York: Berghahn, 2018), 199. See also Simon's book *History in Times of Unprecedented Change: A Theory for the Twenty-First Century* (London: Bloomsbury, 2019). The new "het-

The future exists only as potential; it is not actual. It exists to be made, and its making lies in our imaginative reasoning. The future, therefore, makes history indispensable. It will not be dismissed or evaded, any more than music can be dismissed or evaded; it can only be refined and renovated. In history, as in music, imagination is constrained and empowered by rigorous discipline. In the wake of the providential dispensations that we have lost, we have learned a secular faith, the faith that a reasoning historical imaginary helps to prepare a path to social and political redemption.

But ask yourself: how secure, how well-founded, is this faith? History has faced, and continues to confront, many renunciations. I am not referring merely to the *ignoring* of history, but to something more profound – a total rejection. Consider the rejections of the German philosopher Karl Löwith (1897–1973). History, for Löwith, is a specious, anthropogenic rationalization: it can be used to justify monstrous evil.[346] Or consider the rejection of the French poet and polymath Paul Valéry.

> History is the most dangerous product evolved from the chemistry of the human intellect. Its properties are well known. It causes dreams, it intoxicates whole peoples, gives them false memories, quickens their reflexes, keeps their old wounds open, torments them in their repose, leads them into delusions either of grandeur or of persecution, and makes nations bitter, arrogant, insufferable, and vain. History will justify anything.[347]

Or consider Friedrich Nietzsche. He wrote about the "five ways in which the oversaturation of an age in history seems to me hostile and dangerous." Each of his five ways might be applied to our own time, but consider especially the fifth: "an age attains the dangerous mood of irony about itself and, beyond that, an even

---

erogeneity of timescales and temporality calls for completely new forms of historiography," conclude Eva Horn and Hannes Bergthaler, *The Anthropocene: Key Issues for the Humanities* (London: Routledge, 2020), 162.

346 Löwith's *Meaning in History* (Chicago: University of Chicago Press, 1957 [1949]) is well worth reading. To understand his critique of history, we might start with his view of the eighteenth-century idea of progress. Progress said that a moral and political perfection was capable of being realized, and that it can be observed in the historical process. This faith in progress infuses political movements. The outcome is ideology, including the monstrously destructive ideologies of the modern world. Progress involves the belief that all moral norms are manifested in the human-centred historical world, and have no validity beyond a mere "factical" or evidential validity. Such thinking, in Löwith's view, leads directly to the modern revolutions and the wars of the twentieth century. Jeffrey Andrew Barash, "The Sense of History: On the Political Implications of Karl Löwith's Concept of Secularization," *History and Theory*, 37, 1 (February, 1998), 69–82; Willem Styfals, "Evil in History: Karl Löwith and Jacob Taubes on Modern Eschatology," *Journal of the History of Ideas*, 765, 2 (April 2015), 191–213.

347 Paul Valéry, *Selected Writings* (New York: New Directions, 1950), 136.

more dangerous cynicism."[348] Do we not need to answer? Can history indeed *justify anything*? If it can, then how can we justify a practice, a discipline, that serves so well the doers of evil?

Consider another rejection: the view that history is irredeemably compromised as a Eurocentric consciousness and a product of the European Enlightenment. Ashis Nandy argued in 1995:

> Once exported to the nonmodern world, historical consciousness has not only tended to absolutize the past in cultures that have lived with open-ended concepts of the past or depended on myths, legends, and epics to define their cultural selves, it has also made the historical worldview complicit with many new forms of violence, exploitation, and satanism in our times and helped rigidify civilizational, cultural, and national boundaries.[349]

More recently, Priya Satia has argued that European historicism provided ethical sanction for British imperialism.[350] These are profound challenges. In what form or condition can history survive such challenges and rejections?

I try but fail to get rid of another troubling thought: that in the first half of the twenty-first century historical thinking is threatened not so much by rejection as by erasure and displacement. That the "perpetual present" detected by Eric Hobsbawm in 1994 is now fully embedded in our culture.[351] The historical thinking that I have learned over a long career is very much the outcome of the European Enlightenment; it is an intellectual reflexivity that evolved within the complex conditions of the Enlightenment and its entrails. But what if the Enlightenment heritage is waning? What happens to Enlightenment rationalism in our era of orality, electronic communication, and screen capitalism? All around us we witness new forms

---

348 Nietzsche, "On the Uses and Disadvantages of History for Life," from *Untimely Meditations* [1874], trans. Ian Johnstone: https://leudar.com/library/On%20the%20Use%20and%20Abuse%20of%20History.pdf, p. 19. For a recent critique of historicizing see the works of Martin L. Davies, including his *Imprisoned by History: Aspects of Historicized Life* (Abingdon: Routledge, 2010). See also Alexandre Leskanich, "History Doesn't Work: Reflections on Martin L. Davies' Critique of Historicized Life," *Rethinking History*, 22, 1 (2018), 126–36.
349 Ashis Nandy, "History's Forgotten Doubles," *History and Theory*, 34, 2 (May 1995), 27. The subject of history as a European episteme has generated a substantial literature. Of central importance is Dipesh Chakrabarty, *Provincializing Europe: Postcolonial Thought and Historical Difference* (Princeton: Princeton University Press, 2000). See also the Forum on "decolonizing history" in *History and Theory*, 59, 3 (September 2020).
350 Priya Satia, *Time's Monster: How History Makes History* (Cambridge MA: Belknap Press of Harvard University Press, 2020).
351 Too many, said Eric Hobsbawm, "grow up in a sort of perpetual present lacking any organic relation to the public past of the times they live in." Eric Hobsbawm, *The Age of Extremes: The Short Twentieth Century* (London: Michael Joseph, 1994), 3–4.

of fabulism, alchemy, myth, reductionism, and unreasoning eristic combat. Fundamentalisms, religious and secular, flourish. Is it possible that, in this conjuncture, history will be eluded and retired? At the same time, humanity faces existential threats that cry out for immediate solutions. Will we – indeed, can we – pause to think historically, to engage with the complexity that historical thinking contains, when survival is at stake? Even in universities, we see signs of the decline of historical thinking and teaching.[352] We also see politicians, those plunderers of the past for present vindication, avoiding the past (or inventing it ex nihilo) in their sacralization of policy and self. Who now calls upon the "lessons of history"? Is my faith in historical thinking a dream, a wish fulfillment conjured out of a lifelong devotion to my vocation?[353]

The questions are especially urgent for scholarly history. Zoltán Boldizsár Simon asks: "will history as a discipline and a specifically scholarly mode of understanding survive the next decades . . . . ?"[354]

Answers will differ, of course, and many will quarrel with mine. I suggest that it is not enough to answer by referring to the skills that history teaches, or the value of history as education for citizenship. Such answers will do little to meet the rejections of Löwith, Valéry, Nietzsche, Nandy, and others; still less to answer the evasion of history in our perpetual nowness. We must plant our secular faith on stronger foundations.

In my view, we must return to the question of ethics and history. History is never independent of ethics, nor of politics.[355] The Australian historiographer Marnie Hughes-Warrington, in her recent book on ethics in historiography, argues that the difference among histories is largely to do with ethics. She begins,

---

[352] Benjamin M. Schmitt, "The History BA Since the Great Recession," *Perspectives on History* (December 2018); Eric Alterman, "The Decline of Historical Thinking," *The New Yorker* (4 February 2019); "The study of history is in decline in Britain," *The Economist* (16 July 2019); Robert B. Townsend, "Has the Decline in History Majors Hit Bottom?" *Perspectives on History* (March 2021). Daniel Bessner sounds the alarm in "Is This Actually the End of History?" *New York Times*, 14 January 2023. On history and the "monetization" of knowledge in universities, see E.A. Heaman, *Civilization: From Enlightenment Philosophy to Canadian History* (Montreal and Kingston: McGill-Queen's University Press, 2022), 463–5.

[353] This paragraph was composed following a conversation with my colleague, Tom Saunders. I thank Tom for challenging me to address the pessimistic scenario.

[354] Zoltán Boldizsár Simon, "Introduction: Historical Understanding Today," in Simon and Lars Deile, *Historical Understanding: Past, Present, and Future* (London: Bloomsbury, 2022), 9.

[355] Once again, I risk skating over complex issues in the philosophy of history. Consider, for instance, the attempt of Reinhart Koselleck to separate historical knowledge and moral judgment. Is his attempt persuasive? See Zachary Riebeling, "Koselleck and the Problem of Historical Judgment," *Journal of the Philosophy of History*, 17, 3 (December 2023), 380–404.

as do all serious discussions of ethics, with Aristotle. "Aristotle's ethics helps us to see that history is not an endeavour to be got precisely right, once. We should expect there to be histories, plural, and we expect there to be ethics, plural. We will have to look over time and space to see those histories. The ethics of history is thus historical and global . . . ." In the making of history, we are necessarily engaging with ethics as effort and practice. "History making is an unending effort to do good, which Aristotle described as *ethos*. He saw ethics as an unending activity in which we grapple with what we ought to do."[356] It follows from the logic of this ethos and its responsibilities that Hughes-Warrington incorporates the personal and the intellectual in her historiography (as I am attempting, less persuasively, to do here).

Let's return to historical reasoning.[357] That whole section in Chapter 5 about "parts and wholes" emerges from an ethics. There is no such thing as an individual existing apart from the groups or collectivities in which they live. History is not about fictional Robinson Crusoes.[358] It is always about people understood in their relations with others and within the contexts of their being. Parts conjoin and become an emergent whole. This is about community and the creation of community.[359] The individual is realized, as person and identity, only within community. Consilience is also about the perceptions of women, not as a collective singularity or as individuals, but as members and seekers of community. The making

---

[356] Marnie Hughes-Warrington, *Big and Little Histories: Sizing Up Ethics in Historiography* (London: Routledge, 2022), 7. On the ethical and existential dimensions of history, see the essays in Stefan Helgesson and Jayne Svenungsson, eds., *The Ethos of History: Time and Responsibility* (New York: Berghahn Books, 2018).

[357] I said earlier that "logical reasoning is independent of the significance of the statements or truth assignments in that reasoning. To put it another way: logical truth is not the same as evidentially-confirmed truth." I said that when introducing argumentation theory, but went on to argue that historical reasoning takes on different forms.

[358] There is a respectful dissent here from recent statements by Frank Ankersmit: "individual human beings are considered to be the rock-bottom (both ontologically and methodologically) of our social order." From which it follows that "explanations of social human behaviour are acceptable only if expressed in terms of the properties of the behaviour of human individuals." Ankersmit, "Being Realistic about Anti-Realism," *Journal of the Philosophy of History*, 18, 2 (June 2024), 142.

[359] There is a philosophical orientation often referred to as communitarianism, although many who are discussed under that label reject it. Although the philosophy is often traced back to Aristotle, the recent manifestations begin in reactions to John Rawls' *Theory of Justice* (1971) and critiques of Rawls' position on the individual by Alasdair MacIntyre, Michael Sandel, Charles Taylor, Michael Walzer, and others. A useful introduction is Daniel Bell's article on "Communitarianism" in the *Stanford Encyclopedia of Philosophy* (updated 2020). A retrospective account in 2014 is Amitai Etzioni's, "Communitarianism Revisited," *Journal of Political Ideologies*, 19, 3 (2014), 241–60. Communitarianism is a highly varied orientation and not a coherent theory.

of convergences and motifs: it is the historian doing this, but also her subjects, the women who act in search of togetherness, sometimes succeeding and sometimes failing. Perspective tells us that there is no such thing as disinterested knowing. We see and know from a subject-position in our community of believers.

In my history – including in its reasoning – I am repudiating all forms of individualism and solipsism that deny the priority of community. Among other things, I am repudiating the neo-liberalism that has had pervasive and destructive effects for several decades. I would also seek to repel what the American historian Eugene McCarraher has called "the enchantments of Mammon" – the seductive allures of wealth and commodification, and the falsehoods that sustain them.[360] What is property? "Property," I say, "is created by society, as a social right that's serving [and must serve] the social good." What is equality? "Equality goes with community. Community, with its basic reciprocity, creates equality. Equality is the communal practice of reciprocity." What is freedom? Freedom is a right to choose and behave as we wish, a right limited by the obligations of community. Freedom does not exist outside the community in which we live.[361]

Communities are born in history and solidified in memory. There is an important distinction here because history and memory are not the same. In recent decades we may have witnessed an extensive conflation of memory and history in our culture. We hold in memory the Holocaust, other genocides, racism, colonialisms, and (especially in Canada) the Indigenous experience of residential schools. We live in an "era of commemoration," wherein commemoration is the active empowerment of memory and the site of struggle over signs and symbols of collective pasts.[362] While respecting the powerful testimonies of memory, I

---

[360] Eugene McCarraher, *The Enchantments of Mammon: How Capitalism Became the Religion of Modernity* (Cambridge Mass: Harvard University Press, 2019).

[361] Sager, *The Professor and the Plumber: Conversations About Equality and Inequality* (Victoria, British Columbia: FriesenPress, 2021), 76, 100, 121.

[362] Pierre Nora, "L'ère de la commémoration," *Les Lieux de mémoire III, vol. 3 De l'archive à l'emblème* (Paris: Gallimard, 1984–92), 997. The history and politics of memory have been a vital topic in France, especially since it is entangled with issues of identity, especially French national identity, and with what has been called "repentance discourse." Memory, for Nora, is associated with *communautarisme* or communitarianism, which tends, in his view, to be divisive and identity-obsessed, whereas history, by contrast, tends toward the rational, the universal, and the inclusive. For a critical perspective see Kenan Van De Mieroop, "The 'age of commemoration' as a narrative construct: a critique of the discourse on the contemporary crisis of memory in France," *Rethinking History*, 20, 2 (2016), 172–91. See also François Hartog, *Regimes of Historicity: Presentism and Experiences of Time,* trans. Saskia Brown (New York: Columbia University Press, 2015), 101–3, 120–7; Hartog, "The Texture of the Present," in Zoltán Boldiszár Simon and Lars Deile, *Historical Understanding: Past Present, and Future* (London: Bloomsbury, 2022), 17–23.

share the worry that history is often confused with memory, especially when personal testimony is equated with history. But even as I worry, I remind myself that in collective memory there is nothing inherently anti-historical. On the contrary, collective memory signals an abiding consciousness of the past and its necessary presence. Memory, however, is not history in itself, nor is consciousness of the past. Memory is clearly different from history's imaginative reasoning. As we honor the testimony of the memorialist, we must proceed to ask history's questions: where does your memory come from? And what future will you make of it?

History does not justify anything, and it does not justify any perversion of community. It does not justify ethnocentric nationalisms or racism, for instance; these are denials of community and denials of the empathetic perspectivism that is basic to historical thinking. The community perspective demands respect for difference; while avoiding a dangerous relativism, it denies the universalism (all peoples are basically alike) that promoters of "liberal democracy" often assume. And not all history is written from the perspective of winners.[363] Valéry was wrong. The dreams and delusions and torments that he imagines occur not in historical thinking, but in a parody of it, outside it.

There is a politics here. If politics is about governments maximizing individual freedom – that is, the freedom of individuals to exercise the power of autonomous choice – then we are doomed. That politics would allow no safety in pandemics and no solution to the existential threat of climate change. Survival depends on collective action and collective self-understanding. It is our living within a community that creates the choices available to us, and protects us against the cataclysm that would erase even the possibility of choice.

Many readers may not share this ethical-political position. Some may wish to qualify or refine it. So be it. My argument is: historians need to frame and articulate their own foundational beliefs, and to deploy these as enduring acts of resistance.[364]

Now I hear a voice from my past, a voice of warning and censure. Are you not defending presentism? And is not presentism a cardinal sin? But what, I answer, is this "presentism"? We cannot escape our present, after all; it is omnipresent. Everything we say, everything we write, is said and written within our present. Let us remember the Italian historian Benedetto Croce (1866–1952): "The practical requirements which underlie every historical judgment give to all history the character of 'contemporary history' because, however remote in time the

---

[363] Marnie Hughes-Warrington and Daniel Woolf, eds., *History from Loss: A Global Introduction to Histories Written from Defeat, Colonization, Exile, and Imprisonment* (London: Routledge, 2023).
[364] Richard T. Vann argued that historians hide their moral evaluations behind a veil of neutrality and urged a deeper engagement with moral questions: Vann, "Historians and Moral Evaluations," *History and Theory*, 43, 4 (2004), 3–30.

events there recounted seem to be, the history in reality refers to present needs and present situations wherein those events vibrate."[365]

So what is this "tendency to interpret the past in presentist terms" against which Lynn Hunt and others have warned us?[366] It may mean the tendency to impose values on past persons or actions, or to judge them by values we possess but they did not. But what does this mean? Does any historian avoid such a tendency? Are we supposed to discard our values? David Hume was a critic of prejudice and intolerance; he was also a racist.[367] Of course, we must try to understand the values of his time and to understand racism in its contexts. But when we have done so, Hume remains a racist.

Presentism has many meanings, and its meaning has been extensively reconsidered in recent years.[368] In 2022, a furious debate about presentism broke out among members of the American Historical Association, a debate which, if nothing else, revealed the extent to which important issues remain unresolved.[369] Of course, we need to avoid teleology and anachronism. We also want to discourage the presentism that appears when students avoid courses on distant pasts and rush toward very recent or current time periods. But fear of presentist fallacy

---

[365] Benedetto Croce, *La storia come pensiero e come azione* (Laterza, 1938), 5, cited in David Armitage, "In Defense of Presentism," in Darrin M. McMahon, ed., *History of the Humanities and Human Flourishing* (Oxford: Oxford University Press, 2020), n.p.: https://scholar.harvard.edu/files/armitage/files/in_defence_of_presentism.pdf. Croce's book was translated as *History as the Story of Liberty*, trans. Sylvia Spragge (New York: W.W. Norton, 1941) – a title that missed the key words "thought" and "action" in the Italian title.

[366] Lynn Hunt, "Against Presentism," *Perspectives on History* (American Historical Association, 2002): https://www.historians.org/publications-and-directories/perspectives-on-history/may-2002/against-presentism.

[367] John Immerwahr, "Hume's Revised Racism," *Journal of the History of Ideas*, 53, 3 (July–Sept. 1992), 481–6.

[368] David Armitage, "In Defense of Presentism," in McMahon, ed., *History of the Humanities and Human Flourishing*, n.p.: https://scholar.harvard.edu/files/armitage/files/in_defence_of_presentism.pdf; Craig Bourne, *A Future for Presentism* (Oxford: Oxford University Press, 2006); Wai Chee Dimock, "Historicism, Presentism, Futurism," *Publications of the Modern Language Association* 133, 2 (March, 2018), 257–63; Naomi Oreskes, "Why I Am a Presentist," *Science in Context*, 26 (2013): 595–609. An original, lengthier reflection on presentism and temporality is François Hartog, *Regimes of Historicity* (2015). See also Marek Tamm and Laurent Olivier, eds., *Rethinking Historical Time: New Approaches to Presentism* (London: Bloomsbury Academic, 2019); Lars Deile, "Favouring an Offensive Presentism," in Simon and Deile, eds., *Historical Understanding*, 57–68.

[369] James H. Sweet, "Is History History? Identity Politics and Teleologies of the Present," *Perspectives on History* (September 2022); Malcolm Foley and Priya Satia, "Responses to 'Is History History?'," *Perspectives on History* (October 2022); David A. Bell, "Two Cheers for Presentism," *Chronicle of Higher Education* (23 August, 2022); Joan W. Scott, "History Is Always About Politics," *Chronicle of Higher Education* (24 August 2022).

can no longer excuse historians' failure to speak directly to the present and the future. As David Armitage says in a recent essay on presentism: "Human flourishing – the individual's maximization of her capabilities, and our collective endeavour to realize the best for humanity as a whole – is at once present-centered, future-oriented, and past dependent. It is present-centered because it is only within our own shifting horizon of expectations that we can judge what will best contribute to our own flourishing, as persons and as a species. It is future-oriented since within that horizon we form plans, and discard alternative projects, in order to achieve our goals more effectively." And, he goes on to say, it is past-dependent because only history can supply "the imagination to shape our choices, in the present, among multiple potential paths into the future."[370]

Speak in the present, to the future: this is an ethic, an "imperative of responsibility."[371] And in so speaking, we cannot hide behind the camouflage of neutrality afforded by our structures of evidence. Nor can we hide behind the facade of older forms of objectivity and empiricism; these will not serve young historians, nor will they answer the rejections and renunciations that history faces.[372] History bears responsibility to the present and future. This being so, honesty and transparency demand that we declare the moral and political imperatives that our words embrace and affirm.

Today, in the stronger foundations of my historical understanding, some of the epistemology of my youth endures. But out of its remnants has come a different history. The past is no longer a distant, detached realm of being that has now gone. Instead, there are only possible worlds – realms of being and experience that we historians offer unto the shared critical gaze of our communities. Verifi-

---

[370] David Armitage, "In Defense of Presentism," in Darrin M. McMahon, ed., *History of the Humanities and Human Flourishing* (Oxford: Oxford University Press, 2020), n.p.: https://scholar.harvard.edu/files/armitage/files/in_defence_of_presentism.pdf.

[371] I take the phrase from the title of Hans Jonas, *Imperative of Responsibility: In Search of an Ethic for the Technological Age* (Chicago: University of Chicago Press, 1984).

[372] I remain unimpressed by the recurring attempts to sneak an old-fashioned objectivity into history, as when Gordon Wood insists that "conventions of objectivity and documentary proof should continue to guide and control the writing of history," not least because "they have been painstakingly developed in the Western world." Gordon S. Wood, *The Purpose of the Past; Reflections on the Uses of History* (London: Penguin Books, 2009), 104–5. Of course, Wood's position may not be widely shared. But are we not seeing what Gabrielle M. Spiegel refers to as "current attempts to rehabilitate objectivity and empiricism"? Spiegel, "The Limits of Empiricism: The Utility of Theory in Historical Thought and Writing," *The Medieval History Journal*, 22, 1 (2019), 8. On the other hand, see Forland's critique of the postmodernists' situated knowing and his re-visiting of objectivity following intense debates in Denmark: Tor Egil Forland, *Values, Objectivity, and Explanation in Historiography* (New York: Routledge, 2017).

cation – the arrival at possible truths – requires method but is never the product of method alone; it is the instantiation of value. As understanding, history is a mode of thinking comprised of definable elements, constituents of the meaning that historians offer. These elements are not transcendental or metaphysical; they come from the horizon of rational reflection that is embedded in our culture.[373] As a historian, the elements of my thinking stand on the ground of my own historical contingency; my personal and anecdotal introductions are intended to underline the point. It follows that those elements are not fixed; they too will evolve.

A rejection of older notions of objectivity and scientific method does not mean abandoning method or logic or the intuitive power of reasoning. On the contrary, plausible communication of truth and meaning requires these things.[374] We offer

---

[373] This sentence is likely to prompt criticism for its superficial reference to issues rooted in both history and philosophy. Both "horizon" and "rational reflection" are terms borrowed from hermeneutics. Horizon refers to "the range of vision that includes everything that can be seen from a particular vantage point" (Gadamer, *Truth and Method*, 301). The viewer and the vantage point are historical and contextual; there is no such thing as a single horizon or absolute knowledge. As Zygmunt Bauman says, the historian is subject to the history of which he or she is part. She has "no transcendental ground from which to contemplate the process of which he [or she] is part." (Bauman, *Hermeneutics and Social Science*, 7). Thus, I argue that the elements of historical thinking outlined in this book are not transcendental or metaphysical. It may be, however, that my proposed elements are metahistorical: modes of cognition, or even prefigurings, that stand outside or prior to, as well as within, the acts of representation that we call history. This may be so, to the extent that rules of reasoning or logic exist outside the discipline to which they are applied. If there is an analogy here to the metahistory of Hayden White, the analogy is a weak one. The status of historical representations, White says, does not rest on the nature of the data used to support the representations, or the theory invoked to explain the data. On what, then, does the status of differing historical representations rest? It rests on "the consistency, coherence, and illuminative power of their respective visions of the historical field. This is why they cannot be 'refuted' or their generalizations 'disconfirmed,' either by appeal to new data that might be turned up in subsequent research or by the elaboration of a new theory for interpreting the sets of events that comprise their objects of representation and analysis." The "status" of representations depends ultimately on "the preconceptual and specifically poetic nature of their perspectives." Hayden V. White, *Metahistory: The Historical Imagination in Nineteenth Century Europe* (Baltimore: Johns Hopkins University Press, 1973), 4. And so we are a long way from patterns of reasoning and logical inference. Furthermore, the words consistency and coherence embrace far more than poetics; the words should encourage us to ask what forms consistency and coherence take in historical thought.

[374] The hermeneutic tradition has confronted charges of idealism, irrationalism, and opposition to methodology. Jurgen Habermas criticized Gadamer's *Truth and Method* for, among other things, failing to allow room for rational reflection. See Habermas, "A Review of Gadamer's *Truth and Method*," in Fred R. Dallmayr and Thomas A. McCarthy, eds., *Understanding and Social Inquiry* (Notre Dame, Indiana: University of Notre Dame Press, 1977), 335–363. A seminal work is Zygmunt Bauman, *Hermeneutics and Social Science: Approaches to Understanding* (London: Routledge, 1978). See also Robert

possible worlds, but not any worlds. Historical thinking sets standards: it is not by evidence alone, but rather by the reasoned deployment of evidence in argument that a claim to truth has validity. Can I create a triceratops or a unicorn? Can I fashion peace where there is genocide, or economic equilibrium where class conflict rends asunder the social order? Can we create a stable future where climate change destroys the means of survival? No, such creations fail: the elements of reasoning and imagination expose the implausibility of such claims and deny to them the status of truth. Such, then, is my practical understanding, my history as phronesis, my active rhetoric of argument and persuasion.[375]

Historia magistra vitae, wrote Cicero.[376] History, teacher of life, the teacher that leads us from our present pasts into a future. Our destiny lies in history's possible worlds, and these can only be found in the reasoning imagination. Cicero also said: history, witness of time, herald of antiquity, committed to immortality.

Thorp and Anders Persson, "On Historical Thinking and the History Educational Challenge," *Educational Philosophy and Theory*, 52, 8 (2020), 891–901.

375 Rhetoric may seem an antique term, despite its prominence in writings by and about Hayden White. Rhetoric, however, is worth rescuing from postmodernism. As the means of argument and persuasion in verbal communication, it is surely worth adapting to history as understanding. For Cicero, the Roman exponent of rhetoric, reasoning could not be separated from communicative skill; without both, attempts to persuade would fail. Rhetoric, for Cicero, was didactic and practical, and it was closely connected to history. See Robert W. Cape, "Persuasive History: Roman Rhetoric and Historiography," in William J. Dominik, ed., *Roman Eloquence: Rhetoric in Society and Literature* (London: Routledge, 2005), 175–88. See also "Towards a Neo-Ciceronian Approach," in Ivan Jablonka, *History as a Contemporary Literature*, 260–1.

376 Cicero, *De Oratore*, II, 36.

Suggestions for Further Reading

There is much to be learned from the pioneering work of education theorists who have written about historical thinking. The late Peter Seixas worked at the University of British Columbia, where the web site of The Historical Thinking Project lists books and resources. I would begin with Kadriye Erickan and Peter Seixas, eds., *New Directions in Assessing Historical Thinking* (New York: Routledge, 2015); and Peter Seixas and Tom Morton, *The Big Six Historical Thinking Concepts* (Toronto: Nelson, 2012). The pre-eminent American scholar Sam Wineburg is an educator and cognitive psychologist. His many publications include *Historical Thinking and Other Unnatural Acts: Charting the Future of Teaching the Past* (Philadelphia: Temple University Press, 2001); *Why Learn History (When It's Already on Your Phone)* (Chicago: Chicago University Press, 2018). Wineburg has also written about misinformation and reading on the internet. Other important contributions include Michael Douma, *Creative Historical Thinking* (London: Routledge, 2018); and Stéphane Lévesque, *Thinking Historically: Educating Students for the Twenty-first Century* (Toronto: University of Toronto Press, 2009). There are many books on classroom applications and methods, including Tim Allender, Anna Clark, and Robert Parkes, eds., *Historical Thinking for History Teachers: A New Approach to Engaging Students and Developing Historical Consciousness* (New York: Routledge, 2020); and Magdalena H. Gross and Luke Terra, eds., *Teaching and Learning the Difficult Past* (New York: Routledge, 2018).

It is difficult to separate works that focus on historical thinking from studies of historiography, since the latter are always about historical thought. Nevertheless, there are books that focus on logic and reasoning. These include Clayton Roberts, *The Logic of Historical Explanation* (University Park: Pennsylvania State University Press, 1996). Roberts seeks to breathe life into a covering law model of explanation. In his *Our Knowledge of the Past: A Philosophy of Historiography* (Cambridge: Cambridge University Press, 2004), Aviezer Tucker discusses historical reasoning, methodology, and Bayesian probability while urging that history is scientific. See also the chapters on logic in Aviezer Tucker, ed., *A Companion to the History of Philosophy of History and Historiography* (Chichester: Blackwell, 2009). It is worth returning to David Hackett Fischer, *Historians' Fallacies: Toward a Logic of Historical Thought* (New York: Harper and Row, 1970).

Deserving to be better known in North America are the works of Ivan Jablonka: on historical reasoning see his *History is a Contemporary Literature: Manifesto for the Social Sciences*, trans. Nathan J. Bracher (Ithaca: Cornell University Press, 2018), and especially Chapter 7 on "Approaches to Veridiction." On historical logic, reasoning, and method (broadly defined) see also Jonas Ahlskog, *The Primacy of Method in Historical Research: Philosophy of History and the Perspective of Meaning* (New York: Routledge, 2021). Jouni-Matti Kuukkanen introduces argumentation and reasoning in his *Postnarrativist Philosophy of Historiography* (New York: Palgrave Macmillan, 205). In my view, the broadly historiographical work that most explicitly approaches history as thinking is Sarah Maza, *Thinking About History* (Chicago: University of Chicago Press, 2017).

The philosophy of history is a field of its own. Students seeking a lucid introduction can turn to Daniel Little, "Philosophy of History" in the *Stanford Encyclopedia of Philosophy* (revised 2020). A recent collection of essays is Jouni-Matti Kuukkanen, ed., *Philosophy of History: Twenty-First-Century Perspectives* (London: Bloomsbury, 2020). Introductions to hermeneutics include Lawrence K. Schmidt, *Understanding Hermeneutics* (London: Routledge, 2006); Jens Zimmermann, *Hermeneutics: A Very Short Introduction* (Oxford: Oxford University Press, 2015). On hermeneutic historicism see John H. Zammito, "Hermeneutics and History," in Michael N. Forster and Kristin Gjesdal, eds., *The Cambridge Companion to Hermeneutics* (Cambridge: Cambridge University Press, 2019).

For further readings on specific topics, I refer readers to the extensive footnotes.

Index

abductive reasoning 5, 49, 64, 108–119, 120, 121, 123, 127–129, 130
Aboriginal art 33
Aboriginal understanding of time 33–35
Africanus, Leo 42–44, 57
American Historical Association 147
American Revolution 84, 107
analogy 5, 27, 66, 67, 79–94, 106, 126, 149
Annales 12, 37
Anthropocene 11, 35, 40, 41, 66, 69, 139–140, 141
anthropology 16 n.36, 63 n.42, 68, 140
argumentation 16, 19 n.44, 46–49, 51–54, 59, 65–67, 70, 71, 79–80, 83, 84, 88–90, 94, 107, 111, 112, 113, 128, 133 n.326, 144 n.357, 150
Aristotle 20, 59, 79, 96, 125 n.305, 144
Armitage, David 148
artificial intelligence 1, 46, 109, 118
Atlantic Canada Shipping Project 95
Australia 7, 33–35, 38–39

Bacon, Francis 119
Bali 62
Barak, On 40–41
Barrena, Sara 127
Bartha, Paul 80 n.188, 88–89, 94
Bayes, Thomas 53
Becker, Carl 14–15
Belle, Kathryn Sophia 86–87
Ben-Menahim, Yemima 31
Bentham, Jeremy 92
Berger, John 74
Berger, Stefan 2–3
Bevir, Mark 47
Bigelow, Allison Margaret 67–71
Bittner, Sam 23
Bonnett, John 26
Boureau, Alain 29
Bradley, Keith 98–99
Braidotti, Rosi 140
Braudel, Fernand 24–25, 37, 104
Brinton, Crane 84
Brunelleschi, Filippo 72
Burckhardt, Jacob 102
Burke, Peter 29

Bury, John Bagnell 11, 131
Butler, Judith 88, 94

Canadian Historical Association 7
Carignan, Michael 82
Carr, Edward Hallett 10–11, 14, 30, 31, 110–111
causation 4, 10–11, 18, 30, 31, 32, 55–56, 60, 67, 85, 92, 110–112, 122–123, 129–131
Chakrabarty, Dipesh 8, 40, 139
Chatwin, Bruce 34
chronocenosis 39, 137
Cicero 150
class analysis 27, 28, 29, 38, 59, 61, 66, 86, 102, 103, 120, 132, 139, 150
Clio 2, 3, 6, 16, 17
Cobb, Richard 101–103
Cohen, Ariel 96
colligation 56 n.129, 60–61
Collingwood, R.G. 9, 52, 108 n.278, 114 n.274
colonialism 26, 30, 32, 40, 41, 45, 50, 69, 70, 87, 97, 139
community 39, 144–145, 146
comparative analysis 79, 83, 91, 92, 100, 113–114, 116, 117 n.300, 118, 121, 123, 130, 132, 133
complex systems 26–28
complexity 25–27, 38, 39, 41, 60, 63, 113, 123–124, 128, 130, 143
consilience 5, 62–71, 128, 144
context 4, 5, 9, 17, 19, 20, 21, 23, 26, 28–32, 55, 57, 63, 66, 69, 92, 105, 110, 113, 127, 128, 130, 147
contingency 31–32, 113
contrapuntal reading 68–69
Cook, James 28
correspondence theory 10
counter-factualism 30, 31, 44, 116, 125
COVID-19 42 n.94, 91–92
Croce, Benedetto 146
Cruikshank, Julie 45

Danto, Arthur C. 17
Davidoff, Leonore 97
Davis, Natalie Zemon 42–44, 57–58, 110, 126
De Beauvoir, Simone 86

https://doi.org/10.1515/9783111563800-015

Index

decolonization 40 n.91, 139
Deluermoz, Quentin 125
democracy in decline 121-124, 146
description 17, 62-63, 64
digitization 39, 64, 65, 66, 104-105
Dilthey, Wilhelm 19
disruption 9, 13, 45, 46, 121, 125, 127, 130, 140
distanciation 5, 79, 81, 83, 89, 93, 137
Doyle, William 27
Dreamtime 34, 44

economics 7, 68, 82, 85 n.206, 116, 117
Eliot, George 82-83
emotional reasoning 5-6, 66, 74, 75
empathy 6 n.11, 62, 78, 120
empiricism 5, 9-10, 12-13, 47, 148
Enlightenment 11, 29, 45, 142
epidemics 91-92, 146
epistemic humility 121
epistemology 2, 8, 14, 17, 82, 148-149
Ermus, Cindy 41
erotetics 51-52
ethics 4, 14, 15-16, 33 n.72, 36-37, 47, 78, 89, 99, 116-117, 141 n.346, 142, 143-146
ethnocentrism 16, 129, 146
ethnography 38, 63-64, 66, 80, 81
European Fertility Project 25
European history 7, 33, 35, 40-41, 101, 104, 130, 139, 142
evidence 4, 5, 8, 10, 12, 16, 18, 53, 58, 65, 66, 70, 71, 73, 80, 99, 101, 110, 115, 116, 117, 126, 127, 128-129, 132, 133, 148, 150
expectations 108 n. 278, 118, 119, 135, 148
explanation 18, 25, 27, 30, 52, 53, 60, 108-110, 112, 113-116, 118, 123

facts 3-4, 8, 10-11, 15, 16, 17, 19, 66, 68, 80, 106, 107, 119, 121
fallacy 47, 87-88, 107, 128-129, 131, 132, 147
Faulkner, Carol 51
fertility decline 25-26, 54 n.125
fiction 11, 83, 87, 99, 126, 128, 133
Fischer, David Hackett 47, 88-89, 107, 128, 131, 138 n.338
Flinn, Michael 18
Fogel, R.W. 95-96
Foucault, Michel 74, 92-94

French Revolution 9, 27, 55, 83-84
Freud, Sigmund 8
future 27 n.56, 37, 39-40, 44, 118, 119, 121, 135-150

Gadamer, Hans-Georg 3, 20, 105, 149 n.373
Gaffield, Chad 8
Geertz, Clifford 62-63
gender 11, 13, 14, 16, 26, 50, 61, 63, 69, 74, 85-88, 94, 139
Ginzburg, Carlo 103, 127
Glymph, Thavolia 50-56, 58-61, 63-64, 66, 67 n.151, 71 n.163, 73, 77, 139
Gordon, Peter E. 30, 91
Grimmer-Solem, Erik 139

Hage, Ghassan 138
Hall, Catherine 97
Hartog, François 40, 41
Heidegger, Martin 19-20
Helmreich, Stefan 81
Hempel, Carl 51
hermeneutics 17-21, 105-106, 149 n.373
Hermes 17
history teaching 1, 2, 3-5, 7-9, 13, 143
history writing 1, 2, 5, 8, 14, 19, 33, 37, 38, 41, 42, 138, 146
Hobsbawm, Eric 63 n.142, 83, 142 n.351
Hogeland, Lisa Maria 87
holocaust 15, 67, 90-91, 145
hooks, bell 86
hope 135-136
horizon 5, 19, 95, 148, 149, 149 n.373
Hosfstadter, Douglas 85
Hughes-Warrington, Marnie 33 n.72, 143-144
Hume, David 10, 147
Hunt, Lynn 147

identity 3, 14, 16, 22, 42, 43, 57, 71, 103, 140, 144
idiographic history 57, 61
imagination 2, 11, 15, 77, 82-83, 120-134, 138, 140, 141, 146, 148, 150
Indigenous history 2, 36, 45, 67, 69, 70, 71, 145
industrial revolution 18, 37, 84-85, 114, 129
inequality 6, 92, 100, 101, 118, 123, 139
Innis, Harold 26

interactions 26, 111, 113, 116, 118, 119, 130–132
interpretation 5, 8, 9–11, 17–20, 27, 30, 65, 75–77, 96, 97, 102, 129–130

Jablonka, Ivan 3 n.5, 49, 106 n.274, 133–134

Kant Immanuel 124
Kelley, Abby 86
Khaldun, Ibn 43
Kidd, Ian James 124
Kohn, Hans 131
Kondratieff waves 82
Koselleck, Reinhart 37–38, 104, 136–137, 143 n.355
Kuhn, Thomas 88
Kwakiutl nation 45

L'Ouverture, Toussaint 60
Ladurie, Emmanuel Le Roy 55
linguistic turn 46, 62–63
logic 12, 13, 47–48, 51–54, 55, 59, 64, 82, 89, 96, 107, 109, 116, 117, 130–134, 144, 149
Löwith, Karl 141

MacIver, Robert M. 131–132
Mackinnon, Alison 26
Mandami, Mahmood 87
Markova, Ivana 55
Marxism 18–19, 29
McCarraher, Eugene 145
McNeill, William 137–138
media 1, 37, 90, 93, 105, 120–121, 123–124
Megill, Allan 49, 110
memory 2, 16, 62, 79, 80, 145–146
mereology 5, 21, 24, 27, 28, 57–61, 144
metaphor 15, 35, 37, 39, 67, 75, 76, 79, 81–82, 84, 86, 87, 88, 92, 137
microhistory 29, 69, 103
Mill, John Stuart 10, 83
Morton, Tom 4
Mulder-Bakker, Anneke 73
Munich analogy 90
music 34, 61, 62, 68, 109, 141
Myrdal, Gunnar 86

Nandy, Ashis 142
narrative 5 n.10, 13, 15, 19, 36, 38, 45, 48 n.115, 51, 60, 65, 67, 70, 114 n.294, 132, 133 n.327

nationalism 101, 122, 123, 131, 146
Nelson, Eric 107
neoliberalism 145
Nietzsche, Friedrich 75–76, 141–142, 143
nomothetic approaches 57
Novak, Ben 110
Novick, Peter 9

objectivity 9, 15–16, 21, 75–76, 77, 106–107, 148, 149
Observatory on History Teaching in Europe 1
opioids 130
oral history 2, 38–39
Ormsby, Margaret 7

pacifism 6, 27–28
panopticon 92–94
parts and wholes 5, 21, 24, 27, 28, 57–61, 144
Peirce, Charles 108 n.278, 109 n.280, 112 n.285, 119, 127
perspective 5, 21, 24, 27, 28, 57–61, 144
Phillips, Mark S. 79
phronesis 20, 21, 150
Plato 20, 29, 46, 74, 75
plural pasts 2, 14, 15, 28, 29, 30, 41, 44, 76, 77, 119, 137, 144
Pocock, J.G.A. 14 n.29
Polybius 59
Pomeranz, Kenneth 112–118, 121
positivism 12, 47
postcolonialism 16, 40–41, 68–70
posthumanism 140
postmodernism 13, 46, 117, 148 n.372, 150 n.375
poststructuralism 13
potlatch 45
practical past 16, 20, 80, 136, 146, 150
presentism 5, 14, 16, 146–147
probability 30, 53–54, 106, 108, 110, 118–119, 127

quantification 5, 95–107, 121

race 36, 38, 59, 60, 61, 86–88, 97, 132, 139
realism 9–10, 11, 13, 106, 133
reasoning 6, 28, 31, 36, 46–56, 58–59, 66–67, 71, 76, 120–121, 124, 127–134, 144–150
reductionism 26, 27, 88, 97, 120, 123, 124, 128–129, 143

relativism 15–16, 21, 78, 146
religion 25, 59, 60, 61, 122, 123, 131–132
residential schools 30, 145
revolution 9, 18, 27, 35, 37, 51, 55, 60, 83–85, 107, 123
rhetoric 85, 87, 150
Ricoeur, Paul 20
Roediger, David 132
Roman Empire 98–99, 130
Ruggles, Steven 100, 101, 130
Rüsen, Jörn 18, 19, 114 n.294, 136 n.332
Russell, Bertrand 10

Sahlins, Marshall 28–29
Said, Edward 68–69
Sander, Emmanuel 85
sans culottes 101–103
Satia, Priya 142
Sattelzeit 37–38
Schleiermacher, Friedrich 19
Schwartz, Bill 97
science 11–12, 13, 18, 21, 32, 45, 46, 53, 54, 66, 69, 88, 89, 105, 109, 111, 118, 126, 136
Second World War 7
Seixas, Peter 4–5
self 3, 93, 119, 125, 143, 146, 148
Sewell, William 35–36
sight 21, 24, 33, 50, 60, 68, 72–78, 92, 104
Simon, Zoltán Boldiszár 11 n.27, 37, 39, 140, 143
Singaravélou, Pierre 125
skills 1, 4, 5, 120, 121, 143
So, Richard Jean 104
Soboul, Albert 27, 102
social media 1, 90, 93, 120–121, 123–124
social sciences 6, 7, 12, 57, 106, 133
Staley, David J. 27 n.56, 126–127, 138
statistics 25, 76 n.173, 95, 105–106, 107, 130
synchronicity 37, 38, 62, 66, 69

Tamm, Marek 37, 39, 140
temporality 14, 20, 23, 24, 26, 30, 33–44, 51, 66, 81, 83, 85, 89, 104, 113, 120, 121, 123, 132, 137–139

thinking 2–6, 14, 21, 23, 24–25, 26–30, 39, 41–42, 44, 46, 47, 53–54, 55, 59, 61, 62, 64, 73, 74, 76, 78, 80, 83, 85, 87, 91, 94, 95, 96, 99, 100, 103, 104, 110, 112, 119, 121–130, 133, 134, 135–136, 138, 139, 140, 142–150
Thompson, Edward Palmer 29, 97–98
Thucydides 33
Toulmin, Stephen 47–49
Toynbee, Arnold 84–85
Trevelyan, George Macauley 11
truth 9–10, 12, 16, 21, 31, 47, 53–54, 64, 66, 67, 73, 75, 77–78, 109, 110, 112, 119, 124, 128, 133, 149, 150
Tucker, Aviezer 53

understanding 1–3, 9, 13, 14, 17–21, 24, 29, 32, 33–34, 35, 39, 40, 41, 46, 56, 64, 65, 68–69, 70, 72–73, 78, 92–93, 96, 104, 105, 124, 126, 129, 132–134, 125, 137, 140, 148, 149, 150
University of British Columbia 7

Valéry, Paul 141, 146
Venerable Bede 9
Vietnam War 32, 90, 120
Von Humboldt, Wilhelm 79
Vonnegut, Kurt 109

Walton, Douglas 46, 49, 114 n.294
Whewell, William 66
White, Hayden 11 n.26, 13, 15–16, 19 n.44, 149 n.373
Wilson, Daniel C.S. 85
Wilson, Edward O. 66
Windelband, Wilhelm 57
Wineburg, Sam 4
Wollstonecraft, Mary 86
women 26, 50–61, 62–64, 67 n.151, 70, 73, 74, 76–77, 81, 86–88, 94, 139, 144, 145
Wright, Richard 86

www.ingramcontent.com/pod-product-compliance
Lightning Source LLC
Jackson TN
JSHW020715090725
87332JS00002B/64